MARGARET

ESSAYS ON HER WORKS

EDITED BY BRANKO GORJUP

GUERNICA

TORONTO — BUFFALO — CHICAGO — LANCASTER (U.K.)

2008

Editor was unable to locate Jennifer Murray to obtain permission for the essay published in
this collection nor biographical information.

Branko Gorjup, Guest editor
Guernica Editions Inc.
P.O. Box 117, Station P, Toronto (ON), Canada M5S 2S6
2250 Military Road, Tonawanda, N.Y. 14150-6000 U.S.A.

Distributors:
University of Toronto Press Distribution,
5201 Dufferin Street, Toronto (ON), Canada M3H 5T8
Gazelle Book Services, White Cross Mills, High Town Lancaster LA1 4XS U.K.
Independent Publishers Group,
814 N. Franklin Street, Chicago, Il. 60610 U.S.A.

First edition.
Printed in Canada.

Legal Deposit — Second Quarter
Library of Congress Catalog Card Number: 2008928098
Library and Archives Canada Cataloguing in Publication
Margaret Atwood : essays on her works / edited by Branko Gorjup. — 1st ed.
(Writers series ; 25)
ISBN 978-1-55071-267-4
1. Atwood, Margaret, 1939- —Criticism and interpretation.
I. Gorjup, Branko II. Series: Writers series (Toronto, Ont.) ; 25
PS8501.T86Z728 2008   C818'.5409   C2008-902878-3

MARGARET ATWOOD

ESSAYS ON HER WORKS

WRITERS SERIES 25
SERIES EDITORS:
ANTONIO D'ALFONSO AND JOSEPH PIVATO

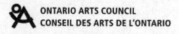

Canada Council Conseil des Arts
for the Arts du Canada

ONTARIO ARTS COUNCIL
CONSEIL DES ARTS DE L'ONTARIO

Guernica Editions Inc. acknowledges the support of
The Canada Council for the Arts.
Guernica Editions Inc. acknowledges the support of
the Ontario Arts Council.

Contents

Acknowledgments 6

Introduction by Branko Gorjup 7

Margaret Atwood's *The Edible Woman* "Rebelling
    Against the System" by Gayle Greene............................ 11

Paradox of Discourse in Margaret Atwood's
    Surfacing by Branko Gorjup 42

Living Literally by the Pen: The Self and Self-Deceiving
    Heroine-Author in Margaret Atwood's *Lady Oracle*
    by Susan Jaret McKinstry 55

"The Roar of the Boneyard": *Life before Man*
    by Barbara Hill Rigney 74

The Here and Now of *Bodily Harm*
    by Lorna Irvine 95

Nature and Nurture in Dystopia:
    The Handmaid's Tale by Roberta Rubenstein 115

Cat's Eye: Elaine Risley's Retrospective Art
    by Coral Ann Howells 130

Questioning the Triple Goddess:
    Myth and Meaning in Margaret Atwood's
    The Robber Bride by Jennifer Murray.............................. 148

I Am Telling This to No One but You:
    Private Voice, Passing, and the Private Sphere
    in Margaret Atwood's *Alias Grace*
    by Stephanie Lovelady 173

The Blind Assassin: Myth, History and Narration
    by Caterina Ricciardi 213

Interview with Margaret Atwood
    by Branko Gorjup 239

Bibliography 254

Contributors 257

Acknowledgments

All but two of the contributions in this volume, "The Blind Assassin: Myth, History and Narration" and "Interview with Margaret Atwood," were previously published in the following books and journals: "Margaret Atwood's The Edible Woman: 'Rebelling Against the System'" in Margaret Atwood: Reflections and Reality, eds. Beatrice Mendez-Egle and James M. Haule, Living Author Series 6, Edinburgh, TX: Pan American University, 1987; "Paradox of Discourse in Margaret Atwood's Surfacing" in Rivista di studi canadesi 11 (1998); "Living Literally by the Pen: The Self-Conceived and Self-Deceiving Heroine-Author in Margaret Atwood's Lady Oracle"; "The Roar of the Boneyard: Life Before Man" in Margaret Atwood, London: Macmillan Education, 1987; "The Here and Now of Bodily Harm" in Margaret Atwood: Visions and Forms, eds. Kathryn VanSpanckeren and Jan Garden Castro, Carbonale: Southern Illinois University Press, 1988; "Nature and Nurture in Dystopia: The Handmaid's Tale" in Margaret Atwood: Vision and Forms, eds. Kathryn VanSpanckeren and Jan Garden Castro, Carbondale: Southern Illinois University Press, 1988; "Cat's Eye: Elaine Risley's Retrospective Art" in Margaret Atwood: Writing and Subjectivity: New Critical Essays, ed. Colin Nicholson, Toronto: Macmillan, 1994; "Questioning the Triple Goddess: Myth and Meaning in Margaret Atwood's The Robber Bride" in Canadian Literature 173 (Summer 2002); "I Am Telling This to No One but You: Private Voice, Passing, and Private Sphere in Margaret Atwood's Alias Grace" in Studies in Canadian Literature 24, 2 (1999).

Introduction

Branko Gorup

Margaret Atwood's literary output has grown in volume
and significance over the past four decades. It has received
during this time sustained popular and critical attention,
contributing more than anyone else's work in Canada to
the development of national literature. Generations of students, myself included, have assimilated "Atwood's representation of the "Canadian Experience" and have witnessed
her fiction, poetry and criticism move to the very heart of
the Canadian literary canon. Much of her large body of
work became part of the master-narrative that has most
powerfully embodied English-speaking Canadians' prototypical search for identity.

Very few contemporary Canadian works of fiction have
caught the readers' imagination as has, for example,
Atwood's second novel, *Surfacing,* in which she examines,
among other things, Western civilization's obsession with
the death-wish as it plays itself out in the primordial
Canadian wilderness. It would be difficult to point out a
single book of poetry that has captured more accurately
Canada's post-colonial mood of the 1960s – the very
beginning of the country's inexorable search for a spiritual and a cultural integration with its physical environment
– than Atwood's *Journals of Susanna Moodie.* And her controversial and immensely influential work in the field of
Canadian literary criticism, *Survival,* has been passionately
praised for its theoretical paradigm within which, as
Atwood's numerous followers have pointed out, the study
of national literature could be undertaken. Much of
Atwood's work, especially her early work, remains a strong
reminder to the fact that literary sensibilities are construct-

ed, not preordained, and are, as such, subject to continual transformation.

Most writers tend to write the same book or poem over and over again, expanding its scope and refining its variants. Margaret Atwood, however, continues to re-invent herself as she re-invents her characters and her poetic personae with every new work. Each novel, each new poetry collection, signals a departure, a turn in an unexpected direction. Each becomes a daring journey that expands the reader's consciousness and defeats expectations. Although Atwood's characters can be anything from cold-blooded torturers of bodies and souls to the determined healers of wounded and dying cultures and environments, they inhabit a world that is contemporary and familiar. Her most common settings are the primordial Canadian wilderness – the great green whale (leviathan) of the Canadian imagination – and the artificial urban enclosures dominated by a rational, narcissistic, language-driven culture. Both provide Atwood with a powerful metaphor for a divided self in a fragmented world.

Atwood's Canadian grounding, however, has never meant insular thinking or indifference to literary and cultural movements outside of Canada and outside of social and political issues. Her writing, especially fiction, which Atwood has described as a "social vehicle" has dealt with a multiplicity of urgent questions – from the destruction of the environment, the role of women in society and the spiritual alienation caused be consumerism, to the desensitizing nature of mass culture, the loss of individual liberties, the role of the writer and the limits of fiction – all of which have been individually and in depth addressed in the present collection of essays.

Ten individuals generously and with sustained enthusiasm participated in this project; they come from several different countries, making the collection truly international in outlook. All the essays – except "*The Blind Assassin*:

Myth, History and Narration" and the interview with Margaret Atwood published here for the first time – can be found in various literary journals and specialized anthologies of criticism, though some of these are now difficult to locate. But the real advantage of gathering these into a single volume goes beyond simple convenience. Since each contributor focuses on and provides a detailed examination of a single novel, the general reader and the students of literature are given the opportunity to follow the various stages in the "novelistic" evolution of Atwood's craft and her ever-expanding thematic concerns. They will witness the process that transformed one of Canada's pre-eminent writers of fiction – admired for her unfailing commitment to social and ethical issues, who never succumbed to art for art's sake, and never severed the connection between art and life – into one of the most relevant and respected writers in the English-speaking world today. Thanks to skilful and wise guidance of the assembled contributors, the reader will marvel at the extent to which Atwood has internationalized Canada and has transformed it into an exciting real and imaginative world.

Margaret Atwood's
The Edible Woman

"Rebelling Against the System"

GAYLE GREENE

The Edible Woman is Margaret Atwood's first novel. It was not well received; its strangeness bewildered, and reviewers dismissed what they could not understand. A summary of its plot from a *Saturday Review* review suggests the nature of this reception:

> Marian MacAlpin becomes engaged to Peter, a "nicely packaged" conservative young lawyer . . . [She] picks up a graduate [student] named Duncan, who finds ironing soothing and tells Marian . . . [she is] "just another substitute for the laundromat." . . . As Marian's wedding day approaches, she begins to lose her appetite . . . A party at Peter's apartment is a disaster, and so is a night in a cheap hotel with Duncan. Eventually Marian bakes a sponge cake and molds it into the shape of a woman. She feeds it to Peter, telling him, "You've been trying to assimilate me." Her engagement broken, she feels better, and manages to eat some of the cake herself.

This reviewer concludes, "in a world where books filled with drama, passion, humanity, humour, fantasy, challenge, or even love are galloping into print, forget it" (Easton 40). Another reviewer describes the material as "thin" but "padded with tedious, irrelevant detail," and the characters as "essentially uninteresting": "There's no reason to purchase *The Edible Woman*."[1]

It is true that this novel does not deliver the customary satisfactions of popular fiction, but a writer as critical of "consumption" as Atwood is could hardly be expected to offer a "consumable" text fit for readers addicted to "stale popcorn," to use her term in "Power Politics" (143). This is not (in Roland Barthes's term) a text that allows the reader to be a passive consumer.[2] Although the novel was – as Atwood herself says – "conceived by a twenty-three-year old and written by a twenty-four-year-old,"[3] it is witty and original. In fact it is "witty" in the seventeenth-century sense of the word, in that it centers on a "conceit," an extended metaphor or series of metaphors. It offers an original combination of Dickensian social satire and black comedy, with a Marxist feminist view of human relations under capitalism. Its characters are caricatures rather than characters because Atwood is making a point about the impossibility of transcending "the system."[4]

I

The narrative is shaped by that most traditional of subjects, marriage. For much of the novel, Marian seems to be headed for a choice between Peter and Duncan, in keeping with the familiar formula described by Jean E. Kennard as "the convention of the two suitors." According to this formula the growth of a woman is marked by her choice of the right suitor over the wrong suitor, the wrong suitor embodying goals she must reject, the right suitor, those which she must accept. The convention is "inherently sexist" because it

> tends ... to imply that the good man – who, after all, held the virtues first, – is superior to the woman who can, with some effort, be taught to emulate him. The very structure of the novel places him as leader, her as follower. (Kennard 10-11, 14)

But Atwood's ending breaks with the convention, for though Marian has been incapable of doing anything except "drift" (a word which recurs) into an engagement with one man and then into an involvement with another, she finally refuses her part in this scenario.[5] The cake lady she offers her fiancé at the end is "a substitute" (278) for herself, as a sacrifice which can undergo the fate she thereby escapes – of being "morselized," in Tony Tanner's term for what happens to Emma Bovary (349-65). Marian concludes her novel not only unmarried to either man, but unpunished for her refusal to follow the forms. Though her offering makes little sense "realistically," it is a powerful symbol, a gesture of resistance to a system that would devour her.

The conservative implications of the "two-suitor convention" – as of traditional narrative resolutions of marriage or death – may be understood in terms of Roland Barthes's analysis of the "realist" ("consumable") text. Far from providing a "neutral" reflection of a pre-existent reality, "realism" is an ideologically complicit form, which appears "realistic" because it produces meaning by evoking and combining codes, which are the received ideas of the culture (*passim*). It is an inherently conservative form, which, assembled from familiar systems, reaffirms the familiar, gaining its credibility by confirming what we already know. Governed by notions of probability and possibility that are actually a tacit agreement, a contract between writer and reader signifying conformity with ideology,[6] it "does the work of ideology" by masking contradictions and containing tendencies toward change.[7] Its conventions are to some extent "determining" – Barthes refers to "the constraints of the discourse" (135) – so that even a novelist who is as critical of society's "code of woman," as is George Eliot, provides her heroines with the most conventional of endings, marriage or death. Moreover, to invoke such resolutions is actually to necessitate them, to perpetuate them as the working myths of our culture, for each invocation of a code is also its reinforcement or reinscription (Hawkes 56).

Contemporary women writers who reject society's "code of woman" seek new conventions to allow women new ways of being in the world. In her essay "What Can a Heroine Do? or Why Women Can't Write," Joanna Russ discusses "the constraints of the discourse" specifically in relation to women. She describes attempts on the part of women writers to create forms that can articulate what has been made unspeakable by the dominant literary conventions. The "lack of workable myths in literature, of acceptable dramatization of what our experience means," accounts for "unlabelled, disallowed, disavowed, not-even-consciously perceived experience, experience which has no embodiment in existing art." Russ asks,

> How to write a novel about a person to whom nothing happens? A person to whom nothing but a love story is supposed to happen? A person inhabiting a world in which the only reality is frustration or endurance – or these plus an unbearably mystifying confusion?

She discusses "two alternatives available to the woman author who no longer cares about How She Fell in Love or How She Went Mad ... (1) lyricism, and (2) life." The lyric mode (that of Virginia Woolf and Sylvia Plath) consists of

> *the organization of discrete elements* (images, events, scenes, passages, words ...) around an unspoken thematic or emotional center ... its principle of connection is *associative* ... A writer who employs the lyric structure is setting various images, events, scenes, or memories to circling around an unspoken, invisible center. The invisible center is what the novel or poem is about. That is, there is no action possible to the central character and no series of events which will embody in clear, unequivocal, immediately graspable terms what the artist means. (158)

The originality of *The Edible Woman* is in such a "lyric" construction. Though Atwood's imagery is actually more "witty" than lyrical, more like that of a metaphysical than a lyric poem, "what the novel is about" is expressed in its texture of images and ideas – in the development of a conceit (an implicit pun on "consume") from which radiates a series of images (relating to hunting and sex) to create a vision of women under capitalism. This is a novel about a person to whom nothing happens, to whom nothing can happen because in conforming to her society's ideal of "femininity," Marian is paralyzed. In the end Marian does summon herself to act, and her action "embodies what the artist means" – but baking the cake lady is effective mainly as a symbol, as a witty conceit whose very outrageousness suggests Atwood's difficulty translating vision into event.[8]

The novel thematizes two kinds of "consumption." "Consuming" is a physiological process, the ingesting and digesting of food, as in Marian's reference to "her body's consumption" (200); and it is a socio-economic process, the purchases and use of commodities, in which Marian is implicated both by being a young woman on "the market" (to use her term for sexual availability) (244) and by her work as a market researcher. As the title "Edible Woman" suggests, the idea of eating is central. Numerous scenes take place over lunch, dinner, drinks; food metaphors are everywhere, as though the novel has been written by a starving person who can think of nothing but food – which is indeed what Marian becomes when her body stops "consuming." The two meanings of "consume" are suggested by Duncan's word play on "system," when he offers his explanation for Marian's inability to eat: "'You're probably representative of modern youth, rebelling against the system; though it isn't considered orthodox to begin with the digestive system'" (197); and it is he who makes the pun explicit when, at the end, he welcomes her back "'to so-called reality'" as "'a consumer'" (286-87). Duncan's term "consumer" implies both physiological and socioeconomic meanings, both eating and participating in the social system. Atwood's analogy between the digestive and the socio-economic "systems" ("machines and mouths," in Ainsley's term) (10) suggests that a society that makes "consumption" the top priority of life – a "consumer society" – makes us prey on one another and finally "consumes" us.

A series of analogies relating "consuming" to hunting and sex creates a vision of male-female relationships in consumer capitalism. Hunting is related to eating most basically in that one hunts to eat – though in a consumer society it is also "conspicuous consumption" in being a sport requiring costly equipment (such as guns and cameras) and involving the validation of "manhood." Eating is related to sex in complex ways: food is commonly confused with love, as the diet slogan "love is not food" reminds us; and more subtly, love can become a form of devouring, as Duncan suggests, in his association of Florence Nightingale with cannibalism (102). Hunting is related to male-female relationships in the obvious sense that both involve predators and prey, and in the subtler sense of symbiosis suggested by the epigraph to "Power Politics": "You fit into me / like a hook into an eye / a fish hook / an open eye" (140). These interrelated analogies create a complex, richly allusive texture, which is as significant as what actually happens in the novel.

Like Plath's *Bell Jar* and Doris Lessing's *Martha Quest*, *The Edible Woman* portrays a world that offers little incentive for growing up. Duncan's exclamation when he sees Marian tarted up for her debut as fiancé – "'Who the hell are you supposed to be?'" (245) – points to a central question. The main characters are at crucial points in their lives when they face the decisions and commitments, personal and professional, which will determine what they "turn into" when they grow up. They are discovering that their society has no use for their best talents, that the positions open to them make them part of a "system" of "production-consumption" that – as Duncan described it – "'makes one kind of garbage into another kind'" (147). "'What else do you do with a B.A. these days?'" (15) Ainsley quips about her job as a tester of defective electric toothbrushes; and Marian echoes her remark, defending her part in the Moose Beer commercials, adding "'We all have to eat'" (55). They are discovering that the work that is available to them, far from allowing expression of their best potentials, subordinates them to a system, which diminishes them.

Marian's work at Seymour Surveys is more permanent than Ainsley's, but for this reason, it is also more threatening. Aside from the daily drudgery, Marian has questions about what she will "turn into" if she continues at it, for given the structure of the company, her options are limited. Seymour Surveys is "layered like an ice cream sandwich," with the men (executives and psychologists) upstairs, the machines below (their "operators . . . frayed and overworked"), and Marian in the all-female "gooey layer in the middle": "What, then, could I expect *to turn* into at Seymour Surveys? I couldn't become one of the men upstairs; I couldn't become a machine person" (18-19).

Besides, she suspects that the company is involved in an enterprise which is immoral and exploitative. Seymour Surveys teaches people to be consumers. By playing on anxieties, which it promises to alleviate through the power of purchasing, it creates needs and trains people to buy. "There really wasn't a single human unpleasantness left that they have not managed to turn to their uses" (177), Marian reflects, wandering like a somnambulist through the aisles of a supermarket, lulled into choosing Kleenex — "precisely what some planner . . . had hoped and predicted she would": "it was dangerous to stay in the supermarket too long. One of these days it would get her. She would be trapped past closing time [and] found in the morning in an unbreakable coma" (177-79). Her terms associate the mind-control exercised by advertising with confinement and death and suggest that she is as alienated from the product of her labour as she is from her labouring activity.

Marian's co-workers, the Office Virgins, represent what Marian will turn into at Seymour Surveys. "All artificial blonds" (20) who are transfixed by their images in mirrors

(28, 239), they await a man to liberate them. They are sketched with exaggerated strokes, differentiated in a Dickensian manner by a few physical tags. Emmy, "whisk-tinted and straggly," "sheds wispy blond hairs and flakes of scalp"; Lucy is "platinum and elegantly coiffured," with mauve eyelids; and Millie is "brassy . . . and cropped" (20-1). These epithets suggest that they are on their way to "turning" metallic or dead. Mrs. Grot of Accounting, her hair "the colour of a metal refrigerator tray" (19), has completed this metamorphosis. In the office workers' similarity to one another is the suggestion of mechanism, which makes – according to Henri Bergson – type characters comic: "wherever there is repetition or complete similarity, we always suspect some mechanism at work behind the living"; and it is this reduction of the living to mechanism that Bergson sees as the source of comedy.[9]

Since it is difficult to husband-hunt in the all-female "gooey middle" of the company, Lucy tries her luck in expensive restaurants:

> She has been lunching out expensively . . . trailing herself like a many-plumed fish-lure, with glass beads and three spinners and seventeen hooks through the likely-looking places, good restaurants and cocktail bars with their lush weedbeds of potted philodendrons, where the right kind of men might be expected to be lurking, ravenous as pike, though more maritally inclined. But these men, the right kind, weren't biting, or had left for other depths, or were snapping at a different sort of bait – some inconspicuous minnow or tarnished simple brass spoon, or something with even more feathers and hooks that Lucy could manage. And in this restaurant . . . it was in vain that Lucy displayed her delicious dresses and confectionery eyes to the tubfulls of pudgy guppies who had no time for mauve. (114)

These terms make clear the relations of sex, hunting / fishing, and catching. "How on earth did you ever catch him?" (115) Lucy asks Marian, when she hears of her engagement to Peter – a question to be asked, for as the above description suggests, the system consigns women to indirect action. Lucy's one hope for escaping Seymour Surveys is to earn enough money to adorn and display herself so that she can attract a man so that he can rescue her – an escape route that enslaves her all the more to the system she seeks to escape. But men also are locked into a cycle which has no object except "getting it over with," as is suggested by Atwood's grim description of the men Lucy imagines as her rescuers:

> – stolid breadfaced businessmen . . . gobbling their food and swilling a few drinks to get the interruption of lunch over with as soon and as numbly as possible so they could get back to the office and make some money and get that over with as soon as possible and get back through the rush hour traffic to their homes and wives and dinners and to get those over with as soon as possible too. (114)

Insofar as the daily reality is drudgery, the promises held out by advertising have the more appeal, and advertising gains power in proportion as life given over to production-consumption is dreary. The contrast between a drab present and the tantalizing promises of advertising is suggested by the juxtaposition, in the grocery store, of the girl on the poster advertising a trip to Hawaii and the cashier behind the counter. On the poster is "a semi-nude girl in a grass skirt and flowers"; behind the counter is a cashier with "a paper garland around her neck; her orange mouth . . . chewing gum. Marian watched the mouth, the hypnotic movements of the jaws, the bumpy flesh of the cheeks with their surface of dark pink makeup, the scaling lips through which glinted several rodent-yellow teeth working as with a life of their own" (179-80) – the life which is drained from the woman's skin and lips, layered and scaling, locating itself in the furiously-working teeth. Women are more targeted than men by this system because they are defined as objects and their bodies exploited in marketing techniques; because, they are valued for their appearance and so must spend vast amounts of money, time, and energy on that appearance; and because as "home-makers" they do more of the consuming. But men are also victimized by a system that defines sexual attraction as purchasing power; that tells us – in John Berger's terms – that "to be able to buy is the same thing as being sexually desirable . . . If you are able to buy this product you will be lovable" (144).[10]

The system promises to fill the hunger it creates by means of "consumption," offering magical transformations through the power of purchasing. As Berger suggests, "It proposes to each of us that we transform ourselves, or our lives, by buying"; it "offers [the buyer] an image of himself made glamorous by the product" (131-32). Advertising promises that consuming will transform us into our society's ideals of masculinity and femininity – and advertising defines these ideals for us. The Moose beer commercials promise to turn "the average . . . slope-shouldered potbellied" beer-drinker into a "real man" – defining "real" as a hunter or fisherman (25), i.e., as predator. Clara in college had a "translucent perfume-advertisement femininity" (35); Peter's appeal is that he is "like the youngish well-groomed faces of cigarette ads" (62). The girdle ad that puzzles and "slightly scandalizes" Marian – "They are so public . . . The female form, I thought, is supposed to appeal to men, not to women, and men don't usually buy girdles" – becomes understandable when Marian realizes that the "lithe young woman" is a "self-image" which promises women a magical restoration of "their own youth and slenderness" (95). As these terms suggest, advertising "steals [woman's] love of herself as she is, and offers it back to her for the price of the product" (Berger 134). Marian speculates on an even more sinister transformation when she relates the "Underwear Man's" perversion (his use of the company's underwear surveys to elicit personal information from women) to the promises of advertising:

> Perhaps [he] . . . had been crazed into frenzy by the girdle advertise-
> ments on the buses: he was a victim of society. Society flaunted these
> slender laughing rubberized women before his eyes, urging, practi-
> cally forcing upon him their flexible blandishments, and then refused
> to supply him with any. He had found when he tried to buy the gar-
> ment in question at storecounters that it came empty of the prom-
> ised contents. But instead of raging and fuming and getting nowhere
> he had borne his disappointment quietly and maturely, and had
> decided, like the sensible man he was, to go systematically in search
> of the underwear-clad image he so ardently desired. (120)

His perversion is only a "systematic" adjustment to a perverse system.

But the real transformation the system accomplishes is
to turn people into objects – a transformation Atwood renders brilliantly by means of her images. The office workers
are metamorphosizing to metal; the women in the bargain
basement have a "patina of lower-middle income domesticity, that weathered surface of slightly mangy fur . . . that
invisible colour that was like a smell, the underpainting of
musty upholstery and worn linoleum" (217) – imagery
which suggests that they become what they do. Like
Duncan, who slaves in "the paper mines" and is described
as papery, or Peter, who associates with "soapmen" and
smells like soap, people become the things of their things.
The woman who married Trigger is, according to Peter,
"predatory" and "sucking," "making [Marian] picture her as
a vacuum cleaner" (65). This vision of people "evolving . . .
to machine," "turning to metal," will be more fully developed in *Surfacing*. But in *The Edible Woman*, Atwood suggests
a reciprocal process, for as the people go dead, objects come
alive. Telephone wires are like snakes (138); the city "coag-
ulates with traffic" (103); the raw materials of Peter's apartment building are "transmuted by an invisible process of
digestion and assimilation into . . . shining skins that
enclosed space" (231); the toilet paper crouches sympathet-
ically with Marian in the ladies room, "helpless and white

21

and furry, waiting passively for the end" (71). This "principle of reciprocal changes between the human and the nonhuman" – in Dorothy Van Ghent's term – is Dickensian: as "people are described by nonhuman attributes, or by such an exaggeration of or emphasis on one part of their appearance that they seem to be reduced wholly to that part, with an effect of having become 'thinged,'" things assume a "malicious sensibility." Van Ghent's suggestive account of Dickens' world casts light on Atwood's. Like Dickens, Atwood renders the objectification of people and animation of things; as with Dickens, the process reflects actual social processes; and with both, the technique bears on the lack of complex inner life in the characters, for life is "transposed to other forms than that of human character."[11] In *The Edible Woman* the transposition of animate and inanimate has further relevance to Marian's anorexia, for in proportion as she goes dead herself, her imagination brings her environment menacingly alive.

II

Marian fears that she will be trapped and stifled in a mold she has not chosen, or that, alternatively, she will simply dissolve and cease to exist. Both possibilities are expressed imagistically, for, alienated from herself as she is, she is incapable of analyzing her feelings. She experiences the first fear (when told that she must join the Pension Plan at Seymour Surveys) as a terror of committing herself to a pre-fabricated self and future which might be, like her signature itself, confined to a small space. She expresses this as

> a superstitious panic about the fact that I had actually signed my name, had put my signature to a magic document which seemed to bind me to a future so far ahead I couldn't think about it . . . a self was waiting, pre-formed . . . [in] a bleak room . . . I thought of signature going into a file and the file going into a cabinet and the cabinet being shut away in a vault somewhere and locked. (20)

Fear of enclosure, "a pervasive imagery of maiming, dwarfing, and suffocating forced upon young girls as part of 'coming of age'" is, as Annis Pratt suggests, recurrent in women's fiction, understandable in terms of the constraints of women's lives (8). Marian's dread is intensified by the Toronto summer atmosphere "condensing around her like a plastic bag" (12), the air like soup (16), like "a layer of moist dough" (37) (an image combining claustrophobia with fear of being eaten). Such images recall the humid New York summer which is the setting of the first part of Plath's *Bell Jar* — as Marian's perception of "the elegant mannequins posturing in their bright glass cages" (174) recalls Esther Greenwood's bell jar.

Marian's second fear, her terror of dissolution, is related to her dissociation from her body.[12] This expresses itself in a dream (though Marian doesn't usually remember her dreams) which combines fear of dissolving with fear of being eaten:

> I had looked down and seen my feet beginning to dissolve, like melting jelly . . . the ends of my fingers . . . turning transparent. I had started towards the mirror to see what was happening to my face, but at that point I woke up. (43)

This sense of her potential for amorphousness accounts for her interest in shells — egg shells, pumpkin seed shells, turtle shells — things that provide shape and protection. Later in the novel, when Marian is soaking in the bathtub preparing for Peter's party, she sees her body as "a curiously-sprawling pink thing" reflected in the "silver globes" of the bath fixtures. At first not recognizing "in the bulging and distorted forms, her own waterlogged body," she has a sense that it is "no longer quite her own," that "she was dissolving, coming apart layer by layer like a piece of cardboard in a gutter puddle" (224). Mirrors and other reflecting surfaces are important to one who is unsure of her existence (66, 155), which is another way she resembles Esther Greenwood – and the distorted images these protagonists receive back are by no means reassuring.[13]

Marian's fears with regard to what she will "turn into" – being forced into a prefabricated mold, or losing shape altogether – have general implications in terms of the relation of self and society. Since identity is defined by relationship with others, on what basis can she define herself if she refuses the molds offered by society? How can she avoid being stifled, on the one hand, or ceasing to be, on the other? Each character in the novel represents a possible resolution to this problem; none is very satisfactory, since each – with the exception of Duncan – avoids one kind of conventional mold only to fall into another.

Clara is what women "turn into" after marriage – wife and mother. Though in college she had an advertisement-perfect femininity, now she is on her third pregnancy; her body, vegetable-like (117, 133), "seemed somehow beyond her, going its own way without reference to any directions of her" (36). The stairs leading to her garden, "overgrown with empty bottles of all kinds, beer bottles, milk bottles, wine and scotch bottles, and baby bottles," are more vital than she is, sitting in her garden "like a strange vegetable growth, a bulbous tuber" (30–31). When Clara urges motherhood on her, Marian recoils, seeing her situation as a trap – "Poor Clara, she was the last person whose advice would be worth anything. Look at the mess she had blundered into" – and she flees with "the sense of having escaped, as from a culvert or cave. She was glad she wasn't Clara" (155). The forces which have taken over Clara are largely physiological, but they have been reinforced psychologically by mass-market romance: her attitude toward her marriage is "complacent and embarrassing . . . sentimental, like the love stories in the back numbers of women's magazines" (134).

Ainsley, as a "quick change artist" (12), is more willing to experiment with her life than either Marian or Clara, seems at first capable of avoiding stereotypical molds. Behaving with Len like "a general plotting a major-campaign" (87) or a siege (121) — or as though she is bird-liming or spearing fish (71) — she is also able to metamorphose to a sweet young thing in pink and blue cotton gingham. But though she seems to know what she wants and how to go about getting it — she knows that "every women should have at least one baby" and that a child without parents has a better chance than a child with parents — she knows these things because she had read paperback books by experts; as she pronounces them, her voice sounds "like a voice on the radio saying that every women should have at least one electric hair-dryer" (40). When she comes across another opinion in her "Motherhood seminar," she decides that a child needs a Father Image and exchanges one trendy idea for another (186). Ainsley, the "free woman," ends married to Fish — settled into the same mold as Clara, that of mother and wife.

Peter is (according to Ainsley) "conventional" (68), but "nicely packaged" (150). Marian takes him at "face value" (62) — a metaphor which suggests both surface and money — and is drawn to his looks and to the security he represents as a young lawyer. But even Peter resists the conventional role that awaits him. At the beginning of the novel he is disconsolate because Trigger, the last of his unmarried friends, has just married: "He and Trigger had clutched each other like drowning men, each trying to make the other the reassuring reflection of himself. Now Trigger had sunk and the mirror would be empty" (26). This zanily mixed metaphor makes the point that Peter, like everyone else, needs mirrors to affirm his identity. Deprived of the person who has provided him with the desired reflection, Peter casts about frantically for another identity. Having sex with Marian in the bathtub – which Marian explains as "an attempt to assert youthfulness and spontaneity, a revolt against the stale doom" of marriage (60) – is his first effort in this direction. Marian outwardly complies, though she feels herself reduced to a "lavatory fixture" (63) and imaginatively transforms the bathtub into that most stifling of small spaces, a coffin (61). But Peter's attempts at spontaneity are in themselves "stale" since "he had read about them somewhere" – in "outdoorsy male magazines," "men's glossies," "murder mysteries" (61). In the same way that Ainsley picks up her ideas from paperbacks and Clara models her marriage on magazine romances and everyone bases their images of themselves upon advertising, Peter's ideas of "manhood" are the clichés of popular culture.

Though marriage to Peter seems to hold out the possibility of escape from Seymour Surveys, there is indication in the very events leading to the engagement that it will turn out to be another trap. Twice in the course of this evening, Marian bolts like a hunted animal, which suggests that on some level she senses that the "femininity" this marriage will require of her – "small and oval, mirrored in his eyes" (84) – is life-threatening. Twice Peter follows her into the night and retrieves her. Finally she defers to his "manly" assertions and transforms him imaginatively to her liberator: "he was changing form . . . turning from a reckless young bachelor into a rescuer from chaos, a provider of stability. Somewhere in the vault of Seymour Surveys an invisible hand was wiping away my signature" (91).

Their engagement produces a "shower" of things – "tea-towels and ladles and beribboned aprons," "china and crystal and silverware" (217). More importantly, it turns Marian into a thing: "I gave him a tender chrome-plated smile" (90); "I heard a soft flannelly voice I barely recognized, saying, 'I'd rather leave the big decisions up to you'" (92). From lavatory fixture she progresses to ashtray holder (208, 213);

on the night they become engaged, she feels like a "stage-prop . . . two-dimensional" (72), "limp as a damp Kleenex" (84); the next morning, her mind is "as empty as though someone had scooped out the inside of [her] skull like a cantaloupe and left [her] only the rind to think with" and her clothes are "scattered" and "crumbled" "like fragments left over from the explosion of some life-sized female scarecrow" (85) – the images suggesting both the mindlessness and the fragmentation which accompany her new role as object. On her way to becoming an object, she is also transforming Peter into an object – "So this object, then, belonged to *me*" (92, 150) – as indeed he is transforming her: "he sounded as though he'd just bought a shiny new car" (90); "now that she's been ringed he took pride in displaying her" (180).[14]

Ironically, her objectification as Peter's fiancée – her sense of her body as (in de Beauvoir's terms) "an object destined for another" (360) – has many of the same effects as her alienation in the world of work. With her "engagement," her alienation actually increases; and the shift in perspective from "I" to "she" indicates that her sense of herself as sexual object makes her the object of someone else's discourse.[15] This similarity between woman's position in the alienated world of work and her sexual objectification – "for women there is no distinction between objectification and alienation" – has been the subject of recent marxist-feminist discussion.[16] Moreover, Marian's acceptance of "femininity" entails a paralyzing passivity, so that rather than "getting organized" as she resolved to do at the end of Part I, she begins Part II sitting "listlessly at her desk" (109). This is why she will need to "reject her femininity" in order to survive; Peter and Ainsley both caution her against such a rejection (82, 280), and indeed, it seems to be as dangerous as the system she is rejecting, since it incurs, initially at least, the anorexia which has become epidemic since Atwood wrote this novel.

Marian's first overt rebellion occurs at dinner, while she and Peter are eating half-raw steak and discussing bringing up children. Taken back by Peter's harsh view, she senses potential violence in him and notices him watching her – "Lately he had been watching her more and more . . . as if he was trying to memorize her." She feels "mechanized":

> He was sizing her up as he would a new camera, trying to find the central complex of wheels and time mechanisms, the possible weak points, the kind of future performance to be expected: the springs of the machine. He wanted to know what made her tick. (153-54)

As he cuts his meat, she suddenly sees the steak as "flesh and blood," "part of a real cow."

Marian's starvation is both protest against and correlative to her repression of herself to fit a mold of "femininity" that requires her objectification. As she goes dead with the effort of repression, she imaginatively brings her environment alive and her refusal to consume the living things around her suggests that she has a compassion for them that she denies herself. At first her body rejects only things "that had once been, or . . . might still be living"; (183) and her concept of "living" extends to carrots, cake, and the mould growing in her sink and refrigerator. Her reduction of self to the inanimate and animation of things around her makes her incapable of distinguishing self from environment. The most powerful intimation of this occurs at the office Christmas party, an event which "consisted largely of the consumption of food and the discussion of ailments and bargains," (166), discussion of "consumption" occurring over "consumption." Marian "examined the women's bodies," observing "the mouths opening and shutting, to talk or to eat":

> What peculiar creatures they were; and the continual flux between the outside and the inside, taking things in, giving them out, chewing, words, potato chips, burps, grease, hair, babies, milk, excrement, cookies, vomit, coffee, tomato juice, blood, tea, sweat, liquor, tears,

28

and garbage. . . she was like that too, her body the same, identical, merged with that other flesh

. . . she felt suffocated by this thick sargasso-sea of femininity. She drew a deep breath, clenching her body and mind back into her self like some tactile sea-creature withdrawing its tentacles; she wanted something solid, clear: a man; . . . Marian focused on the golden bangle on [Lucy's] arm . . . drawing its hard gold circle around herself, a fixed barrier between herself and that liquid amorphous other. (171-72)

Repulsion from her own female flesh is compounded by a terror of dissolution, a sense that what the body takes in is as living as the body itself, that the environment is as alive as the organism that is ingesting and digesting it – which means that to "consume" is to be "consumed." Marian focuses on the gold bracelet as a "barrier" against dissolution, as she will later concentrate on her engagement ring (225) – a more appropriate talisman, in view of her desire for "a man" to rescue her from this "sargasso-sea of femininity." She has yet to realize that "a man" is the cause rather than the cure of this dissolution. Since, as MacGinnon suggests, "accepting one's femininity" means identifying oneself "as a sexual being, as a being that exists for men," gender for a woman is a form of non-being, an absence, a void (531) – so that to "accept one's femininity" is in some sense to realize the dissolution Marian fears. Moving from work to "love" from "public" to "private," Marian has progressed from alienation to an objectification which is also alienation: she has exchanged one trap for another, one form of non-being for another.

III

The one counter to these processes is Duncan, who is in every way Peter's antithesis. If Peter is a stereotype, Duncan is a shape-shifter, someone who deliberately changes his reality and disorients others. If Peter stays on the surfaces, Duncan "'can't concentrate on the surface'" (193). If Peter confines Marian to a stereotype, Duncan leaves her free since he simply ignores her most of the time. A graduate student, he is from another world – though Atwood presents the academic world not as contrasting to the business world, but as participating in the same futile system of production-consumption ("publish or perish") (202), which reduces people to mechanisms. Duncan is himself thingified: from slaving "in the paper-mines" (100), his skin is "the tone of old linen" (48, 148), like "tissue paper or parchment" (103); as Fish, his roommate and fellow graduate student, is reduced at the dinner party to a comically mechanized input-output system, taking in food and giving out words.

Still, it seems that Atwood intends Duncan to be, if not "authentic," at least "original," and intends us to accept that his fantasies, unlike Marian's, are "'more or less my own. I choose them and I sort of like them, some of the time'" (270). Knowing that the self and reality are fictions, he invents his rather than accepting others'. He has a genuine aversion to the "imitations" that the other characters in the novel accept or become, which is why he cannot maintain his interest in women: they become "trite," "'all those scenes have been done already. I mean *ad nauseum* . . . [women] sort of get limp and sinuous and passionate . . . and I start thinking oh god it's yet another bad imitation of whoever it happens to be a bad imitation of'" (195) – his terms suggesting that where we imagine ourselves to be most "private" and original, we are the most stereotypical.

But if Duncan is Peter's antithesis, he is in an odd way Marian's double, representing the side she has repressed in the interests of "normalcy." He comments on their physical resemblance (148); he understands her refusal to eat as "rebellion against the system"; he, too, has a sense of the power of mirrors – though unlike the other characters, he has a mirror of his own, one that he trusts. Like Marian, he feels caged; and for him, as for Marian, who feels like "a manipulator of words", (112) "'words . . . are beginning to lose their meanings'" (97). This is why he seeks nonverbal expression, ironing, which "straightens things out" – because "'I get tangled up in words'" (146).

For a while, Marian sustains a double life, her two potentials expressing themselves in her "two suitors," as is characteristic of the convention. But the night of Peter's party, she brings her lives together to precipitate a crisis. On this evening, her terror of dissolution intensifies to a hallu-cinatory panic, her sense of objectification makes her expe-rience herself as a "target in red," and she flees Peter for the third and final time.

As in the events leading to the engagement, so in her preparations for the party are indications of all that is wrong with her relationship with Peter. Soaking in the bathtub, she experiences terror of dissolution, "of losing her shape, spreading out, not being able to contain herself any longer" (225), against which she opposes "the hard circle [of the engagement ring] . . . as a protective talisman that would help keep her together" (225). She has a surreal vision of herself in the mirror between two dolls, "as though she was inside them . . . looking out," seeing herself as they would see her,

> a vague damp form in a rumpled dressing-gown, not quite focused, the blonde eyes noting the arrangement of her hair, her bitten fin-gernails, the dark one looking deeper, at something she could not quite see, the two overlapping images drawing further and further away from each other; the centre, whatever it was in the glass, the thing that held them together, would soon be quite empty. (225-26)

Again she transposes life to the environment, but in this case, her rage seems to leak out into the things around her, endowing the dolls with destructive and malevolent power; and so extreme is her dissociation that she allies herself with them against herself.

It is appropriate that a hairdo and dress that make her feel like a "callgirl" (216) is the right costume she chooses for her first public occasion with Peter, and that Peter's response is "yum, yum." At the beauty salon, she feels that she is being operated on "like a slab of flesh, an object," and notices the women "under identical whirring mushroom shaped mechanisms . . . Inert, totally inert . . . [being turned to a] compound of the simply vegetable and the simply mechanical. An electric mushroom" (215). The terms of this description jumble the human and mechanical, the animate and inanimate, sentient and insentient, in a way that fulfills Marian's terror of dissolution. The images Marian glimpses of herself in these scenes also suggest that her worst fears, of confinement as well as of dissolution, have been realized: she feels "prisoned in the filigreed gold oval of the mirror" at the beauty parlor (215); and in the mirror on Peter's closet door, she cannot see herself whole. "Only able to see one thing at a time," she cannot grasp "the various parts of her face" (235), and the sense of fragmentation that began with her engagement intensifies. She no longer even knows what part of her is real: her arms, "the only portion of her flesh that was without a . . . covering . . . looked fake, like soft pinkish-white rubber or plastic" (235). She resents Peter's clothes "hang [ing] there smugly asserting so much invisible silent authority" (236). As a woman, such "authority" is not available to her: her options have been to use clothes as "camouflage . . . protective coloration" (12), as she does at the beginning, or to adorn herself as sexual object, as she does after her engagement. The latter has proved the more dangerous, reducing her to a "tiny two-dimensional small figure in a red dress, posed like a paper woman in a mail-order catalogue, turning and smiling, fluttering in the white empty space" (250) – diminished, dissolving, tawdry, for sale.

At this point Peter's attempt to "shoot" her throws her into a panic. The word "shoot" (238) brings together the functions of cameras and guns, Peter's dual obsessions. These are related in that both entrap, one framing and the other killing; and both are associated, here, as in *Surfacing*, with the imposition of men's wills upon nature and women. Marian now perceives the one to be as lethal as the other, realizing that the stereotype she is about to be fixed in will kill her: "Once he pulled the trigger she would be stopped, fixed indissolubly in that gesture, that single stance, unable to move or change" (252). The Peter who had promised liberation from the vaults of Seymour Surveys now threatens to pinion her in another frame, which she envisions as a billboard; "she sensed her face as vastly spreading and papery and slightly dilapidated . . . a huge billboard smile, peeling away in flaps and patches, the metal surface beneath showing through . . ." (251). All her paranoiac fantasies now focus on Peter, the enemy, hunter, killer (perhaps even the Underwear Man), "tracing, following, stalking her" (253). Nor are these terrors extreme, in view of what MacGinnon describes as the fine line between "abuses of woman and the social definition of what a woman is" (532).

As she flees Peter's party to find Duncan in the laundromat, her escape route takes the not very original form of leaving one man for another. She imagines that she is seeking "reality" in Duncan, but this "reality" shapes itself to another stereotypical mold, as she tries to become his rescuer: "'You need me more than he does.'" Duncan assures her that he does not need to be rescued – or to rescue her (254). Though he has encouraged her fantasy ("every woman loves an invalid. I bring out the Florence Nightingale in them" [p. 102]), he explodes it by telling her, after they make love, that she was not his first woman, thereby invalidating the only self-image remaining to her: "The starched nurse-like image of herself she had tried to preserve as a last resort crumbled like wet newsprint" (271).

Though the next morning Marian shows signs of capitulating and returning to Peter, her body prevents her by "cut[ing] itself off" (264) from all foods. Her way home is blocked by her intimation of life lurking in the sink, something "living, hidden and repulsive, down there among the plates and dirty glasses" (265) – her imagination transforming the mould to a menacing force. When Duncan withdraws, she is left to her own device – a device that she knows must be nonverbal, "something that avoided words . . . Some way she could know what was real" (274).

The image of the cake lady takes shape in the supermarket. As she bakes it (choosing a simple grey frock for the task), she submits it to the same processes to which she herself has been submitted. She prepares "to operate" (276) as she herself was operated on in the beauty parlor, "passive," "anaesthetized," "inert," "etherized" (215-16). She nips in the waist, as she herself was "corseted" (227), and turns the icing to hair, a mass of "intricate baroque scrolls and swirls," as her own hair was "treated like a cake . . . iced and ornamented" (214). She "scoops out part of it and makes a head" (276), as her own head was "scooped out" the morning after she became engaged to Peter (84); she sticks "all the separate members together" (276), indicating her awareness that her own fragmentation has verged on dismemberment. She then cooks the cake, as she was herself "gently fried" (216), addressing it, "'You look delicious . . . Very appetizing. And that's what will happen to you; that's what you get for being food'" (277-78).

When Peter flees, she concludes that "As a symbol it has definitely failed" (279). But she is wrong, for as a symbol of Marian's control over processes which have been controlling her, it succeeds; and as a "reality" it has a certain therapeutic value, for in the final section, Part III, Marian is able to return to the first person pronoun, to clean house, to become sufficiently interested in herself to be bored by Duncan's self-involvement ("Now that I was thinking of

myself in the first person singular again I found my own situation much more interesting than his" [284]). Most important, she can eat again, and she looks, as Duncan says, "'jaun-
ty and full of good things'" – though his association of her
eating with a return to consumerism is somewhat ominous.

IV

Though Atwood has expressed certain ambivalences about
feminism, *The Edible Woman* is profoundly feminist in its
exposure of attitudes that legitimize and mystify women's
status. In 1973, Atwood expressed a reluctance to ally herself with "ideological" positions on the basis of a distinction
between "art" and "propaganda":

> The aim of propaganda is to convince and to spur people to action;
> the aim of fiction and poetry writing is to create an . . . imaginative
> world . . . to concentrate on life not as it ought to be, but as it is, as
> the writer feels it, experiences it . . . not what, according to the ide-
> ology, ought to exist.

Skeptical of what she calls "someone else's ideology –
indeed of any ideology – she implies that "imaginative" literature is without ideology; that it reflects life "as it is"
rather than "as it ought to be"[17] But as Barthes's analysis of
the realist novel suggests, all literary forms imply ideological positions; and to claim that they do not is in itself to take
an ideological position. And Atwood knows this, for whatever her protestations about "imaginative" literature, what
she actually does in this novel is modify novelistic conventions in ways that suggest her awareness of the ideology of
forms; and whatever her reservations about feminism, what
she actually shows is that gender is constructed by a system
that exploits both sexes in its need to sell. People are shaped
so predictably by this system that they are reduced to comic
clichés, mechanized in a way that is, according to Bergson,
the cause of laughter.[18]

Marian's cake lady is a gesture of defiance, a way of saying no to a system that defines women as commodities and devours them. It is a refusal of her role as "sugar and spices" – "sugar," "sugar pie," "sweetheart," "sweetie," "sweetie-pie," "honey," "dish," "tart" or "tomato" – and of the fate to which female characters have succumbed through the ages. No Cressida she, who, defined by the men in her play as "cake" to be "leavened," "kneaded," "baked," and "made" (1.1.15–16), ends in Troilus's final designation, as "fragments, scraps" (5.2.159), "food for fortune's tooth" (4.5.293). Nor will she be Miss Havisham, who, indistinguishable from her mouldy wedding cake, waits to be devoured;[19] nor Emma Bovary, who "by the end . . . is in every way *morcelee*," by the males in her novel, by her writer, by her world.[20] But it is difficult to see what Marian *will* be when she grows up, what she will do – what, in the terms of the novel, she will turn into." Her gesture works at the level of symbol, but it is difficult to see how this symbol will translate to action.[21]

Like other contemporary women writers who have rejected the old rules, Atwood is concerned with finding new conventions to express new possibilities. As the narrator of *Surfacing* says, "The word games, the winning and losing games, are finished; at the moment there are no others but they will have to be invented" (223). But – and this is the case with other novels by contemporary women writers – the difficulty of conceiving of alternatives is apparent in the ending.[22] As Duncan suggests the return to "reality" makes Marian "a consumer" again, and though this is satisfactory in immediate physiological terms, in terms of her body's health it is not satisfactory in the long-term psychological or socio-economic sense. Not only does it not resolve the larger problems the novel has raised, but it suggests a certain contradiction in terms of Atwood's conceit, for in becoming a consumer in the socio-economic sense, Marian resumes her place in a system that threatens her life.

In becoming a consumer, Marian evolves — in the terms of the novel — from prey to predator. As the narrator of *Surfacing* says, "there ought to be other choices" (220) — and like that protagonist, she ends poised on the edge of an uncertain future.

NOTES

1. These comments are made by Avant. Easton also calls the novel "tedious . . . rambling" and refers to its "trite characterization and lack of plot." Her summary is quoted by *Book Review Digest*, 1970. Stedmond similarly calls "the characters . . . fairly stock," and the novel's "potentialities . . . disappointingly unrealized."

2. "Barthes terms the realist text "*lisible*" and describes it as an object for consumption that makes the reader a passive consumer. He contrasts this to the "*scriptible*" text, which is "process" rather than "product," open to being "written" rather than merely read, and which is capable of providing a genuine challenge to ideology.

3. Atwood adds that the novel's "more self-indulgent grotesqueries are perhaps attributable to the youth of the author, though I would prefer to think that they derive instead from the society by which she found herself surrounded." See *Second Words*.

4. Sandler describes the characters as "outgrowths of their society" (24).

5. For "drift" see *The Edible Woman* (106, 108, 118-19). Atwood comments on her variation of convention, though of a different sort of convention, in her description of the novel as "anti-comedy": "In traditional comedy, boy meets girl. There are complications, the complications are resolved, and the couple is united. In my book the couple is united and the wrong couple gets married. The complications are resolved, but not in a way that reaffirms the social order" (Sandler 13-14).

6. Miller discusses notions of probability and possibility as determining the shapes of fictions, specifically in relation to women's fictions. She refers to Genette's discussion of "plausibility" and "probability," "*vraisemblance*" and "*bienseance*" (74. 36).

7. See Belsey (46, 52, 72).

8. Atwood acknowledges this disjunction: Marian "commits an action, a preposterous one in a way, as all pieces of symbolism in a realistic context are" (Gibson 20-21). See Grace's description of the novel's "mixed style" — its mixture of realism and "the extravagant, and primarily symbolic" — and her account of the novel as a somewhat unsuccessful combination of "the conventions of realism and romance" (91, 95, 87).

9. Bergson describes the laughable as "a certain mechanical inelasticity" (67), "something mechanical encrusted upon the living" (92): "We laugh every time a person gives us the impression of being a thing" (97); "The attitudes, gestures, and movements of the human body are laughable in exact proportion as that body reminds us of a mere machine" (79 and 82).

10. Atwood's affinity with Berger's work, which was published a few years after *The Edible Woman*, is suggested by her epigraph to *Bodily Harm*, quoted from it: "A man's presence suggests what he is capable of doing to you or for you. By contrast, a woman's presence . . . defines what can and cannot be done to her."

11. See Van Ghent, *The English Novel: Form and Function, Great Expectations*, especially pp. 158-61. See also "The Dickens World: A View from Todgers's."

12. Such concern with dissolution is, like the terror of confinement, also frequent in women's literature. Analyses by Chodorow and Gilligan suggest that women's ego boundaries are less fixed than men's. The works of contemporary women writers reflect this, but what is terrifying to Marian (and presumably to Atwood) is for other novelists a cause of celebration. In Lessing's *The Golden Notebook*, Anna Wulf's breakdown is a break through to new areas of herself, and in *The Waterfall*, Jane Gray is delighted when sexual passion provides a release from the confines of personality.

13. See *The Bell Jar* (14, 92, 142), for Esther Greenwood's distorted reflections.

14. "What a crazy binge of objects a wedding produces," as Frances Wingate marvels in. Drabble's *The Realms of Gold* (124); and her speculations on the function of things in the marriage ritual are relevant here.

15. Drabble's *The Waterfall*, written the same year as *The Edible Woman*, uses the same narrative device, also to explore the various relations of the protagonist to herself.

16. See MacKinnon (540-41).

17. See Atwood's "Paradoxes and Dilemmas, the Woman as Writer," in *Woman as Writer*. Atwood does qualify this two years later, admitting that "feminism" can encompass "telling it like it is" as well as "telling it like it should be" (186).

18. Shakespeare's *Troilus and Cressida* is nearly as full of food imagery as is this novel, and in that work also, such imagery is commentary on "the spirit of capitalism" which "busily reduces life to the demands of the belly" (in Southall's terms [226]). See my "Shakespeare's Cressida: A Kind of Self," References are to *The Riverside Shakespeare*.

19. Van Ghent cites Miss Havisham as exemplary of the process of conversion she sees as typical of Dickens: guilty of using people as things, she is "changed retributively into a fungus"; and "'When the ruin is complete,' Miss Havisham says, pointing to the cake but referring to herself, she will be laid out on the same table and her relatives will be invited to 'feast on' her corpse'" (161).

20. "Morselization" begins with "the first description of [Emma's] appearance amidst an environment of "textures and elements" in which she is "effectively, incubated," and which "in different forms . . . determine the shape of her subsequent life, which is endlessly involved in permutations of clothes, 'metallicism' or threatening male 'instruments' of various kinds" (349). "She is 'morselized' by Charles's eye and by Flaubert's text. Alike, they register the parts with careful and minute attention, but . . . miss the whole, which is not to be found in the sum of the separate items" (351). "The male world is constantly looking at Emma in various kinds of detached, calculating fashions" (353); "She must and can only 'bend' under [its matrix] to the shapes, postures, and positions that it offers, imposes, or dictates. Thus her bodily curves offer themselves for the curvings (social and sexual) of the men who will form (and deform) her life" (354-55).

21. Rule calls the cake "a metaphorical trick rather than a real resolution" but does not see anything wrong with this because she sees the novel as "farce," "not meant as a vehicle for too much serious criticism of consumer society or of the war between the sexes"; if the "author's intent [were] serious," it would be "dangerous" to offer a "metaphorical resolution to a real problem." But I think Atwood's intentions are serious and her ending is unsatisfactory – though this can certainly be understood in terms of the difficulty of conceiving of alternatives to the problems she had depicted.

22. Cf. Atwood's description of the ending: "It's noteworthy that my heroine's choices remain much the same at the end of the book as they are at the beginning; a career going nowhere, or marriage as an exit from it" (*Second Words* 370). Other novels by contemporary women writers have similarly unsatisfactory endings, indicating a similar inability on the part of the author to imagine resolutions to the problems they have analyzed. Some end abruptly with the sense that not much of anything has been worked out (Jong's *Fear of Flying*); some end where they begin, their circular movement suggesting little or no development (Godwin's *Odd Woman*, Lessing's *The Grass Is Singing*); others consign their heroines to situations they have exposed as untenable (Lessing's *The Summer Before the Dark*).

WORKS CITED

Atwood, Margaret. *The Edible Woman*. New York: Warner Books, 1983.

——. Introduction to the Virago Modern Classic Edition of *The Edible Woman*. 1981. Rpt. *Second Words: Selected Critical Prose*. Boston: Beacon, 1984.

——. *Margaret Atwood: Selected Poems*. New York: Simon and Schuster, 1976.

——. "Paradoxes and Dilemmas, the Woman as Writer." *Woman as Writer*. Eds. Jeanette L. Webber and Joan Grumman. Boston: Houghton Mifflin, 1978. 178–87.

——. *Surfacing*. New York: Fawcett, 1972.

Avant, John Alfred. Rev. of *The Edible Woman*, by Margaret Atwood. *Library Journal*. 15 Sept. 1970: 2934.

Barthes, Roland. *S/Z*. New York: Hill and Wang, 1974.

Belsey, Catherine. *Critical Practice*. London: Methuen, 1980.

Berger, John. *Ways of Seeing*. London: BBC and Penguin, 1977.

Bergson, Henri. "Laughter." *Comedy*. Ed. Wylie Sypher. New York: Doubleday, 1956.

Chodorow, Nancy. *The Reproduction of Mothering: Psychoanalysis and the Sociology of Gender*. Berkeley: U of California P, 1978.

de Beauvoir, Simone. *The Second Sex*. Trans. and ed. M. Parshley. New York: Vintage, 1974.

Drabble, Margaret. *The Realms of Gold*. New York: Knopf, 1975.

Easton, Elizabeth, Rev. of *The Edible Woman*, by Margaret Atwood. *Saturday Review*, 3 Oct. 1970: 40.

Evans, G. Blakemore, ed. *The Riverside Shakespeare*. Boston: Houghton Mifflin, 1974.

Genette, Gerard. "Vraisemblance et motivation." *Figures II*. Paris: Sueil, 1969.

Gibson, Graeme. "Margaret Atwood." *Eleven Canadian Novelists*. Toronto: Anasi, 1973. 5–31.

Gilligan, Carol. *In A Different Voice: Psychological Theory and Women's Development*. Cambridge: Harvard UP, 1983.

Grace, Sherrill. *Violent Duality: A Study of Margaret Atwood*. Montreal: Véhicule, 1980.

Greene, Gayle. "Shakespeare's Cressida: 'A Kind of Self'" "The Woman's Part": *Feminist Criticism of Shakespeare*. Ed. Carolyn Ruth Swift Lenz, Gayle Greene, and Carol Thomas Neely. Urbana: U of Illinois P, 1980. 133–49.

Hawkes, Terrence. *Structuralism and Semiotics*. London: Methuen, 1977.

Kennard, Jean E. *Victims of Convention*. Hamden, CT: Archon books. 1978.

MacKinnon, Catherine A. "Feminism, Marxism, Method, and the State: An Agenda for Theory." *Signs*. 7.3 (1982): 515-44.

Miller, Nancy K. "Emphasis Added: Plots and Plausibilities in Women's Fiction." *PMLA* 96 (1981): 36-48.

Plath, Sylvia. *The Bell Jar*. New York: Bantam, 1981.

Pratt. Annis. *Archetypal Patterns in Women's Fiction*. Bloomington: Indiana UP, 1981.

Rule, Jane. "Life, Liberty, and the Pursuit of Normalcy: The Novels of Margaret Atwood." *Malahat Review*, 41, (1977): 42-49.

Russ, Joanna. "What Can a Heroine Do? or Why Women Can't Write. *Images of Women in Fiction*. Ed. Susan Koppelman Cornillon. Bowling Green, OH: Bowling Green U Popular P. 1972. 3-30.

Sandler, Linda. "Interview with Margaret Atwood." *Malahat Review*. 41 (1977): 7-27.

Southall, Raymond. "*Troilus and Cressida* and the Spirit of Capitalism." *Shakespeare's Changing World*. Ed. Arnold Kettle. New York: International Publishers, 1964. 217-32.

Stedmond, John. Rev. of *The Edible Woman*, by Margaret Atwood *The Canadian Forum* Feb. 1970: 26.

Tanner, Tony. "The Morselization of Emma Bovary." *Adultery in the Novel: Contract and Transgression*. Baltimore: Johns Hopkins UP, 1979. 349-65.

Van Ghent, Dorothy. "The Dickens World: A View from Todgers's." *Sewanee Review* 58 (1960): 419-38.

——. *The English Novel: Form and Function*. New York: Harper and Row, 1953.

Paradox of Discourse
in Margaret Atwood's *Surfacing*

BRANKO GORJUP

Margaret Atwood's second novel, *Surfacing*, has been around for more than twenty-five years. During this time it has received considerable popular and critical attention, and has undoubtedly contributed more than any other of Atwood's subsequent novels to her central position in contemporary Canadian writing. Generations of students of Canadian literature, myself included, have accepted the work as one of the canonized texts that most powerfully represents English Canada's prototypical search for identity. Because of its uncomplicated and symmetrical structure, it's carefully positioned characters − each a reflection and a refraction of a simultaneously contemporary and archetypal reality − *Surfacing* easily falls into the category of a novel-cum-text book − a wonderful tool for showing how a sensibility is constructed and how elements in literature work. Yet, in spite of its seeming simplicity, *Surfacing* has continued to fascinate with its tendency to elude the reader's desire for conclusion, with its mysterious quality for further exegesis.

I have been drawn to revisit *Surfacing* in part by this elusiveness of the work itself, and in part by having repeatedly in my various readings stumbled on the trope of an over-dressed woman as a pictorial representation of rhetoric. It was this "woman" − this excessively made-up, superfluously costumed image of speech that took me back to Atwood's unnamed protagonist in *Surfacing*, and to her obsession with the denuding of the language that she felt had suffocated her essential self. The paradox of representation of rhetoric as female − historically a male invention and activity −

became immediately obvious to me. While, on the one hand, this female is equated with a harlot, an archetypal seductress whose tool is linguistic deceit, she is on the other hand – and this is where the paradox resides – condemned to silence, to serving as a substitute for the homo rhetoricus, the silver-tongued patriarch.

In this essay I will argue that in *Surfacing* the protagonist's prime task is to disrupt the male discourse as it parades itself in the "female clothes" and to investigate its narrative "reliability" by turning it upon itself, showing its narcissistic posturing. It is of considerable significance that the protagonist / narrator, while controlling the text as she shapes it, works in two directions: she deconstructs the homo rhetoricus – the rational Western verbal cosmology – and reveals her own unreliability as the teller of her own tale. At once, she delegitimizes the "autonomy" of the text and the self-sufficiency of the subject. Thus, *Surfacing* can be read as a predominantly ironic tale, in which irony is used as a destabilizing factor, rendering the narrator's construct inconclusive.

I will begin by discussing the meaning of the protagonist's escape and / or displacement from a rhetorical / rational civilization, which has historically denied women a full discursive identity, and conclude by offering an interpretation of the novel's ambiguous resolution – the protagonist's reentry into the world of speech after she had briefly opted for a pre-language state of elemental nature. While the protagonist physically sets out to "correct" the future, the shift in her perception is metaphorically represented by a journey backward in time and into the primordial wilderness – a world yet to be articulated and named. The point of arrival seems the same as the point of departure, identified with the moment in which the protagonist is poised[1] to recover her essential self by giving birth, one presumes, to a female child, to herself, and to the new female, all at once. Atwood's discourse in *Surfacing* presents itself as the crisis of identity, as anxiety that lay concealed behind the protagonist's dramatic and well-dramatized rejection of and withdrawal from a socially interactive life. She is continually caught between two powerful forces that shape her worldview, between the rhetorical and the essential selves. The rhetorical self that also shapes the narrative, tells, on the one hand, the tale of a linguistic deconstruction by a woman who proceeds to escape the confusing, meaningless and demeaning reality of signs, words, and metaphors. She responds to what Anne McClintock describes as a typically Lacanian vision of women – being "unrepresentable," being "forbidden citizenship in the Symbolic, exiled from archives and encyclopedias, the sacred texts and algebras, the alphas and omegas of history" (192-193). On the other hand, the rhetorical self tells the story of how the same woman, after she had disavowed language and narrative as a means of communication – albeit only temporarily – succeeds in creating the conditions for her essential self to break free. The protagonist's disavowal of speech is significant because it identifies social discourse not as something sanctioned by nature, fate or God, but rather as a deliberately constructed artifice open to re-evaluation and change.

The protagonist initiates the transformation from the rhetorical to the essential self by drifting into the dark dimension of an incantatory animalistic ritual which, once she has made her point and has had her vision, must itself be transcended if the essential self is to be fully realized. Being foremost a socially responsible writer, Atwood dismisses the elemental alternative, the classical Canadian wilderness. Like the pastoral, the elemental, its opposite – which Atwood has systematically subverted throughout her entire body of work – cannot be a permanent home; it can only serve as a stop-over point to somewhere else. Atwood knows well that the elemental or the primitive is only a part of a larger Western paradigm to which the rhetorical or the rational also belongs. Thus, if the elemental alternative were accepted, the essential self would correspond to a woman turned beast or, even worse, to a being condemned to reside within an ontological void.

For this obvious reason, there must be recovery, a recovery made possible through language — "new" language? "new" discourse? — so that the struggle between the two selves, each dependent on the other, can be transformed into a continual critical dialogue. From the ashes of the burnt words, a new narrative will be reconstructed. The protagonist knows that to abandon the world of communication is to divest herself of what alone makes life tolerable — her social human condition. Ultimately, she knows that she cannot be entirely freed from the rhetorical self because it represents half of human being, that half which maintains society in a working state. But she also knows that the rhetorical self must be demystified, that it must undergo decisive change in order to more accurately represent the inclusion of the female into general discourse.

Let us proceed from the assumption that in *Surfacing* language articulates itself around the central theme of the atrophy of communication. This may seem itself a paradox — "articulation" and "atrophy of communication" occurring simultaneously. But, in effect, it is not. What it suggests is that Atwood "describes" experiences of her protagonist using the same language the protagonist discards as deceptive, which is, of course, a form of complicity. Atwood's approach to writing in *Surfacing* is one of verbal reductionism. The novel is conceived in such a way as to follow a line of regression. The protagonist's rhetorical self begins by moving out and away from a verbal universe towards an ambiguous non-verbal, elemental world. This movement, or a move from one into another representational world, establishes the novel's binary structure which, according to J. Brooks Bouson, has made some feminists uneasy. He quotes

Jessica Benjamin's remark: "Every binary split creates a temptation to merely reverse its terms, to elevate what has been devalued and denigrate what has been overvalued." What has been, for Bouson, elevated in *Surfacing* is "nature-defined femininity" and what has been devalued is "masculinity, culture, and the rational" (50).

But *Surfacing* also relies on the structural mechanism of a quest novel and its central mystical objective of rebirth. Disguised in the twentieth century sensibility, however, the outward manifestation of the quest structure requires that the protagonist's rhetorical self shed its rational consciousness as it advances towards rebirth. As soon as the rational universe is affected, language, its outward and visible sign, is affected as well. The "transformation of consciousness and the transformation of language," as Northrop Frye has remarked regarding this phenomenon of mutual attractiveness, "can never be separated" (226). The derationalizing of the language, one has to remember, has been in one way or another one of the most powerful cultural impulses in the twentieth century.

The novel's emotional centre is the protagonist's profound distrust of language, which gradually transforms itself into an obsession with discarding the word altogether. The language she inherits at birth, with all its subsumed cultural conventions, ceases to be an adequate discursive vehicle. It is perceived, to use Hofmannthal's expression, as a "myopic shorthand" (178), hollow rhetorical constellation of meaningless signs. In fact, the protagonist goes a step further: she identifies the established language as her enemy — the tool of alienation and isolation, the prison of her essential self. At the outset of the journey, the split between words and what they represent emotionally and conceptually is immediately noticeable. While the protagonist attempts to make sense of the chaotic language of advertisements and graffiti lining the road that is supposed to lead her back to her ancestral past, she realizes, and not without irony, that these same signs, if x-rayed, "would be the district's entire history"(Atwood 15).[2] However, a more profound sense of linguistic alienation occurs when the protagonist admits her ignorance of the French language – one of the two official languages of Canada. She describes herself as a misfit in a context in which she should feel at home:

> Now we're on my home ground, foreign territory. My throat constricts, as it learned to do when I discovered people could say words that would go into my ears meaning nothing. (11)

The metaphor of constriction is further enhanced when she discovers she is unable to communicate with her companion in her native English. The words she uses seem "imported, foreign . . ." The act of speaking turns unnatural, physically distorted as her "mouth jump[s] like a stutterer's" (150).

Language is presented not only as the impediment to discourse, but also, and more important, as Frank Davey noted, as a powerful means to "humiliate each other, seduce one another, or to betray bigotry and ignorance" (77). The characters' discourse remains on the level of reciprocal frustration, imposture and deceit. The words in circulation are hard, uncompromising, described as dangerous arms aimed at destruction. For example, for Joe, one of the male characters, speech is a task and the words he uses are "heavy and square like tanks"(77). Although not as fully aware as the protagonist is of the futility of the spoken word, Joe is nevertheless described as being in a perpetual state of *lapsus linguae*. Speech for him remains a task.

Not so for David, the other male character, whose role is to act as an archetypal embodiment of everything that went wrong with the twentieth-century rhetorical man. His body decays with the infection of words:

47

> He [is] an impostor, a pastiche, layers of political handbills, pages from magazines, affiches, verbs and nouns glued on to him and shredding away the original surface littered with fragments and tatters. (152)

In order to get him "where he was true," to find in him "his own forgotten language" beneath the surface of its "copy," the protagonist feels she will have to "scrape" him down, "unearth him"(152). Here she reveals the notion that the transformation of an individual is possible through a regression to a pre-lingual state, thus foreshadowing her own rebirth. David's other function is to remind the protagonist of the enormity of the task she has undertaken in order to unearth her own essential self.

To reinforce the *papier-mâché* image of David, the protagonist comments on his "slap-dash" documentary Random Samples, which intensifies the already existing subject-object alienation inherent in the use of speech. Like language, film collects and randomly freezes life experiences into images capable of neither capturing nor communicating their mystery. David's cinematic expression is as trivial as his verbal one. However, beyond the trivial often resides something much more sinister than expected. When David refers to Anna's disloyalty he suppresses his pain by degrading her – objectifying her as "a cunt on four legs," "a pair of boobs," "a twatface." While David's speech shows how discrimination and oppression are effectively encoded into language, the narrator increasingly, as Bouson detected, "expresses indignation at the masculinist culture which reduces woman to a voyeuristic, pornographic spectacle and to fetishized fragmented body parts" (50).

Having thus foregrounded the sterility and the manipulative character of language, Atwood sends her protagonist to revitalize the power and the magic of the word, a task easily identified with that of the author herself. The process involves the gradual shedding of her rhetorical identity

48

which, like David's, may reveal the "forgotten language." Returning to the origins of language, she may rediscover its integrity. Like Frye, Atwood believes that in *illo tempore*, at the root of civilization and one's life (childhood), meaning and sign form an indivisible unity. This explains the protagonist's journey backwards through the debris of what once was a unified humanistic – read also patriarchal – verbal universe to the point in time before "the ancient metaphor [became] inert and the numinous energies bone-dry" (Steiner 178). Hence in *Surfacing*, the importance of the pictograph that the protagonist drew as a child is obvious. A pictograph, like a hieroglyph, establishes unity between image and word, between pictorial and verbal representation.

The journey of recovery of her verbal origins and beyond, towards an altogether non-verbal system of symbols, assumes eventually not only a physical manifestation but also an intensely hieratic and ritualistic one. The protagonist ceases to be an observer who merely contemplates the given reality of human experience and begins to actively participate in the deconcealment of its essential values. She strips away the multiple layers of masculinist conventions which are designed to rationalize the meaning of life, epitomized by, to borrow Frye's words, an egocentric or Cartesian consciousness. This consciousness is, both in Atwood and Frye, equated with "Americanism" and its mechanistic, technological civilization.[3]

Her primary attack is however aimed at the printed page. It is not surprising that she starts by discarding her latest typescript, "a caseful of alien words" (164), thus canceling out a potential link to the existing verbal universe. She continues the ritual of destruction, this time aimed at her father's library books: "I rip one page from each of the books..., to burn through all the words would take too long...[T]hese husks are not needed any longer, I abolish them, I have to clear a space" (177). "I rip one page from each of the books" is a symbolic gesture, for each page stands for all language. The fact that action takes place in the present tense — "I rip" — underlines the timelessness of the ritualistic act.

The next stage of the quest is an inward descent, an intensely private search for some hidden internal verbal structure, analogous to David's "forgotten language," communicated in a rigorously subjective mood, cryptic and fragmentary in response to the linguistic demands of the others. The protagonist's eventual collapse into verbal apathy and muteness suggests the limits of language, its inability to externally formulate her inner turmoil. This is the point at which the protagonist moves from a verbal to a non-verbal consciousness, from a rhetorical to an essential self, while the novel, on the level of narrative, struggles to formulate her experience from without. As she passes beyond the inner verbal domain towards a primordial, unspeakable, wordless state of being, her outward expression dissolves into a ritualistic frenzy. The language of the novel becomes almost undone, almost a non-language — hence the empty spaces between words and broken sentences — approximating a ceremonial mumbling. The sentences break up into repetitive expression that attempts to utter what cannot be said. Frederic Jameson's notion that such subjective experience cannot be really conveyed through language, but only designated "like a symptom," illuminates Atwood's difficulty in pushing her narrative along (143).

The protagonist's rejection of language is analogous to her desire to discard her humanness and slide into natural otherness:

The animals have no need for speech, why talk when you are a word
I lean against a tree, I am a tree leaning...I am not an animal or a tree,
I am the thing in which the tree and animals move and grow, I am a
place. (181)

At this crucial moment in the novel, Atwood takes her heroine into an area of experience where the subject and the object, the perceiver and the perceived become one – "I lean against a tree, I am a tree leaning . . ." Although the unity of the self with the outer world has been temporarily achieved on the elemental level, and the essential self proclaimed as being "a place," the demands of the rhetorical self seeking verbal expression are still felt. Atwood answers these demands by rendering the protagonist's experience on the level of metaphor. According to Frye's definition of metaphor, the identification of the protagonist in *Surfacing* with the tree or the place – can be treated as a "functional metaphor," which can not be "understood" unless we "surrender precision for flexibility" (56). When the protagonist says or (thinks) "I am a place," the reader is confronted with the same ambiguity as when Christ says "I am the wine." At such point, Frye maintains, it is up to the reader to either accept the metaphorical or "polisemous" meaning, or to seek explanation by "translating" the metaphor into "metonymic language" (51-57).

Had the novel ended at this point, when the protagonist achieves the magic union with her environment – "I am a place" – and when the author has transformed descriptive language into metaphorical, the ending would have been ambiguous in a polisemous sense, open to an infinite number of responses. But the novel does not end here. Atwood manipulates her protagonist out of her state of trans and back into a state of consciousness in which she must confront a more prosaic dilemma: either "the hospital or the zoo." Not surprisingly, she opts for the "hospital."

The reader is left, however, with Atwood's explanation justifying the protagonist's choice of joining the human "hospital," a justification that can be stated as follows. From the beginning of the journey, the protagonist is consci...

of the fact that the moment a word is used to name or describe something other than oneself, a distance between subject and object appears. To bridge the gap between these two, analogous to obliterating the distance between the word as sign and the word as meaning, the two must be identified as one. Having rejected the empty language of her time, symbolized by the rhetorical effigy – this time in the shape of a masculine "hag," the bullying David – made of borrowed words and phrases, she begins the process of linguistic reduction, a process that would facilitate the reconstruction of the essential self. However, in spite of her better judgment, as we are led to believe, she discovers that reduction to the essentials, to a pre-rhetorical self, can equate with a reduction to absurdity. Thus, in the confrontation with the mirror, almost at the end of the novel, the protagonist recognizes that the "natural woman" (190) cannot exist in a social context. What the mirror points out is the split between herself as an animal and as a human being rather than the integration of the two: "that is the real danger now, the hospital or the zoo" (190). The paradox of the rhetorical and essential self remains as the protagonist re-enters her own time and accepts "the intercession of words" (192) as a neccessary requirement for participation in society.

The split between language and non-language can be best explained in terms of a split between the author and the protagonist. Incidentally, it is within this duality that the novel's affirmative aspect is implicit. The author's conviction that language has a social function is shown in her concern to communicate to the reader what the protagonist cannot – she creates a meaningful system of referral out of the protagonist's "unsayings." Whereas Atwood's language (the novel) is directed outward, towards a community of listeners, the protagonist's rejection of the word moves inward, into a world of private codification where it can refer only to inner mental states and be comprehended only by her. In the reader's mind these two aspects finally coalesce as the protagonist and the author are joined in the belief that speech and writing can be used as a vehicle for reconstruction and recovery of self.

NOTES

1. The "crucial" moment of intensified self-consciousness on the part of the protagonist, identified with her refusal to read "victim" as fate, is actually presented twice towards the end of the novel – once, when she decides to become pregnant, thus declaring her situation reversible and, then again, when she is poised at the edge of the lake and confronted (as Atwood has described in her interview with Graeme Gibson, in *Margaret Atwood: Conversations*, ed. Earl G. Ingersoll, pp. 15-16) with three choices: "You can stay standing on the edge of the lake, you can jump in and if you don't know how to swim you'll drown, or you can learn to swim..." The protagonist's "jump" – perhaps the most liberating jump in Canadian literature – is the novel's metaphorical center.
2. Margaret Atwood. *Surfacing* (Toronto: McClelland and Stewart, 1972). Future page references in this chapter are to this edition.
3. In several of his essays, particularly in "Haunted by Lack of Ghosts," Frye contrasts the representations of the American and Canadian environments by means of the Cartesian notion of nature as object. Such nature, Frye explains, is governed by an egocentric consciousness that sees the natural world as something external, as an extension to the individual's power to reason. The American consciousness, unlike its Canadian counterpart, assimilated this principle to itself. It is in this sense that Atwood's "American" hunters, who turn out to be actually Canadian, are "Americanized," representing an attitude rather than nationality.

WORK CITED

Atwood, Margaret. *Surfacing.* Toronto: McClelland and Stewart, 1972.

Bouson, J. Brooks. *Brutal Choreographies.* Amherst: The University of Massachusetts Press, 1993.

Davey, Frank. "Atwood Walking Backward." *Open Letter* 5 (Summer 1973).

Frye, Northrop. *The Great Code.* Toronto: Academic Press Canada, 1982.

Jameson, Frederic. "World Literature in an Age of Multinational Capitalism" in *The Current in Criticism.* Ed. Clayton Koelb and Virgil Lokke. West Lafayette: Purdue University Press, 1986.

McClintock, Anne. *Imperial Leather.* New York: Routledge, 1995.

Steiner, George. *After Babel..* Oxford: Oxford University Press, 1975.

Living Literally by the Pen

The Self-Conceived and Self-Deceiving Heroine-Author in Margaret Atwood's Lady Oracle

SUSAN JARET MCKINSTRY

> (One day
> I'll touch the warm
> flesh of your throat, and hear
> a faint crackle of paper
>
> or you, who think
> that you can read my mind
> from the inside out, will taste the
> black ink on my tongue, and find
> the fine print written
> just beneath my skin.)

Margaret Atwood,
"On the Streets, Love"

Margaret Atwood's *Lady Oracle* is read as a parodic Gothic *bildungsroman* that repeats both the generic conventions of the Gothic and the parodic method of Jane Austen's *Northanger Abbey*. Like Austen's Catherine Morland, Joan Delacourt Foster is not apparently "born to be an heroine."[1] She is an unattractive child; she confuses art and life, using fiction as a model for interpreting the baffling men and women around her; and she becomes, like Austen's Catherine, ironically more correct than her readers initially supposed in her assumptions about the relationship between Gothic literature and life.[2] But Atwood's parody goes beyond the problem of reader's interpretation to deal with authorial creation – and re-creation – as Joan Foster

55

narrates the revised vision of her life. Joan shows her readers not only the dangers of misreading the world of Gothic fiction but the dangers of writing such fiction. *Lady Oracle* is Joan's confessional tale of her growth as heroine and writer, her *kunstlerroman* disguised as female Gothic and *bildungsroman*, search for love, adventure, identity, and interpretation. She attempts to prove through her various writings that she was, indeed, born to be an heroine and writer of her own story, to be creation and creator.

Costume Gothics portray that search for female self-definition in a world of romantic certainty. These novels allow Joan to be a writer and retain her role as heroine precisely because they demand so little of her imagination: "I thought if I could only get the clothes right, everything else would fall into line. And it did" (175). And this paradoxical self-expression through traditional repressive narrative is central to Joan's story. Atwood writes in *Survival* that "literature is not only a mirror; it is also a map, a geography of the mind." And literature reflects both the reader's imaginative world and the writer's, for "a piece of art, as well as being a creation to be enjoyed, can also be . . . a mirror. The reader looks in the mirror and sees not the writer but himself; and behind his own image in the foreground, a reflection of the world he lives in" (12). Formulaic romantic fiction apparently functions as both a satisfying escape from oppressive female reality and a seeming celebration of the romance that confines women by showing cunning heroines who manage to have a moment of heroism before their lives become domestic and dull. In an effort to insure female chastity, women are imprisoned morally, socially, and sexually — the Victorian Angel in the House becomes the Gothic heroine in the haunted mansion, both fighting to protect the sexuality that is the key to their power, romance, and success. As Joanna Russ points out, such fictions are, paradoxically, necessary, because "the Love Story is — for women – *bildungsroman*, success, failure, education, and the only adventure possible, all in one" (686).[3]

For Joan, writing Costume Gothics – ironically entitled *Escape from Love* and *Stalked by Love* – under the pen name Louisa K. Delacourt fulfills this female desire to escape through an imaginative act. Such romantic fictionalizing allows her to play the duplicitous role of heroine-with-secrets and author-with-control:

> These books . . . would be considered trash of the lowest order . . . Worse than trash, for didn't they exploit the masses, corrupt by distracting, and perpetuate degrading stereotypes of women as helpless and persecuted? They did and I knew it, but I couldn't stop . . . [Arthur] wouldn't have been able to understand in the least the desire, the pure quintessential need of my readers for escape, a thing I myself understood only too well . . . Escape wasn't a luxury for them, it was a necessity. They had to get it somehow. And when they were too tired to invent escapes of their own, mine were available for them at the corner drugstore, neatly packaged like the other painkillers . . . Now I could play fairy godmother to them, despite their obvious defects . . . I had the power to turn them from pumpkins to pure gold . . . The Truth was that I dealt in hope, I offered a vision of a better world, however preposterous. Was that so terrible? (33-35)[4]

And that is the question that Atwood's novel – Joan's confessional life story and Louisa's Gothics – tries to answer. For Joan, female power is precisely the power to awaken the female imagination and allow readers to escape from their mundane lives into a romantic Gothic world "where happiness was possible and wounds were only ritual ones . . . where love was as final as death" (316).

But that fictional world is death to independent female identity. The formula demands female victimization in order to create a family romance in which the woman is a child trying desperately to interpret the powerful and dangerous adults around her, trying to decipher, in Tania Modleski's phrase, "the mystery of masculine motives" in the puzzling, contradictory behaviour of men and the competitive tactics of women" (439).[5] Romances must emphasize male / female difference to distinguish and justify the fixed roles of the melting maiden and rapacious men who threaten her innocence. Joan as both writer and heroine reproduces the sexual chasm: her Gothics – *Stalked by Love, Escape from Love*, and *Love, My Ransom* – portray the inherent danger of romance and relationships, while her marriage reenacts the gender struggle that her novels imply between the direct male and the devious female. "That was the difference between us: for Arthur there were true paths, several of them perhaps, but only one at a time. For me there were no paths at all. Thickets, ditches, ponds, labyrinths, morasses, but no paths" (189).

For Joan, and her readers, female Gothics covertly celebrate protective female cunning. Love entraps female characters in this direct, powerful male world; they escape through innocent trickery, circumstantial luck, and fast talk – their strongest weapon, as Janice Radway notes: "It is essential for women to develop the ability to use words adroitly if they are to impose their own wills" (69). Like her childish heroines, Joan as author learns to manipulate the language of romance by revising the same plot over and over, capitulating to romance while recapitulating the tales of heroines' small victories over the men that threaten them.

But, like her heroines, Joan becomes trapped in the maze of romantic vision. She cannot be both controlling author and victimized heroine, for those roles are not compatible: one demands independent imagination, the other passive obedience to sexual and social conventions of heroinism.[6] Joan's narrative becomes a confessional attempt to organize her two selves – Joan and Louisa, victimized heroine and victimizing author – into conventional and therefore comprehensible characters with revised pasts and predictable

58

roles. "I don't think I'll ever be a very tidy person," she sighs at the conclusion of her narrative, but her Gothic plots reflect a totally ordered world (380.) And her narrative attempts to mirror the certainty and fixity of Gothics rather than the messiness of her reminiscences. Creating herself as a character in "a pretty weird story" told to an injured reporter, she justifies her present situation through a *revision* of her past.

Precisely. Her story is an imaginative recreation in the language of a Gothic writer, "as escape artist" anxious because "every one of my fantasies turn[s] into a trap" (367). That is the lesson told by Joan's narrative and Louisa's Gothics as well as Atwood's novel: the rules of convention-al romance entrap Joan by transforming fantasy – escape – into a reality that repeats formulaic plots and romantic repressions. Joan creates conventional female roles and is, in turn, created by them as she becomes the heroine-victim of her own Gothic terrors.

Initially Joan exploits the vicarious escapism of the Gothic forms, for "the heroines of my books were mere stand-ins: their features were never clearly defined, their faces were putty which each reader could reshape into her own, adding a little beauty" (34). Odd that her heroine's villainous rival in *Stalked by Love* has Joan's unusual long red hair, green eyes, small teeth. Clearly Joan casts herself in her Gothics as victimizer and in her confessional life story as victim. In both texts the roles are specifically defined; in both texts the victim utilizes cunning capitulation as power. As an obese child in the role of helpful, sexual con-fidante, Joan is the "sponge" who "drank it all in but gave nothing out, despite the temptation to tell everything, all my hatred and jealousy, to reveal myself as the duplicitous . . . monster I knew myself to be" (102). She rejects her mother as "the manager, the creator, the agent" and herself as "the product" (70) by turning her body into a grotesque "disputed territory" and swelling "visibly, relentlessly . . . In this at least I was undefeated" (73). Ironically, Joan escapes her mother by obeying her: "The only way I could have helped her to her satisfaction would have been to change into someone else" (56).

And she does. By drastic dieting (helped, symbolically, by being shot with a carnival arrow and inheriting money, thus combining the Gothic heroine's physical danger and financial escape with a comic reminder of Joan's decidedly *modern* cupidity), she creates a new body, role and name for herself. Beautiful, innocent, alien, poor, and seduced by a count, she becomes a conventional heroine. Unfortunately, she lives the life of a real woman, and, out of money and bored with her count, she needs vicarious escape: Louisa K. Delacourt, Costume Gothics writer, is born. And Joan's split into incompatible roles — author and heroine — is completed. She rejects her past self as inappropriate to her present life, as "implausible"; as a writer, she is concerned only with fictional probabilities. No longer fat, she turns that obese self into "Aunt Deirdre" and herself into an ex-cheerleader; no longer innocent, she transforms her seducer into a boy at summer camp, a scene complete with the details she learned from the girls she observed so closely in high school. Joan has, indeed, been transformed — into a heroine.

Joan's delight in her dual identity results from her careful separation of — and creation of — two plausible characters who are real enough for plausibility and fantastic enough for escapism. "Escape literature . . . should be an escape for the writer as well as the reader," claimed the Polish count (173). Joan uses her fictions to escape both her past and her present.

> I was two people at once, with two sets of identification papers, two bank accounts, two different groups of people who believed I exist-
> ed . . . As long as I could spend a certain amount of time each week
> as Louisa, I was all right, I was patient and forbearing, warm, a sym-

pathetic listener. But if I was cut off, if I couldn't work on my current Costume Gothic, I would become mean and irritable, drink too
much and start to cry. (238)

Although both identities give Joan pleasure, both are just
characters from her admittedly romantic imagination.

Joan's attempts to fictionalize herself into these clearly
delimited roles fail because she stereotypes herself and those
around her, following the models of the Costume Gothics,
claiming that "there were two kinds of love . . . I kept Arthur
in our apartment and the strangers in their castles and man-
sions, where they belonged." Proud that "when it came to
fantasy lives I was a professional," she still "began to feel
something was missing" (241). Yet she fails to realize that the
omission is her identity as a woman with a past and not a
heroine within a fiction. Ironically, by her decision to live
literally by the pen Joan has transformed herself into a perfect Gothic heroine who must learn in the course of the
novel that the past is inescapable, that all secrets are revealed,
and that romance is dangerous. Heroine Joan and author
Louisa are merely her fictions.

> It was true that I have two lives, but on off days I felt that neither of
> them was completely real. With Arthur I was merely playing house,
> I wasn't really working at it. And my Costume Gothics were only
> paper; paper castles, paper costumes, paper dolls, as inert and lifeless
> finally as those unsatisfactory blank-eyed dolls I'd dressed and
> undressed in my mother's house. (242)

Self-created in language informed by trashy novels and
movies, Joan is caught in her own fictions, unable to unite
the selves she has purposely divided to give herself a "plausible" heroine's past — "this was the reason I fabricated my
life, time after time: the truth was not convincing" (167).
Perhaps, by the rules of Gothic fiction, heroines cannot
have been fat children. Jane Austen played with that con-

61

ventional expectation in *Northanger Abbey*. But with a life made up of plausible fictions, Joan has no route of escape through implausible romances, and she entraps herself in the very medium that she uses to free other women – albeit temporarily – from their lives.

The line between Joan's fictionalized past, Joan's present life, and Joan's (Louisa's) Gothics becomes increasingly thin as the novel progresses. Joan's narrative mirrors both the Gothic formula and the specifics of her latest romance, *Stalked by Love*. The first eight pages of her manuscript are missing, "though it wouldn't be too difficult to reconstruct the opening pages" (31); the opening of Joan's life story is also missing, for the novel opens abruptly with an announcement of her death, and the rest of *Lady Oracle* is an attempt to reconstruct those opening incidents. And her narrative begins, like all good Gothics, with several crimes and secrets, including her own "death," the major motivating secret of the narrative, and several symbolic killings: "the regret for years of murdered breakfasts" (7), the sacrifice of Joan's long red hair ("they'd start looking for the arms and legs and the rest of the body") (12), the burial of her clothes ("still I felt as though I was getting rid of a body, the corpse of someone I'd killed . . . a forgotten rite, a child murder or a protective burial") (18).[7] The body is not real, but the imagined – and dreaded – corpse of the old, fat Joan is indeed a murdered victim that returns to haunt its killer, the Joan who revised her past and deleted that self.

Joan's careful division between self-as-creator and self-as-created collapses. She loses control of the fictional process and becomes part of the Gothics she writes. Not with authorial distance, however. Early in the novel she literally walks through her characters' dilemmas to find solutions. Initially, she succeeds; she meets her husband Arthur while acting as heroine, and becomes a renowned poetess by publishing her reenactment of her Gothic heroine's experiment with Automatic Writing under the title *Lady Oracle*. Ironically her imagination-turned-real provides precisely the situation necessary to a Gothic plot – physical danger, a dreadful secret from the past, and domestic imprisonment.

Transforming herself into *Lady Oracle's* author, Joan finds herself trapped in a plot even more complicated than the Gothics that parented it. Joan herself is unable to interpret *Lady Oracle*; she claims that it "isn't about anyone . . . It's all sort of, well, imaginary" (263), while her husband and critics assume that it is "modern love and the sexual battle, dissected with a cutting edge of shocking honesty" – the autobiography of her marriage (260). She does not recognize that her fictions are, to a degree, mimetic, and the characters in *Lady Oracle* are her disguised, murdered past returned, in appropriate Gothic fashion, to haunt her.

The inserted Gothics in Joan's narrative become nightmarish evidence of Joan's dangerous, besieged position as victim of her husband, her lover, her blackmailer, and of her life filled with "the shapes of my fear, a dead animal, the telephone breathing menace, a killer's notes cut from the Yellow Pages, a revolver, anger . . ." (12). Like her heroines, Joan is forced to confront men who play the dual roles of romance, men "with hard rapacious mouths, but also tender and worshipful" (241). As a child taught to fear strangers, she is confused by the possible kindness of an exhibitionist, wondering whether he "was a rescuer or a villain? Or, an even more baffling thought: Was it possible for a man to be both at once?" (67). In her romances, men always play these implausible dual roles; now in her life they do.

And she, heroine *and* author, finds it frightening. She claims that Arthur is "single-minded, single-hearted, single-bodied," while herself she "was a sorry assemblage of lies and alibis, each complete in itself but rendering the others worthless." Her recognition of Arthur's multiple selves is limited to believing that "I was simultaneous, while Arthur was a sequence" (236). Wrong. Joan's efforts to create men as conventional Gothic heroes who are transformed by love from puzzling, cruel beasts to gentle lovers fail because men do not keep their hero and villain roles separate, as fictional characters must: Arthur, both husband and hunter; the daffodil man, pervert and rescuer; her father, murderer and savior; her lover, the romantic Royal Porcupine and boring Chuck Brewer; the Polish count, escaped hero and dull businessman (and romance writer). "Was every Heathcliff a Linton in disguise?" she asks in despair (300). Men are not as simple as the characters she creates, nor are they as controllable – but they are equally incomprehensible and dangerous to the heroine self that she has made.

This duplicity is mirrored in women, of course. Joan sees her mother as tidy woman in a navy-blue suit and as a three-headed monster, Marlene as her childhood Brownie tormentor and an efficient political mother, Leda Sprott and Miss Flegg as victimizers and guides. Nothing in Joan's past disappears; all the characters in her life (and her fictions) have dual roles. And so, of course, does she. But only when Joan learns to read *Lady Oracle* as "a Gothic gone wrong" (259) does she recognize her own dual role as victim and victimizer. She has entrapped herself in her fictions. She is imaginatively and physically a prisoner. Unable to write her heroine Charlotte safely out of *Stalked by Love* and thus unable to resolve the plot and sell the book, she is herself unable to leave Terremoto because she is broke, pursued by unknown enemies, and publicly dead. Like her heroine, she is a victim of the rules of fiction.

And those rules demand a female sacrifice. Joan has always identified with the heroine, like her readers, but now she sees the villainess, Felicia Redmond, as both victimizer and victim, the "wife who would have to die; such was the fate of wives" (348). Felicia becomes a stand-in for Joan, the real victim of Gothics, as she struggles against her fixed role: "Perhaps she could foresee that life would be arranged for the convenience of Charlotte after all, and that she herself would have to be disposed of" (351). Joan is linked to Felicia by more than their red hair, green eyes, and velvet dresses; she is also a wife, an adulteress, and even a murderess of herself for the sake of romance.[8] "Gazing up at herself from beneath the surface of a river" in imitation of Joan's faked suicide, Felicia moans that "all she wanted was happiness with the man she loved. It was this one impossible wish that has ruined her life; she ought to have settled for contentment, for the usual lies" (351). Joan as author confronts Joan / Felicia as character, the two women whose lives are sacrificed for the rules of fiction:

> Sympathy for Felicia was out of the question, it was against the rules, it would foul up the plot completely. I was experienced enough to know that . . . In my books all wives were eventually either mad or dead, or both. But what had she ever done to deserve it? How could I sacrifice her for the sake of Charlotte? I was getting tired of Charlotte with her intact virtues and her tidy ways . . . Maybe I should try to write a real novel about someone who worked in an office and had tawdry, unsatisfying affairs. But that was impossible, it was against my nature. I longed for happy endings, I needed the feeling of release when everything turned out right and I could scatter joy like rice over all my characters and dismiss them into bliss. (352)

Joan's readerly need for happy endings demands the formula; the formula demands the death of Felicia. But the relationship between creator and creation is too strong. The characters Charlotte, Redmond and Felicia are acting out Joan's secret life, and the Gothic order is overthrown. Beautiful Felicia becomes "an enormously fat woman" who "drowned in an unfortunate accident" and yet returns, grotesquely dripping and calling her husband Redmond "Arthur" ("Who is Arthur?" he responds – the imperturbable Gothic male is puzzled, for once); the romance becomes sexually explicit as she tries to tear off her own soggy clothes (355). Joan warns her heroine that "I'm no longer dependable," but Charlotte "paid no attention to me, she never did" (365). And the danger of misreading the signs around her, getting lost in the maze, is more real for Joan than for her heroine, for there is no Gothic rule protecting her.

"Why had I concocted this trashy and essentially melodramatic script, which might end by getting us all killed in earnest?" Joan wonders (335). She is held captive in Terremoto, stalked by an unknown killer, shunned as witch by the townspeople, and afraid her first "death" was a failure that she must revise so that "this time I would be free completely, no shreds of the past would cling to me" (367). But the past is unavoidable. With Felicia she enters the maze, the "central plot," and finds the characters she has imprisoned there, the discarded selves and multiple men – Redmond, her father, the count, the Royal Porcupine, the hero of *Lady Oracle*, Arthur, and a skull. As Felicia, she opens a door and faces the terrors of the conventional Gothic; as Joan, she opens a door and hits a reporter over the head with a Cinzano bottle.

The comic deflation is obvious. Yet the message is clear; Joan is victim and victimizer. She trapped those women in passive roles, she transformed those men into monsters, she injured the reporter. Her happy ending has failed her. Her multiple identities have been transformed from delightful fictions into nightmare fragments of herself as fat lady, doomed wife, threatened heroine, and embittered suicide, perhaps already dead and "unidentified" or "cut up for spare parts" and blind because "some other body got my eyes" (341). She has lost, metaphorically and artistically, her limited vision of the world as a Gothic romance and herself as Gothic heroine.

Seemingly the moral of the novel is the danger of fictions and fictionalizing. But I think Atwood's novel demands careful reading on the multiple levels she has provided: the Gothic *Stalked by Love*, Foster's autobiography *Lady Oracle*, and Atwood's novel *Lady Oracle*. For the danger lies not in the imaginations of fiction but in the conventions of fiction: in the ways that fictional heroines are "squaw-shed" (to use the Royal Porcupine's appropriate pun) into roles that kill them. Joan's images of herself as the fat lady tightrope walker and ice skater, ideal butterfly and real mothball, writer Louisa and wife Joan, reflect her awareness of the basic capitulation required by public female roles, epitomized by "The Red Shoes," the story of "a ballet dancer torn between her career and her husband" (87) who chooses suicide as her only option.

Near the end of her own story Joan decides to "dance for no one but myself," dances through cut glass, and discovers the danger of romanticizing that conflict.

> The real red shoes, the feet punished for dancing. You could dance, or you could have the love of a good man. But you were afraid to dance, or because you had this unnatural fear that if you danced they'd cut your feet off so you wouldn't be able to dance. Finally you overcame your fear and danced, and they cut your feet off. The good man went away too, because you wanted to dance. But I chose the love, I wanted the good man; why wasn't that the right choice? (367-68)

Only the world of Gothic romance provides clear choices and just rewards, and the cost is high: wives die, pasts are hidden, villains are destroyed, and heroines are condemned to passive, obedient childishness for the sake of the happy ending. Joan's failure with *Stalked by Love* is precisely her successful realization of the dangerous limitations of those fictions and her own part in them: she has cut off her own feet to become a heroine. And she has been telling her readers what they wanted to hear about heroines punished for the wrong choices. She learns, as Leda Sprott says, that as creators they make a dangerous choice, for "you may think it's harmless, but it isn't" (230). Each woman has been forced to change her identity to escape her audience. The stories that please readers and writers can entrap and maim them.

Wilfred Cude argues that "Joan is not deluded by romance; she is deluded by reality" because she suffers from the dehumanizing Miss Flegg Syndrome that teaches Joan to selfishly manipulate situations and people, and thus avoid being hurt herself.[9] Joan's actions have hurt others, presumably. But I would disagree with Cude that she is a dangerous character and argue that she is, precisely, a character: the Joan we read in Atwood's novel is supposedly telling her story in order to justify her behaviour, and she is turning herself into an object of comedy in order to integrate the past fat child with the present woman. Joan's narrative implies that transformations are not only possible but likely, at least in her tale. She has turned herself into a central character in a wonderfully complicated Gothic-comic-murder mystery with feminist overtones, after all. In the process of telling her tale, Joan has revealed clearly the dangers of these limited definitions of selfhood and adventure for women. Even as she denies her unromantic past to turn herself into a text, an ideal heroine like those she reads and writes about in fiction, Joan creates an even more fantastic real woman.

But Gothic readers demand Gothics as an ordered escape from the real world that includes villains and plots, adultery and blackmail, but neglects happy endings and just rewards. Such realism is no romance, certainly. Joan bravely renounces Gothic because "I think they were bad for me. But maybe I'll try some science fiction. The future doesn't appeal to me as much as the past, but I'm sure it's better for you" (379). She is still "hooked on plots" (342). Ironically, her narrative falls into a new genre, hospital romance, as she nurses the injured reporter and considers falling in love with him. She cannot give up her addiction to romance

68

because of its value as escape and representation: where else are women always central, always exciting, always thinking and talking their way out of difficulties? And where else do they have the chance at both the good man and the dance? And – most importantly – where else can women get everything they desire?

Joan's narrative teaches her readers precisely the power of words to free or confine their users. In fiction, she has killed herself; in fact, she resurrects herself. She uses nothing new, but recycles names (Joan Foster, Louisa Delacort) and incidents (her mother at the triple mirror) in several different genres until she is satisfied as an artist with the effect. The doubling, the repetitions, are necessary to revise the tale and its effect on the hearer; even Joan's bitter history can turn to comedy: "At first, every time I repeated this story to myself . . . it filled me with the same rage, helplessness and sense of betrayal I'd felt at the time. But gradually I came to see it as preposterous, especially when I thought about telling it to anyone else" (53). Telling her story, she can turn it into a plausible fiction and remedy for her past hurts. Fiction is truly helpful: Joan's heroine Charlotte protects herself from an attacker with a heavy volume of Boswell's *Life of Johnson* (another fictionalized biography), and the real dynamite becomes a useful fiction to cover Joan's affair with the Royal Porcupine.

The danger is that fiction can kill as well as cure. Joan's reviewers turn her faked death into a conventional suicide caused by a female artist's conflict between art and life:

> I'd been shoved into the ranks of those other unhappy ladies, scores of them apparently, who'd been killed by a surfeit of words. There I was, on the bottom of the death barge where I'd once longed to be, my name on the prow, winding my way down the river. Several of the articles drew morals: you could sing and dance or you could be happy, but not both. Maybe they were right, you could stay in the tower for years, weaving away, looking in the mirror, but one glance

69

out the window at real life and that was that. The curse, the, doom. I began to feel that even though I hadn't committed suicide, perhaps I should have. They made it sound so plausible. (346)

If plausibility were all Joan asked, her fictions would not be so rich. But the narrative of her story has shown that the reality is not plausible – and is it not the wish-fulfillment implausibility of romance a source of its appeal as escape? As long as the ending is ordered, the tale's disorder delights us.

And Joan gives us a happy ending. She manages to revise "The Lady of Shalott" so the choice is no longer between art and life; this heroine gets both. The curse does not kill this artist. In reconstructing the past that she previously destroyed, Joan does fix herself into those roles and destroy several of those secret selves, but there are more versions to come. Joan's rich imagination saves her from the limits of her own fictions; desiring Gothic romance, the unpredictable moments with predictable endings, she must write: "Details would distract me," she sighs. "In a fairy tale it would be one of the two stupid sisters who open the forbidden door and are shocked by the murdered wives, not the third, clever one who keeps to the essentials: presence of mind, foresight, the telling of watertight lies" (170). Her narrative is just such a lie, perhaps, for even as it presents a Joan who is the victim of others, it reveals a Joan inventive enough to free herself. Atwood uses the name of Joan's poem for her novel, playing with the process of revision: Atwood's *Lady Oracle* could be an explanation of Joan's poem "Lady Oracle," a parodic modern Gothic, or a prophecy that the creator need not be destroyed by her desire to have both the man and the dance, romance and art. "Every myth is a version of the truth," Joan claims (99). In *Lady Oracle*, the Gothic myth of beset womanhood is transformed into a celebration of the female imagination as Joan resurrects herselves into new stories.

NOTES

1. In Austen's novel, the comedy lies in the reader's recognition of Catherine as a heroine despite her unconventional looks and behavior, not (as in *Lady Oracle*) because of them. Such is the life of Atwood's modern heroine: the conventions themselves are confusing for Joan, so she returns to an earlier – simpler – form of heroism for her definition and her irony.

2. For further discussions of this confusion between art and life (a common problem for fictional characters from *Don Quixote* to *Madame Bovary*) as it is used as parody and lesson in Austen's novel, see Baker. And for a broader discussion of the problem as it relates to women readers, see Brownstein.

3. See also Modleski, Radway, and Snitow for more discussion on the function of the Gothic Romance in the lives of its female readers.

4. This plea to the reader for understanding echoes Austen's claim in *Northanger Abbey* that female novelists "are an injured body" and that their product is socially condemned (even if it is widely read and enjoyed). Clearly Joan is justifying the use of the Gothic fantasy as escape, even as Atwood is poking fun at her readers; as Russ points out in her article, female readers are embarrassed to admit that they read romances. When pressed to list "fiction read exclusively by women," the female reader "finally relents and hands you three genres: confession magazines, nurse novels – and the Modern Gothic" (666). Ironically, those are the three genres that *Lady Oracle* – or, more precisely, Joan Foster – writes in and enjoys. What these genres share is an emphasis on implausible plots that have plausible – thus conventional – endings, as the women who have struggled independently turn to marriage for social position and fulfillment. Miller writes that "the peculiar shape of a heroine's destiny in novels by women, the implausible twists of fate so common in these novels, is a form of insistence about the relation of women to writing: a comment on the stake of difference within the theoretical indifference of literature itself" (44). These novels clearly do focus on gender difference and, until the ending of the novel, value female difference as the source and cause of the adventures in the plot itself.

5. This aspect of the male as dangerous to the female is also discussed in amusing detail by Russ and Snitow.

6. Stewart argues that "the female novelist suffers disintegration" because those roles conflict: "To be a heroine, she must nurture, help, inspire; by defending her independence as an artist, she turns into a Gorgon." To create a heroine that is a positive and unconflicted fig-

ure, the female novelist "must either rewrite the old myths or create,
a new mythos" (107). Seemingly the conventions for women as created and women as creator do not allow the dual roles that Joan
desires.

7. Joan's "murders" of hair, clothing, and food parody the Gothic
emphasis on such female, domestic paraphernalia in the formula
novel: "hair in the female was regarded as more important than
either talent or the lack of it," claims Joan (11). See Russ for a full
discussion of the ways in which "Occupation: Housewife is simultaneously avoided, glamorized, and vindicated" (675) in romances.
Ironically, Joan Foster does identify herself by her red hair, velvet
costumes, and cooking failures; the self she "murders" is as false – fictional – as the ideal female constructed through those props.

8. Joanna Russ writes, "The eeriest plot element in these books is the
constant "doubling" of the Heroine – she is always in some fashion
a "stand-in" for someone else, usually someone who has been killed"
(683). Atwood's precise use of the Gothic convention in Joan's story
reflects this doubling, as not only the heroine but her tale is retold
and repeated.

9. Cude claims that Joan is a victim of the Miss Flegg syndrome and
"has no recognition of the lethal quality of the malady" and her own
resulting cruelty (47). He argues that Joan accepts mediocrity in her
life, novels, and men, because escapism through mediocre fictions
captivates her and excuses her manipulations of her art and of others. I think he fails to see the dual function of such romantic escapes
for women and thus the implications of Joan's choice of genre. As a
heroine, she can only manipulate through language. Not mediocrity
but artistic necessity demands Gothics, the only form for the female
adventure or *bildungsroman*. (See note 3, above). And certainly Joan as
narrator is ironically aware of the parodic aspects of her tale.

WORKS CITED

Atwood, Margaret. *Lady Oracle*. New York: Avon. 1976.

———. *Survival: A Thematic Guide to Canadian Literature*. Toronto: Anansi, 1972.

Austen, Jane. *Northanger Abbey and Persuasion*. Vol. 5: *The Novels of Jane Austen*. Ed. R. W. Chapman. 3rd ed. 1933. Oxford: Oxford UP, 1980.

Baker, Sheridan. "The Comedy of Illusion in *Northanger Abbey*." *Papers of the Michigan Society of Science, Arts, and Letters* 51 (1966): 547–58.

Brownstein, Rachel M. *Becoming a Heroine: Reading About Women in Novels*. New York: Viking, 1982.

Cude, Wilfred. "Bravo Mothball! An Essay on *Lady Oracle*." *The Canadian Novel Here and Now*. Ed. John Moss. Toronto: NC Press, 1978. 1:45–50.

Miller, Nancy K. "Emphasis Added: Plots and Plausibilities in Women's Fiction." PMLA 96 (1981): 36–48.

Modleski, Tama. "The Disappearing Act: A Study of Harlequin Romances." *The Journal of Women in Culture and Society* 5 (1980): 435–48.

Radway, Janice. "Women Read the Romance: The Interaction of Text and Context." *Feminist Studies*. 9 (Spring 1983): 53–78.

"The Roar of the Boneyard"

Life Before Man

Barbara Hill Rigney

Who locked me
into this crazed man-made
stone brain
where the weathered
totempole jabs a blunt
finger at the byzantine
mosaic dome

Under that ornate
golden cranium I wander
among fragments of gods, tarnished
coins, embalmed gestures
chronologically arranged,
looking for the exit sign

but in spite of the diagrams
at every corner, labelled
in red: YOU ARE HERE
the labyrinth holds me.

***

and I am dragged to the mind's
deadend, the roar of the boneyard, I am lost
among the mastodons
and beyond . . .

Margaret Atwood
"A Night in the Royal Ontario Museum"

Although written at least ten years before her novel *Life Before Man*, Atwood's nightmare poem "A Night in the Royal Ontario Museum" is a companion piece. Both poem and novel centre on the museum as a metaphor for modern life, which Atwood sees here as a vast tomb or an elaborate labyrinth, a maze in which human beings are lost, entrapped, looking for the EXIT sign. All the maps are obsolete, tradition is no longer a guide, and mirrors have lost their magic power to reveal truth. Pervasive in the novel, as in the poem, is a sensation of panic at the possibility of madness, of being "dragged to the mind's / deadend." And always there is the realization of inevitable death, the sand running through the "glass body" (*Life Before Man*, 78).

Unlike *Lady Oracle*, *The Edible Woman* or even *Surfacing*, *Life Before Man* is almost unrelieved by humour except in its most ironic form. The three protagonists — Lesje, Elizabeth and Nate — live relentlessly depressing lives, their states of mind reflected by a surreal cityscape characterized either by intense heat and the smog of pollution or by leaden skies and "fish-grey" snow. Dominating the novel as it dominates the lives of the protagonists, is the forbidding image of the Royal Ontario Museum, that grey monument to an irretrievable past, a temple of death, a massive "animal morgue" (55). Lesje, who spends her life cataloguing pieces of bone and teeth, "shards of the real world," winds her way through the labyrinth of hallways and exhibits:

> She climbs the grey steps of the Museum, walks past the ticket-takers, hurries up the stairs to the Hall of Vertebrate Evolution, tracing again her daily path: the human skull, the saber-toothed cat in its tar pit, the illuminated scenes of undersea life, with their hungry mosasaurs and doomed ammonites. The door that leads to her office is reached through this portion of the ancient sea floor. (191)

The biblical quotation written across the domed "golden cranium" of the lobby, "THAT ALL MEN MAY KNOW HIS WORK" (54), is surely ironic in the context of Atwood's study in extinction.

The characters in this novel are also, like the stuffed dinosaurs and mastodons in the museum, classified and catalogued. Nate, Lesje and Elizabeth are scientifically categorised and arranged in chapters as on file cards, according to name, date, habitat and present activity: "Elizabeth is lying in bed . . . " "Nate sits in the Selby Hotel . . . " "Lesje is doing something seedy . . ." The impersonal and objective third-person narrator, scientist-like, makes no evaluative comments; the lives of the three protagonists are simply the subjects of a report covering a representative two-year period from Friday, 29 October 1976 to Friday, 18 August 1978. Often a single date is repeated, as the activities and perceptions of the subjects on that date will differ; occasionally there is a flashback to 1975, at which point another major character, Chris, shot his head off.

The reader is not invited to empathise with any of the characters; none is likable or perhaps even redeemable. We remain detached yet fascinated as they interact. As Lesje passes her time wondering about the breeding habits of various dinosaurs, so we view the behaviour of the subjects in the novel: there are two suicides, three contemplated suicides, two faked suicides, two funerals, two rapes, numerous seductions, abundant mental cruelty. None of the sexual acts is even vaguely erotic. Rather Atwood gives us case histories, records of "sex among the ossified" (128). The characters are fossils of human beings, guilty of "embalmed gestures," incapable of love and spiritually exhausted. Atwood's poem, "Letters," explores a similar set of characteristics: "I do not know / the manner of your deaths, daily / or final, blood / will not flow in the fossil / heart at my command, I can't / put the life back into those / lives, those lies . . ." (*Two-Headed Poems*, 31).

As the characters are classified within the structure of the novel, so they attempt to classify and categorize each other, fit each other neatly into labelled boxes. Lesje attempts to relate to Nate, "Elizabeth's husband, the husband belonging to Elizabeth. Possessive, or, in Latin, genitive" (53). Nate is, indeed, Elizabeth's husband, father to Nancy and Janet, lover to Lesje, father to Lesje's unborn baby, former lover to Martha, son to Mrs Schoenhof and to a father dead in World War II, former lawyer turned toymaker, former idealist turned cynic. Tall, thin, bearded, shabby, having only recently discarded his love-beads, Nate is a refugee from the 1960s lost in the maze of the 1970s, homesick for his own youth. Nate has no actual home, we are repeatedly made aware; the house he lives in belongs to Elizabeth, even though it is Nate who cleans and cooks and mothers the children. He cooks liver and plays his Harry Belafonte records from the 1960s, two activities hateful to Elizabeth, only when Elizabeth is not at home. Later, he moves to Lesje's apartment, where he also cooks and cleans and mothers Lesje. Always he is nostalgic for a home, an impossible and absurd vision of a "shared harmonious life, left over from some Christmas card of the forties, a log fire, knitting in a basket, glued on snow" (212). Ironically, "Schoenhof translates from the German as "beautiful farm."

Nate cleans and cooks and serves women out of a prevailing and intense sense of guilt, guilt because his surname is German (the protagonist of *Surfacing* at one point remarks, "The trouble some people have being German I have being human"), because he cannot live up to the heroic image he has of the father he never met, and, more acutely, because he is male in what for him is a female world. Nate is, in fact, terrified of the women who dominate his life. Raised by a mother who is a dedicated if ineffectual political activist, Nate is guilty for failing in his role as "radical lawyer," defender of the oppressed. Married to Elizabeth, "Queen Elizabeth," who will "stop at nothing. Or, put another way: when she reaches nothing she will stop" (133), Nate only tolerates her lovers and serves her tea in bed. He has imagined her at her office in the Royal Ontario Museum, "sitting like a Madonna in a shrine, shedding a quiet light . . . He would think of himself running towards her as she receded in front of him, holding a lamp in her hand like Florence Nightingale." Even when Nate has become disenchanted, even when he realizes that Elizabeth is less the "lady with the lamp" than "the lady with the axe" (41), he still runs towards her, seeking approval, seeking absolution. Nor can he expect forgiveness from his two daughters who will soon be women, "and that recognition runs through him like a needle." "[T]hey will criticize his clothes, his Job, his turn of phrase." "[T]ey will judge him. Motherless, childless, he sits at the kitchen table, the solitary wanderer, under the cold red stars" (265).

Absolution is what Nate also hopes from Lesje, "Our Lady of the Bones" (71), "unattainable, shining like a crescent moon" (115). Nate's sexual fantasies about Lesje, as about all women, are firmly grounded in arrested adolescence, having to do with his viewing of the film *She* "when he was an impressionable twelve and masturbating nightly" (62). He imagines the following scenario:

> Holding Lesje would be like holding some strange plant, smooth, thin, with sudden orange flowers. *Exotics*, the florists called them. The light would be odd, the ground underfoot littered with bones. Over which she would have power. She would stand before him, the bearer of healing wisdom, swathed in veils. He would fall to his knees, dissolve. (62)

However, as Atwood points out in her essay "Superwoman Drawn and Quartered: The Early Forms of *She*," the image of "She" is associated by H. Rider Haggard in his novel, with "She-Who-Must-Be-Obeyed" (*Second Words*, 38). Like all the women in Nate's experience, even the innocent young Lesje turns out to be manipulative and domineering, yet another "lady with an axe." Like Elizabeth and Martha,

Lesje also requires that Nate grow up, accept the role of fatherhood, commit himself to her, return to his legal career, abandon his toys. Nate, however, remains a child, unable to truly commit himself to any person or thing. In imagery typical of Atwood's earlier descriptions of failed artists, Nate sees himself as divided, amputated, his own toys effigies of himself: "The head screwed on, holding the man together. A clown's smile he used. This is his body, stiff fragments held together by his spine and his screwtop head. Segmented man" (223).

Clearly Nate nurtures a vision of himself as victim; like the female protagonists of Atwood's earlier fiction, he uses his sense of himself to mitigate his guilt, to absolve himself of complicity in the violence which he sees as implicit in sexual relationships in general. Yet, he is an accomplice, at least in his imagination: he envisions Elizabeth in the grip of her maddened lover, beaten and helpless, "white flesh buckling under those fists, powerless, whimpering," but the vision is "only momentarily erotic" (214). Nate creates Chris as the male monster, an alternate self permitted the excesses which Nate represses in himself. Imagining Chris as the brutal rapist and savage beast enables Nate to remain the chaste knight in the service of his ladies, a role which renders him psychologically and sometimes physically impotent, always ineffectual. He thinks of himself in terms of "a lump of putty, helplessly molded by the relentless demands and flinty disapprovals of the women he can't help being involved with" (33). Like numerous other of Atwood's characters, Nate is an "escape artist," but a failed one. His obsessive jogging only traps him more hopelessly within the labyrinth as he runs in circles around Toronto's Parliament Buildings, running from women, from himself, for his life: "His shadow paces him, thin and pinheaded, stretching away to his right, a blackness flickering over the grass. A premonition, always with him; his own eventual death" (287).

Elizabeth is also preoccupied with death. Those chapters of which Elizabeth is the subject frequently open with her lying on her bed, arms at her sides, staring at the ceiling, simulating death. Her carefully-decorated parlour, in which she frequently sits "as if waiting for a plane" (15), is funereal in its atmosphere. The walls and furniture are a uniform grey / mushroom colour, devoid of personality and of light save for a quality of "underwater light." She derives most pleasure from the two porcelain bowls on the sideboard, "good pieces," but empty, without use: "they were meant for offerings. Right now they hold their own space, their own beautifully shaped absence" (16). Elizabeth is also an absence, mechanically eating and bathing, "servicing" her body "for the time when she may be able to use it again, inhabit it" (74). Within the scope of the novel, such a time does not arrive.

Elizabeth is also concerned about the actual and possible deaths of others. Her two daughters, she fears, could disappear, could "drown in two inches of water," could die in any number of terrible and bizarre ways. She repeatedly dreams that she is searching for her missing babies through deserted streets, but she knows that the lost babies in the dreams are also her mother, burned to death in a drunken stupor by the fire started from her own cigarette, and her sister, Caroline, who, mad since childhood, drowned herself in a bathtub. These ghosts preoccupy her: "She's shut them out, both of them, as well as she could, but they come back anyway, using the forms that will most torment her" (171). Equally persistent is the ghost of her former lover, Chris, whose suicide is the ostensible reason for her present severe depression. Elizabeth, too, endures yet another death, that of her seemingly indestructible and witch-like foster mother, Auntie Muriel, who is dying of cancer.

Elizabeth's demons, both real and symbolic, haunt her throughout the novel. The opening pages depict the children's preparations for Hallowe'en, but even this image of innocence becomes sinister as the little girls perform "some grotesque and radical form of brain surgery" (28) on their pumpkins, one of them dressed as a devil. Other children come to the door, disguised as Frankenstein's monsters or as rats. To Elizabeth they represent All souls. Not just friendly souls but all souls. They are souls, come back, crying at the door, hungry, mourning their lost lives. You give them food, money, anything to substitute for your love and blood, hoping it will be enough, waiting for them to go away. (45) Predictably, the next holiday recorded in the novel is Remembrance Day, set aside in memory of the dead.

Elizabeth resurrects her demons out of guilt, a guilt which seems a great deal more justifiable than Nate's self-indulgent suffering. She understands that her mother died as if by her own hand, that her mother, in fact, had "sold" her two little daughters to Auntie Muriel. Yet the mother's death is also somehow due to Elizabeth's rejection and denial, her refusal to recognize her mother as the pathetic figure beneath the street lamp, gazing hungrily up at the window of her daughters' bedroom. Elizabeth has also prevented the younger Caroline from reconciliation with the mother and has thus contributed to Caroline's tragic breakdown and eventual death. On the night that Caroline symbolically leaves her body, enters into a state of catatonic collapse, Elizabeth has left her alone in order to seek her own thrills and lose her virginity to a boy she picks up on the street. She has also precipitated Chris's death by refusing to marry him, by ordering him from her house. Even the death of the evil Auntie Muriel is somehow partly her fault: she has hurled one of her precious bowls at Auntie Muriel, who has melted as a result. Lying in the hospital, the cancer consuming her body, Auntie Muriel appears to be "falling in on herself, she's melting, like the witch in *The Wizard of Oz*, and seeing it Elizabeth remembers: Dorothy was not jubilant when the witch turned into a puddle of brown sugar. She was terrified" (258).

Perhaps Elizabeth's guilt is, in a convoluted way, responsible for her punishment of others, punishments almost as cruel as those she metes out to herself. She is the sadist in the sado-masochistic relationship with both Nate and Chris, the long leather gloves she wears and removes so deliberately, finger by finger, an emblem of her role. All her sexual relationships, which she interprets as tests of her dominance and power, manifest forms of perversity. Her parlour becomes a kind of web into which she seduces such victims as William, Lesje's lover before Nate. According to Elizabeth, William is comparable in bed to "a large and fairly active slab of Philadelphia cream cheese," but he may also contain "pockets of energy, even violence" (196), an accurate interpretation as we know from Lesje's experience of William. The real challenge for Elizabeth, however, has been Chris, "a dangerous country, swarming with ambushes and guerrillas, the center of a whirlpool, a demon lover" (196). Even Elizabeth's youthful escapades are flirtations with rape and violence; her adult forays into sleazy bars are equally degrading and dangerous. While Marian in *The Edible Woman* only fantasizes about "the Underwear Man," Elizabeth actually arranges a date with a travelling salesman of fetishistic underwear for women. "We both know what you're here for" (209), he says just before he rapes a now-frigid Elizabeth while holding the microphone of his two-way radio against her throat in order to give his listeners "a thrill."

There is also an element of voyeurism in Elizabeth's relationships with Nate's lovers. She invites their confidences and confessions, and her manipulation of both Martha and Lesje is almost sexual in its cruelty. Again,

Elizabeth is the Spider Woman who invites the innocent flies into her parlour, takes them to lunch, snickers as they spill their coffee and expose their weaknesses. Lesje is not so terribly erroneous in her classification of Elizabeth as "CLASS: *Chondrichthyes*; ORDER: *Selachii*; GENUS: *Squalidae*; SPECIES: *Elizabetha*. Today she classifies Elizabeth as a shark; on other days it's as a huge Jurassic toad, primitive, squat, venomous; on other days a cephalopod, a giant squid, soft and tentacled, with a hidden beak" (245).

As always, however, Atwood does not permit her readers such a simple interpretation of character. Elizabeth cannot be so easily categorized and dismissed. For one thing, she is subject to unexpected expressions of tenderness, towards her children especially, but also towards Auntie Muriel, whom she has good reason to hate. At their last encounter in the hospital, Elizabeth wishes to run, to leave Auntie Muriel to the fate she deserves, but she recalls her mother's death, and the good, the vulnerable part of her prevents her flight:

> . . . she leans forward and takes Auntie Muriel's blinded hands. Desperately the stubby fingers clutch her. Elizabeth is no priest: she cannot give absolution. What can she offer? Nothing sincerely. Beside her own burning mother she has sat, not saying anything, holding the one good hand. The one good fine-boned hand. The ruined hand, still beautiful, unlike the veined and mottled stumps she now cradles in hers, soothing them with her thumbs as in illness she has soothed the hands of her children.
>
> Sickness grips her. Nevertheless, nevertheless, she whispers: It's all right. It's all right. (260)

A similar gesture, that of touching, will prove the salvation of the protagonist of *Bodily Harm*.

Elizabeth is like Auntie Muriel in many ways, domineering, spiteful, with "the backbone of a rhinoceros." Yet there is a positive aspect to Elizabeth's strengths. She is a survivor, a "homemaker" in a world where homes are not possible. Literally homeless in childhood while the other characters in *Life Before Man* are only symbolically homeless, Elizabeth has created, by the end of the novel, a home against all the odds. She will go to her home and make peanut butter sandwiches for her children:

> It suddenly amazes her that she is able to do this, something this simple. How close has she come, how many times, to doing what Chris did? More important: what stopped her?
>
> . . . But she's still alive, she wears clothes, she walks around, she holds down a job even. She has two children. Despite the rushing of wind, the summoning voices she can hear from underground, the dissolving trees, the chasms that open at her feet; and will always from time to time open. She has no difficulty seeing the visible world as a transparent veil or a whirlwind. The miracle is to make it solid.
>
> She thinks with anticipation of her house, her quiet living room with its empty bowls, pure grace, her kitchen table. Her house is not perfect; parts of it are in fact crumbling, most noticeably the front porch. But it's a wonder that she has a house at all, that she's managed to accomplish a house. Despite the wreckage. She's built a dwelling over the abyss, but where else was there to build it? So far, it stands. (278)

In the final analysis, Elizabeth is the only adult in the novel. She has, as she says, "been down the yellow brick road" (86), and she knows well enough that the Wizard does not exist. Her own escape fantasy, inspired by Chinese paintings she commissions for a showing at the museum, involves the idealization of peasant life, the intensely artificial beauty of fruit and vegetables, the sentimental assertion that "Everyone Helps in Building each Others Houses." But Elizabeth knows that no one helps, that "paradise does not exist," that the Chinese paintings do not represent reality but only desire: "Like cavemen, they paint not what they see but what they want" (291). Elizabeth is not an heroic figure in any ordinary sense, but she is strong in her loneliness, ready to face a reality that is unmitigatedly hostile. She resolves the existential dilemma evaded by all of Atwood's earlier heroines: she has pitted her own free will against the absurd, and she survives.

Lesje, on the other hand, is one of Atwood's more familiar perennial child / women, and, as Lesje classifies her fossils, other people, and the world in general, so we are tempted to classify her among Atwood's Diana figures patterned after the archetypes discussed in *Survival*. Like a Marian in *The Edible Woman* and like Alice in Wonderland, Lesje avoids growing up or confronting reality by becoming a tourist "underground." Lesje's chapters, including the first one of which she is the subject, frequently describe her wandering through the Jurassic swamp of her imagination: she is in prehistory, "Under a sun more orange than her own has ever been, in the middle of a swampy plain lush with thick-stalked plants and oversized ferns, a group of bony-plated stegosaurs is grazing . . . She mixes eras, adds colors: why not a metallic blue stegosaurus with red and yellow dots?" (10). Lesje is a paleontologist, a scientist, compulsively objective just as Joan Foster in *Lady Oracle* is compulsively romantic. Yet Lesje's views on prehistory are derived from the imagination rather than from textbooks. Her "passion for fossils" originates with her reading of Sir Arthur Conan Doyle's *The Lost World* when she was ten, and she has never outgrown the idea that, like the hero of the novel, she might also discover some lost world in which prehistoric life survives.

When that event occurs, as she still imagines it inevitably will, she will name her country after herself, a plan which poses a problem because, also like Joan Foster, Lesje has multiple names. Her last name would have been Etlin had not her Ukrainian grandfather changed it to Green when he arrived in Canada, and "There already was a Greenland, which wasn't at all the sort of place she had in mind. Greenland was barren, icy, devoid of life, whereas the place Lesje intended to discover would be tropical, rich and crawling with wondrous life forms" (82). Lesje is Ukrainian for Alice, a name Lesje uses for a time, but she finally prefers Lesje because "Aliceland" simply "wasn't right." Nevertheless, Atwood here establishes her familiar theme: Lesje is another Alice travelling in a "green world" of her own creation.

Although Lesje's fantasies are redolent with lush sexual imagery – steaming swamps, phallic shapes, dinosaurs with two penises – and although she spends an inordinate amount of time musing on the sexual habits of her prehistoric creatures – the "gargantuan passions, the earth actually moving . . . sighs of lust like a full-blast factory whistle" (128) – these fantasies actually represent an evasion of sex in any real context. Lesje is not a participant in life, prehistoric or otherwise, but a voyeur watching from behind a large fern, "invisible" to the dinosaurs to whom she is "so totally alien that they will not be able to focus on her. When the aborigines sighted Captain Cook's ships, they ignored them because they knew such things could not exist. It's the next best thing to being invisible" (10). As the heroine of *Surfacing* prays to be made invisible, as Joan Foster in *Lady Oracle* regards her excess weight as "a magic cloak of invisibility," and as Marian in *The Edible Woman* seeks to disappear by refusing to eat, so Lesje in this novel finds it convenient to temporarily eliminate herself.

Invisibility in Atwood's terms is a complex symbol: at times, it represents a refusal to deal with reality, a means of escape from a necessary confrontation, but invisibility is also the prerogative of the artist. Atwood writes in *Second Words* that one of the things she used to wish when she was very young was "the cloak of invisibility, so I could follow people around and listen to what they were saying when I wasn't there . . ." This is what novelists do, says Atwood, "every time they write a page" (429). But, like Joan Foster and Marian McAlpin, Lesje may have the soul of an artist, but she misuses and misinterprets her talents. Like other of Atwood's heroines, she is a "failed artist," solipsistic and incapable of translating the imagination into language. To remain invisible in the green world is to escape "real life," adulthood, the sexual recognition that implies, and the moral implications of the role of the artist as well.

For Lesje, "men replaced dinosaurs, true, in her head as in geological time; but thinking about men has become too unrewarding" (11). The men in Lesje's life are in fact remarkably unrewarding. At first she lives with William, who is a double to Peter in *The Edible Woman*, a "good man," theoretically safe but unutterably boring. "William Wasp," as Lesje thinks of him, is "pink-cheeked" and "hairless" (20), and an incurable optimist who believes that "every catastrophe is merely a problem looking for a brilliant solution" (19). William, he and Lesje both believe, will save the world in his professional capacity as a specialist in environmental engineering, translate "sewage disposal": ". . . they're all in danger of drowning in their own shit. William will save them. You can see it just by looking at him, his confidence, his enthusiasm" (19).

But, as is almost always the case in Atwood's novels and poems, beneath the clean white shirt beats the heart of a Bluebeard; the facade of an Albert Schweitzer hides the reality of a Hitler; the redeemer inevitably becomes the famous Underwear Man. Elizabeth has recognized those "pockets of violence" latent in William, but Lesje is shocked to find herself raped, violated: "She always thought of rape as something the Russians did to the Ukrainians, something the Germans did, more furtively, to the Jews; something blacks did in Detroit, in dark alleys. But not something William Wasp, from a good family in London, Ontario, would ever do to her" (169). Like the naive narrator in Atwood's short story, "Rape Fantasies," who believes that rape always happens to someone else and is an event that might be avoided by simply reasoning with the rapist, Lesje does not even know what to call William's act of violence. "The incident," nevertheless, is traumatic enough to precipitate Lesje's departure from their apartment, paving the way for her intensified relationship with Nate.

Whereas William regards Lesje as racially suspect, her Ukrainian-Jewish heritage rendering her unfit in his judgment to meet his parents or bear his child, Nate is attracted to what he considers exotic in Lesje. And Lesje is attracted to Nate because he sees her as exotic: "the fact is that she's addicted to Nate's version of her . . . she wants to be this beautiful phantom, this boneless wraith he's conjured up. Sometimes she really does want it" (247). Lesje is, of course and with good reason, terrified of Elizabeth, and yet there is a perverse desire on her part to "become" Elizabeth, a thing she can best accomplish by marrying Nate: "she wants to belong, to be seen to belong; she wants to be classifiable, a member of a group. There is already a group of Mrs Schoenhofs: one is Nate's mother, the other is the mother of his children" (246). Lesje considers that "maybe she's been thinking too much about Elizabeth . . . If she isn't careful she'll turn into Elizabeth" (247).

In significant ways, Lesje does just this. Whether it is Nate's necessity to create domineering women in order to absolve his guilt, or whether Lesje is innately this and her role of ingénue is merely a disguise, she begins more and more to resemble Elizabeth. Her first sexual experience with Nate takes place in Elizabeth's bed, and her later evaluations of Nate reflect Elizabeth's perceptions: he becomes for her an object of ridicule, an object to be possessed and used. Her very language takes on the qualities of Elizabeth's hard-edged tone: Lesje tells Nate, "I've got news for you . . . Elizabeth doesn't need any support. Elizabeth needs support like a nun needs tits" (268). Lesje comes to regard Nate with "ball-shriveling looks," as if "he was a teeny little dog turd"

(237). And, she begins to understand Nate's real value in terms that were Elizabeth's as well; he can provide a classification for her; he can make her a mother.

Atwood's great fertility myth as a symbol of rebirth and artistic creativity, as it figures so prominently in all her novels and in so many of her poems, is completely inverted in *Life Before Man*. In a doomed world, its inhabitants on the verge of extinction, even childbirth becomes an ironic commentary, a mockery of artistic and biological creativity. Lesje's act of throwing away her birth control pills, an act of liberation for the protagonist of *Surfacing*, is here committed in revenge and with malice. "Surely no child conceived in such a rage could come to much good," Lesje worries. "She would have a throwback, a reptile, a mutant of some kind with scales and a little horn on the snout" (270).

Lesje herself, however, is the real monster. Earlier she has identified herself as an "herbivore," peaceful and benign. But Lesje's teeth, a feature she comments upon at various points in the novel, are too big; they indicate an ominous hunger. On the morning following the conception of her baby, Lesje is "gnawing a bran muffin, hair falling over her face"; she looks at Nate "like Fate, sullen, gauging." She wants him to know that she has not been "caged" (270). Three months later, her pregnancy confirmed but Nate still unnotified, Lesje imagines locking herself into one o the museum's display cases, "hairy mask on her face, she'll stow away, they'll never get her out" (284). Always one of Atwood's "dancing girls," Lesje is, at the end of the novel, still dancing, this time among the carnivores: "Here are her old acquaintances, familiar to her as pet rabbits: allosaurus, the carnivore, parrot-beaked chasmosaurus, parasaurolophus with its deer-antler crest" (285). She joins a bizarre parade: "one after another the fossils would lift their ponderous feet, moving off along the grove of resurrected trees, flesh coalescing like ice or mist around them. They'd dance stumpily down the stairs of the Museum and out the front door" (286).

Nate may imagine that he has found a home with Lesje (although his continued presence at the Selby Hotel bar would indicate otherwise), but Lesje at the end is wearing her white coat, symbol, not of wifehood, but of her perennial "virginity" and of her status as museum employee, as scientist. The white coat is Lesje's "label" for herself, her need for labels being analogous to Nate's search for a home. Throughout the novel, Lesje longs for an identity, a label, a category to which to belong. She wishes she were either Ukrainian or Jewish and not a combination of the two, not "multicultural." She tries on fashionable clothes in the stores, but cannot determine into which style of fashion she fits. She decides, finally, that the "Mrs Schoenhof label is not compatible with her role as scientist: "a pregnant paleontologist is surely a contradiction in terms. Her business is the naming of bones, not the creation of flesh" (284). Her real home then is the museum: "She does belong here . . . This is the only membership she values" (283). None of these convictions represents a favourable sign for the success of Lesje's possible marriage to Nate or for the positive symbolism of her future motherhood. Lesje's labels, like the polar thinking in terms of good and evil on the part of the protagonist of *Surfacing*, entrap her in the realm of childhood. She remains, at least psychologically, among the guardians of death, a permanent resident yet still a tourist in an ideal world in which the only life is "a life before man."

The greater number of Atwood scholars would not agree with the above interpretation of Lesje's pregnancy and the novel's final resolution. Linda Hutcheon in "From Poetic to Narrative Structures: The Novels of Margaret Atwood" sees Lesje's pregnancy as a "truly creative act" which becomes "the real paradigm of the novelist's act of creation, an act of moral responsibility for the creation of life."[1] Frank Davey also concludes that Lesje discards her birth control pills "in order to claim her future."[2] Such evaluations are based, understandably, on an accurate interpretation of Atwood's use of fertility symbolism in earlier novels. However, *Life Before Man* marks, not so much a change in Atwood's literary directions, as an intensification of her ironic sensibility and of her political consciousness. Sherrill Grace's predictions in *Violent Duality* that this novel represents "what may prove to be a new stage in Atwood's artistic evolution," that of "social and domestic realism,"[3] were indeed perceptive, although Grace might well have added the term "political" to describe Atwood's areas of artistic concern.

As I have argued elsewhere, Atwood's works have always been "political" in that they represent a social consciousness, a concern for the survival of individuals, particularly women, in a world characterized by hostility and violence that is both latent and overt. *The Edible Woman* is a study of the evils of a consumer society as well as of the psychology of young womanhood; beneath the narrative of *Surfacing* and *The Journals of Susanna Moodie* is a pervading sense of the violation of nature and a concern for ecological balance. In *Life Before Man*, such concerns become paramount: for Atwood, the human race may indeed be confronting its own extinction, its own mass suicide.

The characters in this novel are in fact homeless, for one major reason: their world is no longer habitable. William's sanitation efforts are absurdly futile, but at least he makes an attempt to salvage what is possible. His gloomy predictions are annoying to Lesje, and, through her perceptions, we too see William as a joke. Atwood's jokes, however, are almost inevitably laced with a deadly irony, and, as is often the case in her fiction, the least likely character becomes a speaker of truth. William serves as both fool and prophet in the following passages:

. . . pollutants are pouring into the air, over three hundred of them, more than have yet been identified. Sulfuric acid and mercury are falling, metallic mist, acid rain, into the pure lakes of Muskoka and points north. Queasy fish rise, roll over, exposing bellies soon to bloat. If ten times more control is not implemented at once (at once!) the Great Lakes will die. A fifth of the fresh water in the world. And for what? Panty-hose . . . rubber bands, cars, plastic buttons . . .

. . . birds . . . are eating worms, and stable, unbreakable PCB's are concentrating in their fatty tissues. Lesje herself has probably been incapacitated for safe child-bearing due to the large quantity of DDT she has already stored in her own fatty tissues. Not to mention the radiation bombardment on her ovaries, which will almost certainly cause her to give birth to a two-headed child or to a lump of flesh the size of grapefruit, containing hair and a fully developed set of teeth . . . or to a child with its eyes on one side of its face, like a flounder. (126)

Not only are human beings violating nature, they are also violating each other with a similar destructive intensity. Nate scans the newspaper headlines, and what he sees is "one long blurred howl of rage and pain":

. . . the Pakistani pushed onto the subway tracks . . . The child who strangled while being forced by her mother to stand on one foot with a rope around her neck as punishment. Gossip about Margaret Trudeau, for weeks. An exploding butcher's shop in Northern Ireland. Widening rift between English and French Canada. Murdered Portuguese shoeshine boy; cleanup of Toronto's Sin Strip. Quebec language laws: Greek grocers in all-Greek districts forbidden to put up Coca-Cola signs in Greek. (184)

"What else can be expected," Nate asks himself, and his own impotence is confirmed in his vision of the newspapers as studies in "distilled futility." Language itself, at this point in Atwood's literary philosophy, is suspect, often futile; "the true story is vicious / and multiple and untrue / after all . . ." Atwood writes in *True Stories* (11). Many of the poems in this volume, in *You Are Happy* and in *Two-Headed Poems* are concerned with the inadequacy of poetry, of art, in the face of the destruction and atrocity that constitute reality. How can one write poems or novels about that which is indescribable? "How can I justify / this gentle poem then in the face of sheer / horror?" (*True Stories*, 34). How does one dare, like Elizabeth, to build a house over the abyss?

The alternative is to remain silent, to refuse the confrontation, to hide from reality in fantasy, or to be detached. One of Atwood's great ironic observations about Lesje is that she was named for a famous Ukrainian poet, and yet Lesje either refuses or is unable to speak. She is always "afraid of saying the wrong thing; of being accused" (53); she is always inept in social situations, and she has no close friends. After their first lunch together, Nate is unable to remember what she said: "did she even say anything?" (61). For Lesje, the names of rocks are the only meaningful language: "not many people might know it, but if you found one who did, you would be able to talk together" (83). But the truly monstrous thing about Lesje, Atwood implies, is that she chooses to regard even the inevitable destruction of humankind with scientific detachment. Unlike Nate or even Elizabeth, Lesje chooses to remain emotionally uninvolved: "the real question is: Does she care whether the human race survives or not? She doesn't know. The dinosaurs didn't survive and it wasn't the end of the world . . . the human race has it coming. Nature will think up something else. Or not, as the case may be" (19).

The human race may indeed "have it coming, and yet, in Atwood's own terms, it is still possible to care, to forgive and to redeem. Language is a "fragile protest," but it represents the only salvation possible: "you must write this poem," she says, "because there is nothing more to do" (*True Stories*, 70). In her next two novels, *Bodily Harm* and *The Handmaid's Tale*, and in her poems, *True Stones*, Atwood writes that poem, the one "that invents nothing / and excuses nothing" (*True Stories*, 70): "Here is the handful / of

93

shadow I have brought back to you / this decay, this hope, this mouth- / full of dirt, this poetry" (*True Stories*, 93).

NOTES

1. Linda Hutcheon. "From Poetics to Narrative Structures: The Novels of Margaret Atwood." *Margaret Atwood: Language, Text and System.* Eds. Sherrill Grace and Lorraine Wier. Vancouver: University of British Columbia Press, 1983, 29.
2. Frank Davey. *Margaret Atwood: A Feminist Poetics.* Vancouver: Talonbooks, 1984, 92.
3. Sherrill Grace. *Violent Duality: A Study of Margaret Atwood.* Montreal: Véhicule Press, 1980, 135.

WORKS CITED

Atwood, Margaret. *The Animals of That Country.* Boston: Little, Brown and Company, 1968.

——. *Bodily Harm.* New York: Bantam, 1983.

——. *The Edible Woman.* New York: Popular Library, 1976.

——. *The Journals of Susanna Moodie.* Toronto: Oxford University Press, 1970.

——. *Lady Oracle.* New York: Avon, 1978.

——. *Life Before Man.* New York: Warner, 1983.

——. *Second Words.* Toronto: Anansi, 1983.

——. *Surfacing.* New York: Popular Library, 1976.

——. *True Stories.* New York: Simon and Schuster, 1981.

——. *You are Happy.* New York: Harper and Row, 1974.

The Here and Now of *Bodily Harm*

LORNA IRVINE

I think "feminine literature" is an organic, translated writing . . . translated from blackness, from darkness. Women have been in darkness for centuries. They don't know themselves. Or only poorly. And when women write, they translate darkness.

Marguerite Duras
From an interview by Susan Husserl-Kapit

Isn't the final goal of writing to articulate the body? For me the sensual juxtaposition of words has one function: to liberate a living past, to liberate matter.

Chantal Chawaf
"Linguistic Flesh"

With the opening words of Margaret Atwood's novel *Bodily Harm*, "this is how I got here,"[1] the reader, along with the main character, Rennie, is drawn into a labyrinthine plot that uses the themes and images of earlier Atwood novels, poems, and criticism in order to make a radical statement about female sexuality, the political body, and the female text. It is a terrifying novel, a mystery that systematically confuses characterization, plot development, setting, and even genre. Surrealism imbues the story, making ambiguous its temporal orientation as well as its location. Although the opening sentence implies a specific time (the present) and space (here), the novel in fact refuses clarification in favour of a nightmarish literary landscape that condenses the characters and displaces the affects. Throughout, plots and subplots intermingle, and the repetition of both words and

95

images creates a ritualistic pattern that often suspends movement. A number of italicized language fragments, seemingly disembodied, pierce the text, drawing to the reader's attention the peculiar balance between first- and third-person narration while, at the same time, signaling a possible here and now. It is a heavily coded novel, yet a novel that painfully articulates the female body, that perhaps even liberates it.

The novel's major code is the superficial plot that gives an apparent, although highly deceptive, order of development to a number of recorded events. The central character, Rennie Wilford, a free-lance journalist, is presented as possessing mediocre ability. The narrative appears to be her story, told sometimes in the first and sometimes in the third person, in which a splitting of subject and object is of considerable importance to the mystery of the novel. The story begins with Rennie's recounting of an attempted crime against her body. A man has entered her apartment and as a reminder of his visit has left a coil of rope on her bed. Like the game of Clue, the episode establishes a series of similar patterns that are also based on clues. Not long after this episode, Rennie is offered a chance to do a story for *Visor*, a magazine directed toward male readers. She accepts the assignment, flies to the Caribbean island where she is to do the travel piece and arrives at Sunset Inn, a place more ominously named than at first appears. For the next six days, she travels around the island, meeting people and becoming inadvertently involved in the island's current revolution. During the early morning of her seventh day on the island, and following a night of violent revolutionary outbreak, she is arrested. She then suffers, for about two weeks, in a poorly run Central American prison, from which she is finally rescued by a member of the Canadian diplomatic corps. She is put on a plane back to Canada where, as Audrey Thomas comments in a review of the novel, she has become, like the

Ancient Mariner, "a sadder but wiser person" (9-12). An acceptable, upbeat, Harlequin plot: another story about a victimized woman who wins in the end. A deceptive story!

Of course, we learn much more about Rennie than this plot summary suggests. Because she constantly reflects on the past, large segments of the novel present other stories, other lives. One such story is that of her relationship with Jake, a man with whom she has been living but who has moved out of the apartment shortly before the novel begins. Another story is that of her operation, a partial mastectomy. Daniel, the doctor who performed the operation, figures dominantly in her fantasy life; as she suggests, he has been imprinted on her, the first face she saw when emerging from the unaesthetic. Rennie also talks about her early life in the small town of Griswold, where she and her mother lived with her mother's parents. Memories of her grandmother flit in and out of her consciousness. As well, the stories of two other women are included, one told by Jocasta, a Toronto friend of Rennie's, and, on five separate occasions, those told by Lora, a woman whom Rennie meets on the island and who becomes her cell mate in the last section of the novel. Throughout, the present events and characters of the novel merge with those of the past. Thus, segments of alternating stories are condensed and displaced so that the operation, the grandmothers of the island, the sexually violent men, the doctors, the brutal beating of Lora, all have the resonance of recurrence rather than singularity. As a result, the texture of the novel is peculiarly dense.

Certainly the themes and images of the superficial stories of *Bodily Harm* allow a coherent literary critique and satisfy contemporary demands for extended analysis. The novel addresses itself to the nature of violence, to victimization, to women. The epigraph from John Berger's *Ways of Seeing* focuses immediate attention on these themes: "A man's presence suggests what he is capable of doing to you and for you. By contrast, a woman's presence . . . defines what can and cannot be done to her." Newspaper articles describe "those women they were always finding strewn about ravines or scattered here and there" (23); Jake gets sexually excited by imagining intercourse as pretended rape; taxi drivers and policemen make constant sexual innuendos; a deaf and dumb man on the island seems on the verge of attacking Rennie; the Toronto policemen's pornography museum displays women's bodies as maps of violence; on the island, men freely beat up their wives; attacked by the male guards in the prison, guards to whom she has been giving sexual favors in return for help, Lora is mutilated and possibly killed. Rennie's summary of the situation is inspired by her sexual involvement with Paul, whose boyish pride in his gun fills Rennie with terror: "She's afraid of men and it's simple. It's rational, she's afraid of men because men are frightening" (290).

The sexual battlefield with its various power plays is paralleled in certain nationalistic themes that appear from quite a different perspective in the opening section of *Survival*, Atwood's early book of criticism. There, Atwood discusses the ways in which victimization seems to dominate the Canadian imagination and offers her thematic study as a "map of the territory" (18). More important, she uses as a dominating question Northrop Frye's frequently quoted statement about Canadian literature, that the major question is "Where is here?" The opening sentence of *Bodily Harm* thus alerts the reader to the novel's interest in Canadian nationalism and to certain of its political intentions. The refrain, "the sweet Canadians," reiterated by the shrunken Fisher King, Dr. Minnow, means different things at different points in the novel. Sometimes, it implies the naïveté of Canadians, a theme given physical representation through the character of Rennie, who, like the narrator of *Surfacing*, represents the country in which she lives. Like

98

Canada, Rennie is perceived by many different characters as naïve, as politically uncomplicated, as obscurely old-fashioned. Towards the end of the novel, Paul says about her: "'For one thing you're nice . . . You'd rather be something else, tough or sharp or something like that, but you're nice, you can't help it. Naïve. But you think you have to prove you're not merely nice, so you get into things you shouldn't'" (15). At another point, an old couple questions Rennie: "'You're Canadian, aren't you? We always find the Canadians so nice, they're almost like members of the family. No crime rate to speak of. We always feel quite safe when we go up there'" (186). In this respect, then, the novel ironically attacks Canadian simplicity by dramatizing the massive involvement of Rennie in the political affairs of a country she knows so little about. Far from keeping her safe, her naïveté is responsible for her ultimate victimization. No one, not even the Canadians, can stay outside contemporary political violence or placidly castigate other countries for encouraging such violence. As Dr. Minnow says to Rennie: "'Everyone is in politics here, my friend . . . All the time. Not like the sweet Canadians'" (124) and, later, "'There is no longer any place that is not of general interest . . . The Sweet Canadians have not learned this yet'" (135). Furthermore, even Rennie, who at the beginning emphasizes her own neutrality ("she needs it for her work . . . Invisibility" [15]) is embarrassed by the Canadian official with his safari jacket and attempted neutrality. As she watches him following Dr. Minnow out of the room, she can think of him only as "the neutral-coloured Canadian" (191). Strikingly enough, the text itself represents the colours of the Canadian flag – red and white – by reiterating them in all kinds of different combinations.

Bodily Harm also self-consciously investigates the act of writing, even dramatizes the creative process. Because Rennie is a writer, the spatial and temporal ambiguity that

99

permeates the novel evokes the actual space and time of the writing act. Small spaces and moments of time punctuate the novel like clockwork, suggesting the painful physical problems that accompany composition. Furthermore, at the beginning of the novel, masculine and feminine readers, and by extension writers, are contrasted. Rennie has been associated with the "Relationships" column of a magazine called *Pandora*, and allusions to Pandora's box (thinly disguised as Lora's box) keep constantly before the reader the implications of the myth. Her present employment is with the magazine *Visor*, a magazine whose readership is predominantly male. As for the writer herself, she refuses to be taken seriously, insisting that she is merely interested in writing trendy articles. Her frivolity is, of course, misleading. Like every other stance in this novel, it is a defense. One of the poems from Atwood's *True Stories*, a collection published the same year as *Bodily Harm*, also emphasizes the shift that Rennie experiences, a shift from belief in a "real story" (*Bodily Harm* 64) to a recognition of the unreliability of narrative:

> The true story lies
> among the other stories
> [. . .]
> the true story is vicious
> and multiple and untrue

(*True Stories* 11)

The themes that emerge from the stories of *Bodily Harm* — victimization of women, nationalism, writing — are certainly important and can be related by readers and critics to all of Atwood's work and to that of many other writers. Yet, having said this much, I now insist that they do not, at least in their apparent form, explain this novel, do not clarify its geography and history, do not situate the italicized voice, do not account for the peculiarly evasive shifts of perspective, do not explain the emphasis on the unreliability of narrative, do not, finally, unmask the truly radical statement at the novel's core. In somewhat the same way as suggested by Frank Kermode in his analysis of Conrad's *Under Western Eyes*, "Secrets and Narrative Sequence," *Bodily Harm* is replete with secrets that pull against straightforward interpretation and cloud the major themes. Rennie admits that "she no longer trusts surfaces" (48) and announces that "almost nobody here is who they say they are at first" (150). Her fear of the "faceless stranger" moves in and out of consciousness, sometimes associated with specific characters, for example Paul, at other times merely a focus for free-floating anxiety. Although Rennie's stories dominate the text, as the novel progresses, it becomes increasingly clear that her reading of events is erroneous. In some fundamental way, she is blind. She plays Clue poorly: "What has she done, she's not guilty, this is happening to her for no reason at all" (286). Thus, the reader has great difficulty in accumulating the clues that will lead to the discovery of the space, the victim, and the weapon of the crime. Even the crime itself is unclear.

Most problematic is the time of the novel's action. Partly, as with many novels, this temporal ambiguity results from a reliance on recollection. In *Bodily Harm*, recollected stories interfere with the forward narrative movement and even break up the written page. Like the dismembered bodies referred to, the text itself seems repeatedly deconstructed. But the temporal ambiguity is not only a structural problem; it is also contextually important. Early in the novel, Rennie admits that she has "stopped thinking in years" (11). Indeed, as the novel progresses, it seems likely that she has stopped thinking in terms of time at all. Unable to assume a future ("'I'll tell you about it sometime,' she says, assuming the future; which is more than she can do" [47]), near the end, she admits: "There's the past, the present, the future: none of them will do" (282). Time, always critical for the constructor of stories, disintegrates completely. The opening sentence with its apparently assured present tense is therefore merely a cover, a secret. The concluding "this is what will happen" (293) that parallels the opening "this is how I got here" insists on temporal confusion right to the stopping of the novel by casting the narrative into the future tense. Indeed, even such narrative closure as is allowed by projected fantasy is questioned, for present, past, and future continue to cross through each other: "She will never be rescued. She has already been rescued" (301). Time is like the time of dreams. In "Postcard," similar ambiguities exist:

> Time comes in waves here, a sickness, one
> day after the other rolling on;
> I move up, it's called
> awake, then down into the uneasy
> nights, but never
> forward.
>
> (*True Stories* 18)

Vertical rather than horizontal movement perplexes the novel throughout.

This last observation introduces the other principal ambiguity of *Bodily Harm*, its space. To repeat the question asked of Canadian literature by Frye and Atwood: "Where is here?"[2] Certainly, the reader's attention to space is visually insisted on by repeated references to enclosed spaces that are being threatened or that reflect damage. The small apartment bedroom that contains the first of the novel's stories has been violated, a violation that is emphasized by Rennie's offering to show the investigating policemen her mastectomy scar. The enclosed cabin of the plane to the island is also connected with Rennie's damaged body for, as she enters, "she's afraid to look down, she's afraid she'll see blood, leakage, her stuffing coming out" (22). Lying in her room in the Sunset Inn, her hands across her chest, Rennie listens to the sounds from the next room, an eavesdropping insisted on by spatial constriction. The neighbouring couple's lovemaking eerily combines torture and sex, a sado-masochistic ritual that is emphasized here by the disembodied, italicized "*Oh please*," a cry repeated in other places in the novel, an ambiguous fragment (Who is speaking? To whom? From what space? At what time?) that becomes an important clue in the clarifying of the novel's locale. Other confined spaces – the cellar Rennie recalls being locked into by her grandmother, the basement apartment that Lora describes – condense into references to boxes (Pandora's, Lora's); and into statements such as Jake's, that women "should all be locked in cages" (73).[3]

Furthermore, the fear of enclosure invokes a claustrophobia that reflects death. Asked by Rennie what he dreams about, Paul answers, "a hole in the ground" (249). Dr. Minnow's coffin is yet another "box." The gravelike jail cell, five feet by seven feet, in which Lora and Rennie are incarcerated also figures dominantly in the measurements of the novel. Here is a space from which the stories of the text often seem to emerge, a central space in the novel. Such a space would help to account for the kind of story telling that occurs in *Bodily Harm* and also for the confusion of time: virtually unpunctuated days, one space, the creating of stories the only protection against insanity. It would account, too, for the thematic centrality of physical brutality, dominantly the fear of rape, and would explain the insistence on the spatial metaphors that connect enclosure and death. The ambiguous italicized words are given terrifying resonance if the reader answers the confusions and false leads of the novel by believing that *Bodily Harm* culminates with Rennie's physical crises, brought on by seeing a man

(Paul? the Prince of Peace? the deaf and dumb man?) being tortured by the prison guards in the yard of the prison: "She has been turned inside out, there's no longer a here and a there. Rennie understands for the first time that this is not necessarily a place she will get out of, ever. She is not exempt. Nobody is exempt from anything" (290). If the novel's spatial parameters are the prison cell and its temporal parameters the day of Lora's beating, Lora's dismemberment would become the dominant metaphor of the novel, and Rennie's inability to separate here and there, inside and outside would help to account for the way in which she reports Lora's beating. Furthermore, such a scenario also implies a combination for the textual Clue game: the guards in the prison with the penis / gun; the victim, Lora; or, in a possible displacement, Rennie.

Yet the disembodied voice of the novel, its splits, its mysteries, its secrecy, remains insistent. "This is how I got here." Is it possible for there to be another space, another time, another story? Certainly, one other space figures dominantly in the stories of the novel – the hospital room where Rennie undergoes her operation for breast cancer. So pervasive is this space in the themes and images of the novel that it gives considerable resonance to the ambiguous "here." It gives resonance also to the novel's time, and helps to account for the repeating of dreams, the recurrence of the question, "What do you dream about," the dream-like organization.

Rennie's stories seem, then, to imply a slipping in and out of consciousness that roughly corresponds to her experiences in the operating room. Even her dreams condense and displace anxieties about the operation. Her grandmother, a major actor in these dreams, looking for her hands, becomes a projection of Rennie herself, a foremother who, like Rennie, suffers fears about dismemberment. For example, in a dream occurring apparently at the Sunset Inn,

Rennie dreams of gardens, of her mother (who "can't take care of everything" (115), of hummingbirds, and, most important, of her grandmother. As she struggles to wake from the dream, she describes herself in "a long white cotton gown," although she insists that she is not in a hospital. Like her grandmother, she is looking for her hands. Again, she drifts into sleep, and again struggles into consciousness: "It's dawn; this time she's really awake, the mosquito netting hangs around her in the warm air like mist. She sees where she is, she's here, by herself, she's stranded in the future. She doesn't know how to get back" (116). Such combinations of waking and sleeping, of dreaming and experiencing, of sensory condensation and displacement disguise absolutely both time and space. The anaesthetic, the mosquito netting, and the mist illustrate Rennie's confused senses and clouded eyes. Furthermore, the sign system used implies yet another variation on the metaphoric game of Clue: the doctor in the hospital room with the knife, the victim Rennie.

Like the "picture-puzzles" of Freud's dream texts in *The Interpretation of Dreams*, *Bodily Harm* thus creates perplexity by disguising time and space and by representing the same thoughts in a number of different ways. Lost gardens and grandmothers, somewhere in the past, mingle with an indecipherable present and future. Towards the end, space and time become increasingly ambiguous and the characters condense, split, and reform with ever greater frequency. Apparently in the jail cell, Rennie allows her thoughts to wander wildly; she wants to end her stories. She thinks of Paul, then of the doctor, Daniel, of Daniel's hands, of "Daniel enclosed in a glass bubble," herself on the "outside looking in": "From here it's hard to believe that Daniel really exists" (284). But the real focus of her attention is, once again, her body, her "nibbled flesh"; she assures her reader-listener that "nothing has happened to her yet, nobody has done anything to her, she is unharmed. She may be dying, true, but if so she's doing it slowly, relatively speaking. Other people are doing it faster: at night there are screams" (284). I do not need to point out the ways in which this passage, like many other passages in the novel, simultaneously evokes the hospital bed and the jail cell; nor do I need to emphasize the obsession with the body. The concluding comments in these thoughts about Daniel are so much like the dream of her grandmother as to seem like an insistent accumulation of clues: "Rennie opens her eyes. Nothing in here has changed. Directly above her, up on the high ceiling, some wasps are building a nest . . . Pretend you're really here, she thinks. Now: what would you do?" (284). Where is here? Obviously, the passage does not answer that question. Yet, whether in a hospital bed or a jail cell, Rennie needs to distance herself from her body, to pretend. In these respects, she behaves like a writer.

Such condensed images inevitably create a surrealistic, rather than a realistic, landscape. The hummingbirds in the dream of her grandmother, the wasps building their nest on the ceiling, the sounds of the air-conditioner in the hospital room (and the draughts from open windows that keep occurring in Rennie's dreams), the concluding ride in the airplane where "there's too much air conditioning, wind from outer space flowing in through the small nozzles" (301) merge into one image – something cold and humming somewhere above Rennie's head. The clothing of the various characters also blends together: the safari jacket worn by the Canadian government official looks like a doctor's uniform; the outfits of the stewardesses on the plane, pink satin with white aprons, and the blue and white uniforms of the waitresses at the Sunset Inn are outfits similar to those worn by nurses. Whenever Rennie mentions her clothing, it is usually white, "a plain white cotton dress" (59), a "white shirt and wrap skirt, also white" (203). The bed she sleeps in with Paul has been "expertly made, hospital corners tucked firmly in" (203). Recalling a dream she has had during her night with Paul, Rennie describes "another man in bed with them; something white, a stocking or a gauze bandage, wrapped around his head" (217). The mosquito netting around her bed at the Sunset Inn blends with her description of crawling through "the grey folds of netting" (173) as she lies on the hospital bed and with the threatened suffocation she describes just before escaping to St. Antoine: "Rennie closes her eyes. Something with enormous weight comes down on them" (259). Daniel's hands blend with those of her grandmother. Her fantasized leaving of the jail corresponds with a patient's leaving a hospital: "Rennie will be taken to a small room, painted apple green. On the wall there will be a calendar with a picture of a sun-set on it. There will be a desk with a phone and some papers on it" (293). The recurring italicized words, "*malignant*," "*massive involvement*," "*terminal*," and the italicized statement overheard at Dr. Minnow's funeral, "*What did she die of? Cancer, praise the lord*," combine to give, in the disembodied voice of the novel, political and bodily correspondence. Blood colours the text.

Bodily Harm seems, therefore, a considerably more complicated text than at first appeared. Although the story as told by Rennie superficially follows narrative logic and gives the reader a plot to hold on to, that plot is in fact profoundly ambiguous. Unlike the cover story, the submerged stories follow no specific chronology nor do they make clear their space. Yet, from the clues gathered and the dreams interpreted, a here and now do emerge: it seems possible that the novel presents Rennie's drugged reflections in the hospital.

But what does the reader gain by discovering that the ambiguous here and now of the novel are in fact its subject? Furthermore, what point is there in establishing the connection between jail cell and hospital bed? The title

helps our search for an answer. The novel is predominantly concerned with bodies, most notably, with Rennie's. It
is also concerned with harm, the symbol of which, on the
body, is the mark of castration. Can we therefore discover,
on a woman's body, the marks that will allow us to read
her story? For much of the novel, Rennie reveals herself
to be a thoroughly manipulated writer, and repeatedly
emphasizes that she is not writing. Nonetheless, that her
body is to be imagined as potential material for inscription is abundantly clear. After Daniel operates on her, he
says: "Think of your life as a clean page. You can write
whatever you like on it" (84). Later, buying postcards to
send home, Rennie recalls this conversation with Daniel
and reflects that "empty is not the same as clean" (85). She
also recalls herself complaining to Jake: "Sometimes I feel
like a blank sheet of paper . . . For you to doodle on"
(105). Rennie even establishes a physical difference
between phallic penetration and female passivity when she
wonders "what it was like to be able to throw yourself into
another person, another body, a darkness like that. Women
could not do it. Instead they had darkness thrown into
them" (235-36). In many of the ways elucidated by
Gilbert and Gubar, for Rennie the pen is phallic, the page
the female body.[4]

The powerlessness of women's inscribing is certainly
attacked by Helene Cixous in "The Laugh of the Medusa,"
when she insists that "woman must write her self: must
write about women and bring women to writing, from
which they have been driven away as violently as from their
bodies – for the same reasons, by the same law, with the
same fatal goal. Woman must put herself into the text – as
into the world and into history – by her own movement"
(875). And, later: "Here they are, returning, occurring over
and again, because the unconscious is impregnable. They
have wandered around in circles confined to the narrow

108

room in which they've been given a *deadly brainwashing*"
(877, my italics). Perhaps, then, Atwood's novel illustrates,
ironically, inscription of the female body and, by connecting hospital room and jail cell, dramatically presents the
injury to the female body that results from its confinement.
Similar bodily harm is described in another of the poems
from *True Stories*:

> But power
> like this is not abstract, it's not concerned
> with politics and free will, it's beyond slogans
> and as for passion, this
> is its intricate denial,
> the knife that cuts lovers
> out of your flesh like tumours,
> loving you breastless
> and without a name,
> flattened, bloodless, even your voice
> cauterized by too much pain.
>
> a flayed body untangled
> string by string and hung
> to the wall, an agonized banner
> displayed for the same reason
> flags are. (51)

The metaphoric relationship between the female body and
the country, Canada, here, as in *Bodily Harm*, insists on the
connection of the politics of sexual power with the politics
of colonial domination, for, like women, Canada is only
now emerging from "deadly brainwashing." Atwood seems
to suggest that such a brainwashing has clearly interfered
with both Canada's history and her literature.

Up to a point, the novel therefore appears to be an intricate analysis of female history (with underlying allusions to
Canada), and a record of the dismembering of the female
body. Inside and outside are radically confused. Rennie's
divided consciousness, like the split space and time of the

narrative, seems to represent both disrupted female history and a confused sense of self. Early in the novel, she imagines "herself from the outside, as if she were a moving target in someone else's binoculars" (40). Both inside and outside are subjects in this novel; so too are the conflicts between appearance and actuality, stereotypes and realistic characters, woman's superficial exterior and the interior text of her self. Rennie struggles with repression. "Her real fear, irrational but a fear, is that the scar will come undone in the water, split open like a faulty zipper, and she will turn inside out" (80). She is physically revolted by Lora's hand: "She doesn't like the sight of ravage, damage, the edge between inside and outside blurred like that" (86). The operation thus seems a metaphor for a radical split in consciousness and for the repression that results:

> There's a line between being asleep and awake which Rennie is finding harder and harder to cross. Now she's up near the ceiling, in the corner of a white room, beside the air-conditioning unit, which is giving out a steady hum. She can see everything, clear and sharp, under glass, her body is down there on the table, covered in green cloth. There are figures around her in masks, they're in the middle of a performance, an incision, but it's not skin-deep, it's the heart they're after, in there somewhere, squeezing away, a fist opening and closing around a ball of blood, (172-73)

The separation between consciousness and the female body-text is here dramatically described. So too is the act of writing. Like all the other hands of the novel (Lora's, the grandmother's, Daniel's, the deaf and dumb man's), the fist that opens and closes around "a ball of blood" seems a metaphor for painful inscription.

Nonetheless, *Bodily Harm* is not, finally, a negative text. As the sign of the father is recognized ("she's afraid of men . . . because men are frightening" [290]), a new sign begins to emerge. For women, this sign seems to be that of the mother, the sign of creativity, freedom, even flight. Thus, this novel also describes the joining of splits that have dominated texts by women. Rennie first imagines joining through positive sexual intercourse, an experience that is paralleled with the separation experienced on the operating table:

> Nobody lives forever, who said you could? This much will have to do, this much is enough. She's open now, she's been opened, she's being drawn back down, she enters her body again, and there's a moment of pain, incarnation, this may be only the body's desperation, a flareup, a last clutch at the world before the long slide into final illness and death; but meanwhile she's solid after all, she's still here on the earth, she's grateful, he's touching her, she can still be touched. (204)

But it is not enough. Sexual joining does not give woman control of the pen. Instead, Rennie has to go further; she has to give birth to herself. In a powerful doubling towards the end of the novel, Lora and Rennie become one: "She turns Lora over, her body is limp and thick, a dead weight . . . She's holding Lora's left hand, between both of her own, perfectly still, nothing is moving, and yet she knows she is pulling on the hand as hard as she can, there's an invisible hole in the air, Lora is on the other side of it and she has to pull her through, she's gritting her teeth with the effort" (298-99). A birth indeed!

A three-part movement seems, then, to define the production of a female text: a recognition of the silence imposed on the castrated body by patriarchal rules; an illustration of the use the male pen has made of the female body as text; a final enlightenment that gives birth to an independent and complete female body. When this birth occurs, the female text is ready to be written. Only then, as Cixous suggests, can women "take pleasure in jumbling the order of space, in dissolving it, in changing around the furniture, dislocating things and values, breaking them all up, emptying structures." Flying becomes "woman's gesture – lying in language and making it fly" (887). When Rennie describes flight at the end of the novel, she stops being text and becomes writer. She can now inscribe herself.

According to Marks and de Courtivron, French feminists "poke fun at the male erection, the male preoccupation with getting it up, keeping it up, and the ways in which the life and death of the penis are projected into other aspects of culture: in the need for immortality and posterity, in the fear of death, in the centralized organization of political systems, in the impossibility of living in the here and now" (36). To a considerable degree, Atwood's text does "poke fun" at the penis, although the humour is very black, and the knowledge of the depths of its destructiveness is paramount. Throughout, the game of Clue implies a kind of conjunction between play and torture, between fun and terror. Yet Rennie can imagine extricating herself from its various combinations, even from the one that most damages her own writing: man with the pen in the text, the victim, the female body. She learns how to write herself and about herself. Furthermore, she learns to deal with the fear of death ("Zero is waiting somewhere, whoever said there was life everlasting; so why feel grateful? She doesn't have much time left, for anything. But neither does anyone else. She's paying attention, that's all" [301]), to question "the centralized organization of political systems," to live in "the here and now." Luce Irigaray insists that woman's dominant pleasure is touching rather than seeing. Rennie learns the importance of touching: "she can feel the shape of a hand in hers, both of hers, there but not there, like the afterglow of a match that's gone out. It will always be there now" (300).

In *Archetypal Patterns in Women's Fiction*, Annis Pratt writes: "Since women are alienated from time and space, their plots take on cyclical, rather than linear, form and their houses and landscapes surreal properties" (11). Spatial and temporal alienation dominates much of Atwood's novel and its landscape, as Rennie herself emphasizes, is insistently surreal. Yet, at the same time, in this moving dramatization of the female body-text, the novel arrives somewhere. Although the time and the space of the novel are limited (a confined area, one day), by the end Rennie has become her own mother, has given birth to herself. Dismembered, fragmented, victimized, the female body has regrouped, has become its own subject. No longer the blank page, it is prepared to write itself, to report. Thus, in a fundamental way, the title, *Bodily Harm*, has been canceled, the sign of castration (the former sign of the female sex) refused.[5] Not surprisingly, Rennie "for the first time in her life . . . can't think of a title" (301). She has discovered herself through a new and subversive language.

NOTES

1. I would like to thank the National Endowment for the Humanities for the grant that made the writing of this paper possible. Page references in the text are to the following editions: *Bodily Harm* (Toronto: McClelland and Stewart, 1981); *True Stories* (Toronto: Oxford Univ. Press, 1981). A shorter version of this essay was presented at the National Women's Studies Association Conference in 1983; a longer, slightly different version constitutes chapter 2 of *Sub/Version*, my study of Canadian women writers published in 1986. Since working through various of the themes in the novel, I have read Elame Tuttle Hansen's "Fiction and (Post) Feminism in Atwood's *Bodily Harm*." As I do, Hansen pays close attention to the opening sentence of *Bodily Harm*, to the subversive feminist argument throughout, and to the connections between politics and narrative. Hansen's emphasis on consciousness raising and on metaphors of healing foregrounds important elements in the text to which I have paid less attention.
2. A number of titles reflect the importance of this question to Canadian literature, for example, Frank Davey's *From There to Here: A Guide to English Canadian Literature Since 1960*; John Moss's *The Canadian Novel Here and Now*; Sandra Djwa's "The Where of Here: Margaret Atwood and a Canadian Tradition."

3. In *The Wacousta Syndrome*, Gaile McGregor argues that, at least from the evidence of their cultural artifacts, Canadians distrust transcendence. Her discussion of Jack Hodgins's *The Invention of the World* strikingly reflects what I have just said about *Bodily Harm*: "In Hodgins's fictional universe, for example, life is a closed system, a *box*, from which – as from the reception hall that stands as its symbolic correlative at the end of the novel – there is only one exit, under the aegis of the Horseman, death" (82). Later, McGregor writes: "From one point of view the 'box' makes a mockery of human aspirations. From another, a demythicized landscape says that anything is possible – at least "inside." Canadian literature in the twentieth century has largely addressed itself to the task of negotiating if not often actually reconciling these two extremes" (90).

4. The whole first section of *The Madwoman in the Attic* is introduced by the now famous question: "Is the pen a metaphorical penis?" Also relevant is Susan Gubar's "'The Blank Page' and the Issues of Female Creativity," in *Critical Inquiry*. She writes that Dinesen's story "can be used to illustrate how women's image of herself as text and artifact has affected attitudes toward her physicality and how these attitudes in turn shape the metaphors through which she imagines her creativity" (247).

5. In *Communities of Women*, Auerbach describes Monique Wittig's work symbolically as follows: "The apparent zero of the vulva, token of traditional and Freudian visions of female incompleteness, is transmuted by female art into the circle of eternity" (186).

Nature and Nurture in Dystopia

The Handmaid's Tale

ROBERTA RUBENSTEIN

I

One might say that Margaret Atwood has always been concerned with issues of survival — first as a condition of Canadian experience and, more recently, as a condition of female experience. In her latest fiction and poetry, she connects the personal and political dimensions of victimization and survival in explicitly female and feminist terms. Moreover, in the course of her fiction the terms of survival have become increasingly problematic. In her fablelike *The Handmaid's Tale*,[1] she stunningly extends, recasts, and inverts two of the most persistent clusters of theme and imagery that originate in her earlier concern with survival: *nature* and *nurture*.

As a number of her commentators have pointed out, Atwood uses the imagery of nature in her poetry and fiction in complex ways, delineating the terms of survival and growth as well as oppression and death. Concurrently, from the beginning of her fictional *oeuvre* in particular, *nurture* — I use the term here as ironic shorthand for motherhood and procreation — is viewed in problematic terms. In *The Edible Woman*, Marian MacAlpin's female friends dramatize extreme attitudes toward procreation as a "natural" function of female identity: Ainsley is obsessed with becoming pregnant while Clara is virtually engulfed by maternity. Marian views both women with skepticism and anxiety. A central problem for the narrator of *Surfacing* is the necessity to come to terms with her denied abortion; the somewhat ambiguous sign of her psychological recovery is her desire to be impregnated by her primitive lover, Joe.

Joan Foster of *Lady Oracle* also feels anxiety about motherhood, principally because for much of her life (as revealed in her story) she has remained psychologically merged with her destructive mother. Her childhood obesity and her adult fantasies of the sideshow "Fat Lady" are grotesque exaggerations of anxieties about maternity. In *Life Before Man* Elizabeth Schoenhof and Lesje Green represent complementary views of motherhood. Elizabeth has appreciative but rather remote relationships with her two daughters; Lesje, unmarried but perhaps pregnant (by Elizabeth's husband, Nate) by the end of the narrative, seeks maternity to confirm her fragile female identity. Rennie Wilford of *Bodily Harm* worries that the cancer in her body, which has already resulted in the loss of part of a breast, will fundamentally alter her reproductive capacity.

In *The Handmaid's Tale*, female anxieties associated with fertility, procreation, and maternity are projected as feminist nightmare and cultural catastrophe. Atwood demonstrates the way in which the profound and irreconcilable split between "pro-life" and "pro-choice" ideologies of reproduction in contemporary social experience corroborate female ambivalence about childbearing in patriarchy. She imagines a world in which women are explicitly defined by their potential fertility (or its absence); procreation and maternity are simultaneously idealized and dehumanized.

Atwood has recently acknowledged her increasingly explicit ideological focus, noting that there is a vital connection between the function of the novel as a "moral instrument," the responsibility of the writer to "bear witness," and politics. As she elaborates, "By 'political' I mean having to do with power: who's got it, who wants it, how it operates; in a word, who's allowed to do what to whom, who gets what from whom, who gets away with it and how" ("An End to Audience?" *Second Words* 353). In her most recent novel to date, the correspondences between "personal" and "political" find brilliant and disturbing expression. Both public and private worlds are radically altered, exaggerating the unresolved cultural and ideological controversy over the circumstances of procreation

In the Republic of Gilead the "natural" world is utterly denatured. Pollution of the environment has resulted in adult sterility and genetic mutation and deformity of off-spring; generativity itself is at risk. Hence fertile females are made vessels for procreation; anatomy is indeed destiny. The physical confining rooms, walls, and other actual boundaries of the Republic of Gilead corroborate the condition of reproductive "confinement" to which the handmaids are subject. Maternity is both wish (handmaids are discarded after three unsuccessful attempts at pregnancy) and fear (the baby, unless deformed and declared an "Unbaby," becomes the property of the handmaid's Commander and his wife). The surrogate mother's function ceases after a brief lactation period following delivery of a healthy child.

The handmaid Offred (the narrator), subjected to sexual exploitation masquerading as religious fervor and worship of procreation, experiences herself as utterly subordinated to the procreative function. In her former life she had regarded her body as an "instrument" under her own control — with "limits . . . but nevertheless lithe, single, solid, one with me" (84). In Gilead, her body, like that of her coequal "handmaids," exist literally to be used against her: "Now the flesh rearranges itself differently. I'm a cloud, congealed around a central object, the shape of a pear, which is hard and more real than I am and glows red within its translucent wrapping. Inside it is a space, huge as the sky at night . . ." (84). Under the pressure of terrifying alternatives, Offred (whose name encodes her indentured sexuality: both "offered" and the property "Of-Fred") "resign[s her] body freely, to the uses of others. They can do what they like with me. I am abject" (298) — and object.

II

From the central issue of procreation to the language and imagery that form the substructure of Offred's narrative, *The Handmaid's Tale* demonstrates multiple inversions and violations of *nature* and *natural*. Not only is the female body used as a tool for reproduction, but bodies in general are objectified and described in terms of parts rather than as wholes. In *Bodily Harm* Atwood implied that the reduction of the body to a "thing" is connected to its violation; in *The Handmaid's Tale* torture and mutilation as well as less extreme forms of manipulation underscore the ruthless and repressive value that shape Gilead. Both men and women who are identified as political "enemies" of the state — guilty of such crimes as "gender treachery" (53) — are sacrificed at public ceremonies called "Salvagings" (the word resonates ironically with *salvage, salvation,* and *savaging*) in which they are mutilated and hanged in public view.

Other images throughout the narrative reinforce the symbolism of disembodiment and dismemberment. When Offred tries to recall her visceral connections to the husband and daughter from whom she has been so abruptly separated, she mourns,

> Nobody dies from lack of sex. It's lack of love we die from. There's nobody here I can love . . . Who knows where they are or what their names are now? They might as well be nowhere, as I am for them. I too am a missing person . . . Can I be blamed for wanting a real body, to put my arms around? Without it I too am disembodied.(113)

Most obviously, Offred and other handmaids are, to those in power in Gilead, merely parts of bodies: "two-legged wombs" (146). The doctor who examines them periodically for signs of pregnancy never even sees their faces; he "deals with a torso only" (70). The ceiling ornament in Offred's room resembled "the place in a face where the eye has been taken out" (17); in fact, there are Eyes – the network of informants (C–Eye–A?) – everywhere. The grappling hooks on the large Berlin Wall-like structure where criminals are hanged resemble "appliances for the armless" (42). An image of people with "no legs" (143) resonates with the unknown but terrible torture to which the rebel handmaid Moira is subjected (102); and with Offred's first intimation of the changing dispensation that has culminated in the Republic of Gilead. When she and other women were fired from their jobs and summarily stripped of political and legal rights, she felt as if someone had "cut off [her] feet" (188). In these latter instances of literal or symbolic mutilation of female feet, the image of Chinese footbinding – another form of social control of women – comes to mind.

In Gilead, Aunt Lydia (one of the "Aunts," who retain power in the puritanical state through their role as indoctrinators of the handmaids) speaks distastefully of women in the recent past who cultivated suntans, "oiling themselves like roast meat on a spit . . ." (65). In her former life, Offred had been aware of the self mutilations practiced by women who, desperate to attract men, had "starved themselves thin or pumped their breasts full of silicone, had their noses cut off" (231). She also recalls more violent crimes against the (implicitly female) body, as expressed in newspaper stories of "corpses in ditches or the woods, bludgeoned to death or mutilated, interfered with as they used to say . . ." (66). In Gilead the handmaids, as part of their "re-education" in submission, are made to watch old pornographic films from the seventies and eighties in which women appear in various attitudes of submission, brutalization, and grotesque mutilation. Extrapolating from these contemporary realities, Atwood extends into the future her critique of female brutalization articulated in *Bodily Harm* and in recent essays.

The imagery of mutilation and dismemberment permeates the narrator's own language. Offred struggles to "reconstruct" (144) her fragmented selfhood and to justify the choices she has made (or which have been imposed on her) under the circumstances she describes. Her past experiences, apparently severed from the "present" time of Gileadean tyranny, are in fact linked by these very images of female brutalization. The terse words she exchanges with other handmaids, who may or may not be trustworthy confidantes, are "amputated speech" (211). Late in her story Offred apologizes to an unknown audience in whom she must believe for her own survival; her story is an act of self-generation that opposes the oppressive obligations of procreation. She describes her narrative as if it were herself, "a body caught in crossfire or pulled apart by force . . . this sad and hungry and sordid, this limping and mutilated story" (279).

III

Among the multiple inversions of normalcy in *The Handmaid's Tale* are frequent references to animals, plants, smells, and other objects or experiences typically associated with "nature." In Gilead the changing seasons bring no solace; spring is "undergone" (160). The month of May, however, is linked with the one possibility of freedom: the password of the resistance movement, "Mayday," with its coded message of "*M'aidez*" (54).

Flowers are among objects of the natural world whose symbolic associations have not been entirely corrupted. Offred frequently describes them in terms of colour and variety and, late in her narrative, confesses that they are among the "good things" she has tried to put in her sordid story (279). More often, flowers and plants suggest the confining circumstances of sexuality and reproduction. Offred struggles to keep the image of crimson tulips (also the colour of the nunlike robes worn by the handmaids) free from association with blood. The blossoms worn by Serena Joy (the ironic name of Offred's Commander's wife) are withered, like her sexuality; flowers are, Offred reminds herself, merely "the genital organs of plants" (91). Elsewhere she describes the reeking "stink" of "pollen thrown into the wind in handfuls, like oyster spawn into the sea. All this prodigal breeding" (190). Handmaids are told to think of themselves as seeds (28); their password to each other is "Blessed be the fruit" (29) – yet seeds and fruit are associated with manipulated, not natural, reproduction.

The narrative is studded with such references to plant and animal life – generally primitive or lower forms – which are often juxtaposed with aspects of the human body / or sexuality. The animals in Gilead are, for the most part, repugnant. A virtual menagerie of insects, fish, fowl, and beasts parades, figuratively, through the narrative: ant, beetle, fly, worm, oyster, mollusk, rat, mouse, fish, frog, snake, pigeon, hawk, vulture, chicken, turkey, pig, sheep, horse, cat, dog, elephant. The handmaids are treated like brood livestock: tattooed with "cattle brand (266), they are kept in line by women called Aunts who wield electric cattleprods.

The "livestock of the narrative is partly of the zoo, partly of the barnyard – the latter figures recalling Orwell's satiric *Animal Farm*. Offred thinks of herself, in the eyes of the powers of Gilead as a "prize pig" (79); another handmaid takes mincing steps like "trained pig" (29). Both usages resonate ironically with the other-gendered "chauvinist pig[s]" (131) and "fucking pigs" (190) of Offred's mother's generation. A number of the animals images are associated with confinement: caged rats in mazes (79, 174), "held birds" (80) or birds with wings clipped or "stopped in flight" (289, 305), and the predatory relationship of spider to fly (89).

Handmaids are both sexual "bait" and "baited," as in the sense of "fishbait" (164) or "throwing peanuts at elephants" (212).

Often, the animal references suggest the debased, dena-tured, dismembered human body as mere flesh. Offred, walking after a rainy night on a path through the back lawn that suggests "a hair parting" (27), observes half-dead worms, "flexible and pink, like lips" (27). In the dehuman-ized sexual act (a *ménage à trois* in the service of insemina-tion: the Commander, his Wife, and the Handmaid), the penis is disembodied: the male "tentacle, his delicate stalked slug's eye, which extrudes, expands, winces, and shrivels back into himself when touched wrongly, grows big again, bulging a little at the tip, traveling forward as if along a leaf, into [the women], avid for vision" (98). Elsewhere Offred imagines sexual encounters between "Angels" and their brides (insipid young men and women of Gilead who actu-ally marry) as "furry encounters . . . cocks like three-week-old carrots, anguished fumbling upon flesh cold and unre-sponding as uncooked fish" (234). Similarly, she imagines a balding Commander with his wife and handmaid, "fertiliz-ing away like mad, like a rutting salmon . . ." (230).

Thus, in the perverse relations of Gilead, the distinctions between "natural" and "unnatural," between human and non-human, are grotesquely inverted or reduced. In a cen-tral passage Atwood suggestively links these levels of imagery and theme, clustering the ideas of institutionalized reproduction, environmental pollution, and the inversions, between animal, vermin, and human that results from these perversions of normalcy. As Offred explains,

The air got too full, once, of chemicals, rays, radiation, the water swarmed with toxic molecules, all of that takes years to clean up, and meanwhile they creep into your body, camp out in your fatty cells. Who knows, your very flesh may be polluted, dirty as an oily beach, sure death to shore birds and unborn babies. Maybe a vulture would

die of eating you. Maybe you light up in the dark, like an old-fashioned watch. Death watch. That's a kind of beetle, it buries carrion.

I can't think of myself, my body, sometimes, without seeing the
skeleton: how I must appear to an electron. A cradle of life made of
bones; and within, hazards, warped proteins, bad crystal jagged as
glass. Women took medicines, pills, men sprayed trees, cows ate grass,
all that souped-up piss flowed into the rivers. Not to mention the
exploding atomic power plants, along the San Andreas fault, nobody's
fault, during the earthquakes, and the mutant strain of syphilis no
mould could touch. Some did it themselves, had themselves tied shut
with catgut or scarred with chemicals. (122)

The chances of giving birth to a deformed infant are, the
handmaids learn during their indoctrination, one in four.
Yet Gileadean ideology prohibits birth control and abortion under any circumstances as "unnatural" and obliges
the handmaids to submit to "natural" childbirth without
medication. The pregnancy that culminates in birth during
Offred's narrative is a manifestation of the revolt by nature,
the blurring of categories of living forms. Before the handmaid Janine delivers, Offred speculates on whether the
baby will be normal or "an Unbaby, with pinhead or a
snout like a dog's, or two bodies, or a hole in its heart or
no arms, or webbed hands and feet" (122). In fact the baby
initially seems normal, but is later discovered to be
deformed and is mysteriously disposed of. Despite the
obsessive focus on procreation, actual children are notably
absent from Gilead. The only child described in the narrative is the young daughter from whom Offred has been
painfully separated.

As part of the inversion of "natural" in the unnatural
Republic of Gilead, Atwood demonstrates the assault on
the senses as well as the body and the psyche. In keeping
with the implicit barnyard references, Gilead *stinks*. The
stench of rotting flesh from corpses of executed political
enemies — including doctors who practiced abortion —
masks the equally humanmade but relatively less repugnant

odours of "Pine and Floral" deodorizing sprays. As Offred phrases it, "people retain the taste" for these artificial scents as expression of "purity" (174) – embodying the false connection between cleanliness and godliness.

Conversely, uncleanliness is associated with sin and – since sex is evil in Gilead apart from procreation – sexuality. The servant Marthas express distaste toward the handmaids, objecting to their smell; the handmaids, to whom baths are permitted as a luxury rather than as a hygienic routine, are regarded as unclean not only in literal but in moral sense.[2] Nuns who are forced to renounce celibacy and become reproductive objects have "an odour of witch about them, something mysterious and exotic . . . " (232). When Offred first observes Nick, her Commander's chauffeur who later becomes her lover, she wonders whether or not he supports the status quo arrangements between the sexes. As she expresses her doubts, "Smells fishy, they used to say; or, I smell a rat. Misfit as odour" (28). Yet, instead, she thinks of "how he might smell. Not fish or decaying rat: tanned skin, moist in the sun, filmed with smoke. I sigh, inhaling" (28). When Offred tries to (and tries not to) imagine what might have happened to her husband, Luke, she thinks of him "surrounded by a smell, his own, the smell of a cooped-up animal in a dirty cage" (115). Later the rebel handmaid Moira describes her contact with the underground resistance movement in similar terms. "'I almost made it out. They got me up as far as Salem, then in a truck full of chickens into Maine. I almost puked from the smell'" (259).

The air of Gilead is stagnant, suffocating, oppressive: literally the polluted atmosphere; symbolically, the claustrophobia and oppression experienced by its unwilling female captives. Offred describes the atmosphere of a "birthing" – a collective ceremony, attended by both handmaids and wives who coach the delivering handmaid – in language that reverberates with other images derived from animals and nature: "the smell is of our own flesh, an organic smell, sweat and a tinge of iron, from the blood on the sheet, and another smell, more animal, that's coming, it must be, from Janine: a smell of dense, of inhabited caves . . . Smell of matrix" (133).

As the sense of smell is more typically assaulted by the unnatural, so is the sense of taste and the experience of hunger. Reference to the smell of food also demonstrates the perverse connection – or disconnection – between sensory stimuli and their objects. The odour of nail polish, improbably, stimulates Offred's appetite (39). Recalling the sexual violation termed "date rape" in her former life, she remembers that the term sounded like "some kind of desert. *Date Rape*" (48).

In fact, like sex in Gilead, food serves only functional, not emotional, appetites. In a parody of the Lord's Prayer, Offred makes the connection between bread and spiritual sustenance, observing, "I have enough daily bread . . . The problem is getting it down without chocking" (204). The yeasty aroma of baking bread, one of the few pleasant smells in Gilead, also recalls comfortable kitchens and "mothers": both Offred's own mother and herself as a mother. Accordingly, it is a "treacherous smell" (57) that she must resist in order not to be overwhelmed by loss. Later she provides another context for these ambiguous associations as she recalls her childhood confusion about the extermination of the Jews: "In ovens, my mother said; but there weren't any pictures of the ovens, so I got some confused notion that these deaths had taken place in kitchens. There is something especially terrifying to a child in that idea. Ovens mean cooking, and cooking comes before eating. I thought these people had been eaten. Which in a way I suppose they had been" (154–55).

Late in the narrative, Offred extends this link between eating and sacrifice. She describes another "Salvaging," the public execution of handmaids accused of treason and sacrificed before breakfast; she and the other handmaids grip a rope that reeks of tar, the reaction to her compulsory complicity in the horrifying event discloses the extent of her emotional numbing and deprivation. The tar odour makes her feel sick; yet at the same time,

> Death makes me hungry. Maybe it's because I've been emptied; or maybe the body's way of seeing to it that I remain alive, continue to repeat its bedrock prayer: *I am, I am*. I am, still.
> I want to go to bed, make love, right now.
> I think of the word *relish*.
> I could eat a horse. (293, Atwood's italics)

Offred's hungers are both literal and symbolic. Earlier, she had been "ravenous for news" (29). When her Commander, having sought her out for forbidden companionship, allows her the proscribed act of reading, she reads like starving person finally given food – "voraciously, almost skimming, trying to get as much into my head as possible before the next long starvation. If it were eating it would be the gluttony of the famished, if it were sex it would be swift furtive standup in an alley somewhere" (194). The pieces in the Scrabble game she plays with her Commander remind her of candies: peppermint, lime, "delicious" (149). In Gilead, the act of intellectual intercourse is the equivalent of sin; as Offred puns, "Quick, eat those words" (191).

"Nature" is also invoked in Gilead as justification for male sexual dominance and female oppression. Offred's Commander advises her that the era of romantic courtship and marriages based on love – the older dispensation – was "an anomaly, historically speaking . . . All we've done is to return things to Nature's norm" (232). This "norm," however, leaves something to be desired for men who still prefer sex in the old manner, as conquest rather than duty. Those with power have access to a nightclub – brothel called Jezebel's. Resembling a Playboy Bunny Club, it is stocked with women in provocative costumes (primarily females "unassimilated" into other Gileadian roles) and private rooms for sexual assignation. To Offred's assumption that such things are "strictly forbidden," the Commander rejoins, "'but everyone's human, after all . . . [Y]ou can't cheat Nature . . . Nature demands variety, for men . . . [I]t's part of the procreational strategy. It's Nature's plan'" (248-49).[3] Even at Jezebel's, the ubiquitous cattleprod-wielding Aunts preside, supervising the women's "rest breaks" and reinforcing the sense of sexual slavery that prevails in Gilead. The "forbidden" is accommodated, but only to serve traditional assumptions about male, not female sexuality.

Offred's dark story of female exploitation concludes with an ambiguous event. A van arrives for her and – like an experience described by one of Kafka's characters – she has no way of knowing whether she is approaching her own "salvaging" or her salvation: whether she is being delivered into the hands of spies or rescuers. Entering the vehicle, she faces either her "end or a new beginning . . . I have given myself over into the hands of strangers, because it can't be helped" (307). The ambiguity corroborates the earlier conflations of death and birth: "And so I step up, into the darkness within; or else the light" (307).

In the narrative's ironic coda, "Historical Notes on *The Handmaid's Tale*," the reader discovers that Offred's story was originally spoken onto audio tapes, presumably after her escape from the Republic of Gilead. From the distant perspective of the year 2195, at the Twelfth Symposium on Gileadean Studies held in Nunavit ("None-Of-It" – presumably somewhere in the Arctic reaches of Canada), anthropologists and historians meet to debate the chronology and authenticity of events detailed in Offred's story. (One imagines Atwood wryly anticipating her commentators at the annual rites of MLA!). In this pseudopedantic coda, the imagery of nature that is so consistently inverted in the handmaid's own narrative is briefly parodied. The conference facilitators bear names (presumably analogous to Canadian Inuit) with associations with nature: Professors Maryann Crescent Moon and Johnny Running Dog. Program participants can avail themselves of special activities, including a fishing expedition and Nature Walk (311).

From the more "objective" perspective of scholarly research, Professor Pieixoto, an archivist whose remarks comprise most of the coda, focuses less on the details of Offred's life than on the *men* who shaped it. Yet, as he concludes, "the past is a great darkness, and filled with echoes. Voices may reach us from it; but what they say to us is imbued with the obscurity of the matrix out of which they come . . . " (324).

Along with the professor's concessions to the limits of interpretation, his choice of words is particularly resonant, given the narrative that precedes his remarks. The "matrix" of Offred's experience – with its linguistic associations with mother and matter – is the matrix out of which Atwood has written her dystopian fantasy of female oppression. If "nature" and "nurture" are the matrices out of which we come, *The Handmaid's Tale*, by inverting both, demonstrates the "broad outlines of the moment in history" (317) in which we live: the inhospitable environment in which female identity must discover itself. Appropriately, the narrative ends with the interrogative, "'Are there any questions?'" (324).

NOTES

1. Margaret Atwood. *The Handmaid's Tale.* Toronto: McClelland and Stewart, 1985. Page references in the text are to this edition.
2. I am grateful to Annette Kolodny for pointing out the "literality" of this detail.
3. In a brilliant and influential essay, "Is Female to Male as Nature Is to Culture," Ortner has traced the phenomenological linkages between "female" and "nature" in terms that illuminate Atwood's narrative. According to Ortner, women are perceived, in virtually all societies, as "closer" to nature. This proximity derives from physiological functions, domestic roles (including childbearing), and psychic makeup. The consequences of the cultural attribution of women as "intermediate" between culture and nature can be interpreted as "middle status" in a hierarchy, as "mediating" between the two categories, or as ambiguous (both "above" and "below" culture).

Cat's Eye

Elaine Risley's Retrospective Art

CORAL ANN HOWELLS

> What's the difference between vision and a vision? The former relates to something it's assumed you've seen, the latter to something it's assumed you haven't. Language is not always dependable either.[1]

This passage from Margaret Atwood's prose poem with its questioning of the reliability of modes of visual perception and of language might serve as preface to *Cat's Eye*, her autobiographical fiction which is itself a challenge to life-writing, that ambiguous literary genre which Shirley Neuman claims lacks any generic unity and which Paul De Man asserts is no genre at all.[2] Incidentally, the hybrid form of the prose poem would seem to prefigure the transgressive form of the novel itself, with its combined discourses of fiction and autobiography, painting and science, in its attempts to represent the subject of / in the text. Arguably we could read *Cat's Eye* as Atwood's own retrospective glance back at the imaginative territory of her earlier fictions,[3] but I do not want to pursue that exploration here. Instead, I shall focus on *Cat's Eye* as Atwood's version of life-writing in the feminine, where her middle-aged protagonist Elaine Risley struggles to define herself as a subject through figuring out her life-story in different versions. Who is she? And what is the significance of the *Cat's Eye* of the title? Elaine is a painter; the story is littered with references to her pictures and culminates in her first retrospective exhibition in Toronto. It is her return to her home town for this exhibition which provides the stimulus for her curiously doubled narrative with its "discursive" memoir version and its "figural'" version presented through her paintings.[4] Indeed, it is this double figuration of the self, projected through the relationship between the discursive and the figural as forms of autobiography, that is the site of my inquiry. I shall pay particular attention to Elaine's paintings and the retrospective exhibition in order to highlight Atwood's distinctive contribution to the problematical construction of female subjectivity in fiction.[5]

The retrospective exhibition positioned at the end of the novel (or almost) might be taken as Elaine's final statement, a *summa* of all the elements of her life already contained in the narrative. The exhibition is presented as a chronicle, with its brief views of earlier paintings and detailed descriptions of five late paintings (the last one with the promising title "Unified Field Theory"), together with a few less-than-helpful interpretations from the catalogue supplemented by / contradicted by Elaine's comments. As readers we have the advantage over the compiler of the catalogue because we already know the private references which are coded into the paintings, whereas she does not. What we also know (if we remember back 318 pages) is that this retrospective statement is not an authoritative one, for Elaine has left the arrangement of the paintings to the gallery's director (87). Her own position at the opening is that of a visitor:

> I walk slowly around the gallery, sipping at my glass of wine, permitting myself to look at the show, for the first time really. What is here, and what is not. (404)[6]

Actually the exhibition has the same kind of provisionality as *The Handmaid's Tale*, where Offred's narrative transcribed from her tapes is presented as the editor's version rather than as her own. In both cases, the recording subject remains elusive; she cannot be defined by the statements made on her behalf. Yet *a* retrospective exhibition (not the one described at the end) is the informing principle of the novel, for it has already been constructed on the Contents page, where the chapter titles are all given the names of paintings mentioned in the text. (That is, all except for the first one, "Iron Lung," which Elaine cannot paint because she is still inside it for as long as she lives, "being breathed" by time.) Throughout the narrative, individual paintings offer a disruptive commentary figuring events from a different angle to the memoir, so that it is only appropriate that they should be collected and shown in a gallery named "Sub-Versions." The doubled retrospective device[7] creates a complex patterning where painted surfaces present a riddling version of the truth. These visual artifacts (always of course mediated through / invented by language) represent the relation between "vision" and "a vision" (what it's assumed you've seen and what it's assumed you haven't), where socially accepted codes of seeing are challenged by the eye of the artist. As Elaine looks through the lens of her *Cat's Eye*, her Third Eye, "the single eye that sees more than anyone else looking" (327), she sees more because she sees differently.

However, for all her insight Elaine remains a slippery subject, difficult to get into focus. Even now at the age of nearly fifty she is a "blur" to herself when she looks in the mirror:

> Even when I've got the distance adjusted, I vary. I am transitional; some days I look like a worn-out thirty-five, others like a sprightly fifty. So much depends on the light, and the way you squint. (5)

And again, "There is never only one, of anyone" (6). It is surely significant that the first and only complete picture of her face is the photograph on the poster near the gallery where her exhibition is to be held: "The name is mine and so is the face, more or less. It's the photo I sent to gallery.

Except that now I have a moustache" (20). Her view of her own face "defaced" is surrounded by images of multiple identities, disguises ("I could be a businesswoman ... a bank manager ... a housewife, a tourist, someone window-shopping" (19), and by a reference to her double, Cordelia – all of which underline Elaine's indeterminacy and multiplicity as a subject.

In order to "read" Elaine's autobiography we could not do better than turn to the theoretical essay by Paul De Man, "Autobiography as De-facement," which would seem to be signalled by the grotesque visual self-image on the poster. Atwood's project in this novel bears a fascinating resemblance to De Man's deconstructive critique:

> Are we so certain that autobiography depends on reference, as a photograph depends on its subject or a (realistic) picture on its model? We assume that life *produces* the autobiography as an act produces its consequences, but can we not suggest, with equal justice, that the autobiographical project may itself produce and determine the life and that whatever the writer *does* is in fact governed by the technical demands of self-portraiture and thus determined, in all its aspects, by the resources of his [her] medium?[8]

This construction of subjecthood would seem to be confirmed by Elaine's response to the poster, which may be, as she says, a feeling of wonder, but which also may be read as a self-reflexive comment on her autobiography: "A public face, a face worth defacing. This is an accomplishment. I have made something of myself, something or other, after all" (20). Elaine's confrontation with her own face defaced, like her return to Toronto, constitutes that "specular moment" which De Man identifies as the autobiographical impulse with its sudden alignment between present and past selves that opens up multiple possibilities for "mutual reflexive substitution" displacements and doublings. These are for him the "defacements" endemic to the autobiographical project, which "deals with the giving and taking away of faces, with face and deface, *figure*, figuration and disfiguration."[9]

Cat's Eye would seem to provide the perfect exemplars of such "defacements" – wittily in the comic-book story of the two sisters "a pretty one and one who has a burn covering half her face" who comes back from the dead to "get into the pretty one's body" (211); and more seriously, in Elaine's portrait of Cordelia which is called "Half a Face" (227). It is Cordelia, her childhood companion and tormentor, for whom Elaine searches incessantly on her return to Toronto, Cordelia who belongs to that city which "still has power; like a mirror that shows you only the ruined half of your face" (410). Lacking, her dark double trapped in an earlier period of time, Elaine remains unfixed, incomplete: "We are like the twins in old fables, each of whom has been given half a key" (411). Cordelia as the absent Other would also confirm De Man's theory of autobiography as a double project of self-representation moving towards self-restoration at the same moment as it marks otherness and deprivation: "Autobiography deprives and disfigures to the precise extent that it restores."[10]

Returning for a moment to an earlier stage of De Man's critique I should like to highlight his question about figures and figuration:

> Does the referent determine the figure, or is it the other way round: is the illusion of reference not a correlation of the structure of the figure, that is to say no longer clearly and simply a referent at all but something more akin to a fiction, which then, however, in its own turn, acquires a degree of referential productivity?[11]

The notion that it is the mode of figuration which produces the referent is crucial to Atwood's subject-constructing project where two modes of figuration are used. While Elaine's discursive narrative remains incomplete (she is still looking at the end for what is lost in the past), her paintings offer a different figuration, acting as a kind of corrective to the distortions and suppressions of memory and offering the possibility of theoretical solutions. Not that autobiography can ever attain completeness:

> The interest of autobiography, then, is not that it reveals reliable self-knowledge – it does not – but that it demonstrates in a striking way the impossibility of closure and totalization (that is the impossibility of coming into being) of all textual systems made up of tropological substitutions.[12]

Though De Man's discussion focuses exclusively on linguistic signifiers here, and Elaine's autobiography offers the variant of (verbalized) visual images, the result is the same. As seeing eye or discursive recorder, she tells her own private history, fragments of Cordelia's story, her brother Stephen's story, the stories of her parents and of Josef, Jon and Ben the men in her life, and the story of Mrs. Smeath. She also presents a historical documentary account of Toronto in the 1940s and 1950s from the perspective of an English-speaking Canadian girl, together with a cultural critique of feminism in Canada in the 1970s and 1980s. Arguably, Elaine succeeds in establishing her position as a speaking / painting subject, but she herself always exceeds her carefully constructed parameters of vision: "I'm what's left over" (409).

Atwood's novel adds one important dimension to De Man's theory of autobiography, and that is the dimension of time. Curiously, he neglects this, possibly because he is more interested in the opposition between life and death implied by life-writing, but Atwood does not. As she said in her *Cat's Eye* discussion at the National Theatre, London, in April 1989, "The thing I sweated over in that novel was Time," for Elaine's story covers a period of nearly fifty years from the early 1940s to the late 1980s. This is

a "space-time" novel (a phrase with precise scientific connotations here) where the narrator tries to establish her
position by using the three spatial co-ordinates plus the
temporal co-ordinate, only to discover that back in
Toronto, though her space might be defined, she is living
in at least two time dimensions at once as she remembers
the past: "There are, apparently, a great many more dimensions than four" (331). Here Elaine transcribes the words
of her dead brother Stephen, who grows up to become a
theoretical physicist and is later killed by terrorists in an
aircraft hijack incident. As so often happens in life-writing, her story is also a memorial to the dead. The narrative
begins with a speculation on time: "Time is not a line but
a dimension, like the dimensions of space . . . It was my
brother Stephen who told me that" (3). It is filled with
echoes of Stephen's voice in allusions to his theories about
space-time, curved space, the expanding universe, light,
black holes, string theory and the uncertainty principle.[13]
In significant ways Stephen's scientific enthusiasms have
shaped Elaine's imagination, so that her paintings and his
theories come to occupy the same area of speculation on
the mysterious laws which govern the universe. They are
both engaged in trying to reconstruct the past, he through
physics and mathematics and she through memory and
imaginative vision. His discourse from theoretical physics
provides the conceptual framework for her paintings, for
Elaine is "painting time": "These pictures of her, like
everything else, are drenched in time" (151), and finally at
the retrospective, "I walk the room, surrounded by the
time I've made" (409). Recording her brother's death, she
recalls his anecdote about identical twins and the high-
speed rocket, part of his youthful disquisitions on the theory of relativity and its effect on the behaviour of time:

What I thought about then was the space twin, the one who went on an interplanetary journey and returned in a week to find his brother ten years older.

Now I will get older I thought. And he will not. (219)

Perhaps the most important single memorial to her brother's influence is her last painting, "Unified Field Theory," to which I shall return in my discussion of the retrospective exhibition.

We should remember that Elaine trained not as a painter but as a biologist, like her father, producing slide drawings of planaria worms that looked like "stained glass windows under the microscope" (247), and that her instructor Dr. Banerji appears in one of her late paintings dressed like a magus holding a round object figured with bright pink objects ("They are in fact spruce budworm eggs in section: but I would not expect anyone but a biologist to recognize them" (406). The boundaries between science and art are dissolved here in what might be seen as an act of gendered transgression, where Elaine's paintings and drawings show one way in which a woman deals with the master discourse of science, transforming it through another medium or "another mode of figuration."[14]

Whether as a trainee biologist or a painter, or as the sister of a budding astronomer, Elaine's primary activity is "seeing." Eyes are important, but so are microscopes and telescopes, and so are lenses, with their ability to magnify and to focus more powerfully than the naked eye. It is in this context that we might consider the significance of the *Cat's Eye* of the title. Certainly the cat's eye marble exists as a referential object in the text, introduced first in the childhood games in the schoolyard with "puries, bowlies, and cat's eyes" ("my favourites"; 62), where it is strongly associated with her brother's superior skill.[15] It recurs many times in an almost casual way, as something to be fingered in Elaine's pocket as a secret defense against her tormentors when she is nine years old (141); later, as something she has grown out of, like her red plastic purse (203); and later still, as an object to be rediscovered among the debris in the cellar:

> The red plastic purse is split at the sides, where the sewing is. I pick it up, push at it to make it go back into shape. Something rattles. I open it and take out my blue cat's eye...I look into it, and see my life entire. (398)

Suddenly the cat's eye marble is transformed into the lens of imaginative vision, becoming that Third Eye[16] through which "each brick, each leaf of each tree, your own body, will be glowing from within, lit up, so bright you can hardly look. You will reach out in any direction and you will touch the light itself" (12).

But is it a sudden transformation? Hardly that, for the cat's eye marble has always had a duplicitous existence: "The cat's eyes really are like eyes, but not the eyes of cats. They're the eyes of something that isn't known but exists anyway . . . like the eyes of aliens from a distant planet. My favourite one is blue" (62). Invested by the nine-year-old girl with supernatural powers to protect her, it becomes for her a talismanic object and the sign of her own difference: "She doesn't know what power this cat's eye has to protect me. Sometimes when I have it with me I can see the way it sees . . . I am alive in my eyes only" (141).

Cat's eyes, planets and stars swirl together in Elaine's power dream, when the cat's eye enters her body:

> It's falling down out of the sky, straight towards my head, brilliant and glassy. It hits me, passes right into me, but without hurting, except that it's cold. The cold wakes me up. My blankets are on the floor. (145)

It functions as the nexus for all those contradictory feelings of fear and longing, love, hatred and resistance that she feels towards Cordelia, Grace Smeath and Carol Campbell "in that endless time when Cordelia had power over me" (113). Indeed, it is already functioning beyond her consciousness as her Third Eye when, deserted by her friends and lying in the snow in the dark, she has her vision of the Virgin Mary, "Our Lady of Perpetual Help," floating over the footbridge in the Toronto ravine. Elaine's reassumption of her own independence after this agony is marked by the sign of the cat's eye: "I am indifferent to them. There's something hard in me, crystalline, a kernel of glass. I cross the street and continue along, eating my licorice" (193). Much later Elaine will recognize it as the sign of the artist's powers of vision, and it will appear again and again in her paintings as her signature (the pier glass, the globe, the cat's eye marble). She will use it to figure curved space where "Nothing goes away."

The cat's eyes disappears entirely from her discursive memoir narrative of her adolescence and early adulthood in a complex process of repression:

I've forgotten things, I've forgotten that I've forgotten them ... I find these references to bad times vaguely threatening, vaguely insulting: I am not the sort of girl who has bad times. (201)

However, in the double mode of figuration employed in this novel, the discontinuous narrative constructed by Elaine's paintings tells a different story about Elaine as subject. She may feel like "nothing" but a "seeing eye," though her paintings display an excess of signification that goes beyond the discursive narrative produced by her conscious mind. They are truly "sub-versions," uncovering that highly complex network of conflicting energies, conscious and unconscious, which make up the human "subject" in its psychoanalytical definition.[17] The presence of the cat's eye is signalled in Elaine's fascination with the effects of glass when she is studying the history of visual styles, and a little drama of substitution is played out for the reader (though not for her) in her particular concern with the pier-glass in Van Eyck's picture "The Arnolfini Marriage," where the "round mirror is like an eye" (327). The cat's eye is there, multiplied, in some of her early still lives, though scarcely visible; "far back, in the dense tangle of the glossy leaves, are the eyes of cats" (337). Arguably, it is through that alien lens that Elaine paints her savage exposures of Mrs Smeath: "One picture of Mrs Smeath leads to another. She multiplies on the wall like bacteria, standing, sitting, flying, with clothes, without clothes, following me around with her many eyes" (388). This is a form of revenge that her conscious mind fails to understand, either at the time of painting or when her pictures are attacked by the ink-throwing woman at the feminist art show in Toronto: "It is still a mystery to me, why I hate her so much" (352). The answer hovers in the reader's mind as the words of Atwood's prose poem whisper, "The third eye can be merciless, especially when wounded."[18]

What is never explained in either the discursive or the figural narrative are Elaine's moments of revelation: her childhood vision of the Virgin Mary or that moment when she looks through the lens of the cat's eye marble and sees her "life entire" (398). Yet these are perhaps the crucial moments which determine her life as an artist and they both figure together in her final painting, where the Virgin Mary holds "an oversized cat's eye marble, with a blue centre" (408). ("[V]ision . . . a vision: something it's assumed you've seen . . . something it's assumed you haven't.") Through the logic of the image Elaine's paintings present "a vision" as "vision," so that as we follow the verbal descriptions of the paintings, reading changes to gazing. We "see" through Elaine's mediating eye which dissolves the bound-aries between the visionary and the visible.

The retrospective exhibition occurs in the chapter, "Unified Field Theory," which, with its echoes of Stephen's lecture, "The First Picoseconds and the Quest for a Unified Field Theory: Some Minor Speculations" (331), places it in a relational context and also signals its function in this auto-biographical narrative. Within the parameters of theoretical physics Elaine traces her figural interpretation of her life-story, which offers a significantly different series of projec-tions from her discursive memoir. By way of explanation for such differences, we might consider briefly Norman Bryson's emphasis on the double nature of painting, which he calls "the divided loyalty of the image."[19] This seems a useful analogy to describe the fissure within Elaine's remembering process, between her conscious mind's dis-cursive narrative and the figural narrative of her imagina-tion. From physics comes the definition of a "field":

> In physics a field can only be perceived by inference from the rela-tionships of the particles it contains; the existence of the field is, however, entirely separate from that of the particles; though it may be detected through them, it is not defined by them.[20]

Unified Field Theory itself (the attempt to formulate a comprehensive theory of the laws that govern the uni-verse) belongs to the discourse of theoretical physics; to a non-physicist like Elaine, her brother's lecture sounds as close to metaphysics as to physics.[21] At the end of it, after his speculation on picoseconds, space-time and matter-energy, Stephen does, however, give her a sentence which is crucial to her project of self-representation: "But there is something that must have existed before. That some-thing is the theoretical framework, the parameters within which the laws of energy must operate" (332). It is this relationship between the cosmic and the humanly particular that Elaine figures in her paintings, none of which offer a totalized representation of her "self," though maybe that "self" is the "field" that might be inferred from the constructions of her pictures.

At the retrospective, we are invited to "read" the pictures in sequence as we are led by Elaine past the "early things" and the "middle period" (all of which we have already "seen"), to her five most recent paintings which she has never shown before. These are described in detail, and we realize first that these paintings have a double significance as representations. There is a personal rationale behind the collocation of images in each picture which Elaine interprets for us, for these are plain statements in her own private narrative of crises, revelations and memories. However, as the wickedly satirical extracts from the catalogue commentary suggest, they also have a public life as paintings in an exhibition, available to the viewer's interpretation, so that plain statements become riddles provoking other people's narrative solutions: "I can no longer control these paintings or tell them what to mean. Whatever energy they have came out of me. I'm what's left over" (409).

The second thing we notice is that these late paintings share a common structural feature: they all introduce further dimensions of meaning into the figural image by their pierglass motifs or their triptych designs, which initiate shifts in perspective. A host of possible meanings are generated through different spatial patternings, different time dimensions, executed in different painterly techniques. As each painting contains several styles of representation, so the referentiality of any single image is undercut. These multiplicities are quite simply illustrated in Elaine's self portrait, "Cat's Eye" ("There is never only one, of anyone," and anyway her portrait, like the one she painted of Cordelia, is only "Half a Face"), while more complex representations of space–time and vision are developed in "Unified Field Theory." The

142

structural feature of the convex lens also highlights artifice, for these paintings reveal themselves as constructions / reconstructions, where realistic images are used to map a psychic landscape in Elaine's project of painting time.

It is important in the double mode of figuration of this novel to note that the paintings effect quite significant revisions in Elaine's retrospective narrative, for they encode insights that she herself only later realizes when she looks at the paintings. Now she reads the Mrs Smeath paintings differently, understanding at last not only "Why I hated her so much" but also how vengeful she was, and how her earlier self lacked the compassionate recognition which she had actually painted into Mrs Smeath's eyes:

> It's the eyes I look at now. I used to think these were self-righteous eyes, piggy and smug inside their wire frames; and they are. But they are also defeated eyes, uncertain and melancholy, heavy with unloved duty. The eyes of someone for whom God was a sadistic old man; the eyes of a small-town threadbare decency. Mrs Smeath was a transplant to the city, from somewhere a lot smaller. A displaced person; as I was. (405)

This process of moving from the blindness of consciousness to the insight of imaginative seeing occurs in Elaine's reading of all her late paintings, with her questioning of the reliability of memory in "Picoseconds," her awareness of mutual limits of understanding in "Three Muses," her ignorance of her brother's last moments in "One Wing," and her recognition of what her childhood torments were and how they were crucial to the development of her artistic powers.

It is the last painting, "Unified Field Theory," which effects the most significant revision of all in its effort at synthesis. Elaine's figuration of her vision of the Virgin Mary holding the cat's eye marble and floating above the bridge of her childhood traumas combines with her brother's cosmic imagery ("Star upon star red blue, yellow and white, swirling nebulae, galaxy upon galaxy"). This representation of the night sky could also be read as a black hole under the ground, as the secret place of her brother's buried treasure, or as "the land of the dead people," one of the many terrors of her childhood. Here the figural presents oppositions as co-existing on the same plane; the past and the present, "a vision" and "vision," the sacred and the profane, science and art, the universal and the particular. This is Elaine's attempt to present her "life entire" in an impersonal vision of wholeness, painting the forces which govern the laws of her being. All this is carefully spelled out by Elaine (there is no comment from the catalogue this time) and as readers we probably believe her interpretation because it gathers up so many anecdotes from her memoir text, offering a possible site for accommodating the Virgin Mary vision. The meanings also work forwards as well as backwards to enhance Elaine's discursive narrative when she will record her last "vision" of Cordelia in language which sets up parallels and echoes with the account of the first vision. However, the painting might also work another way, to problematize further her memoir narrative by highlighting gaps and omissions. In a universe where "Nothing goes away" (3), "What have I forgotten?" (334) always remains an open question.

Of course, the last painting like the retrospective, like the memoir, offers only a theoretical framework for the definition of Elaine's self, providing an illusion of completeness which is dispelled by the final chapter entitled "Bridge," where the narrative takes up once again the quest for Cordelia and Elaine's registration of lack and loss. Our view of Elaine herself remains partial and provisional; though we have learned to see through her eyes, we have only ever seen half her face or her face "defaced." Apparently the human subject is as mysterious as the universe: "The universe is hard to pin down; it changes when you look at it, as if it resists being known" (388).

In this version of life-writing in the feminine with its double project for constructing female subjectivity through the discursive and the figural modes, the emphasis on displacements, doublings and "defacements" underlines the inherent instability of the narrating subject at the same time as it "undoes the model [of autobiography as a genre] as soon as it is established."[22] Though we may be persuaded that Elaine succeeds in locating her distinctive "position" as a subject in her figural constructions of space-time, the discursive narrative as a "textual system made up of tropological substitutions"[23] will always register some incompleteness in the construction of "subjecthood," a lack that is confirmed at the thematic level by Elaine's failure to find Cordelia:

> This is what I miss, Cordelia: not something that's gone, but something that will never happen. Two old women giggling over their tea (421).

Through the multiple modes of narrative representation Elaine, like Offred or Cordelia, "slips from our grasp and flees." By telling the reader so much, Atwood has paradoxically exposed the limits of autobiography and its artifice of reconstruction. The best Elaine Risley or Margaret Atwood can offer is a Unified Field Theory from which inferences about the subject may be made, but the subject herself is always outside, in excess, beyond the figurations of language. The "I" remains behind the "eye." At the end, Elaine recedes back into her seeing eye, voided of personality, as her narrative dissolves into light:

> Now it's full night, clear, moonless and filled with stars, which are not eternal as was once thought, which are not where we think they are. If they were sounds, they would be echoes, of something that happened millions of years ago: a word made of numbers. Echoes of light, shining out of the midst of nothing.
>
> Its old light, and there's not much of it. But it's enough to see by. (421)[24]

NOTES

1. Margaret Atwood. "Instructions for the Third Eye." *Murder in the Dark*. Toronto: Coach House, 1983. 61-2.

2. Shirley Neuman. "Life-Writing." *Literary History of Canada: Canadian Literature in English*, vol. 4, 2nd ed. Ed. by W.H. New. Toronto: University of Toronto Press, 1990. 333-70; Paul De Man. "Autobiography as De-facement." *MLN*, vol. 94, 1979. 931-55. See also *Reflections: Autobiography and Canadian Literature*. Ed. by K.P. Stich. Ottawa: University of Ottawa Press, 1988.

3. This point has already been made by Constance Rooke in "Interpreting *The Handmaid's Tale*: Offred's Name and the Arnolfini Marriage." *Fear of the Open Heart: Essays on Contemporary Writing*. Toronto: Coach House, 1989. 175-96.

4. In its use of paintings *Cat's Eye* focuses on a similar area of inquiry to Norman Bryson in *World and Image: French Painting of the Ancien Régime*. Cambridge: Cambridge University Press, 1981. His discussions about writing and painting have suggested important directions for my inquiry into Atwood's novel.

5. Sharon R. Wilson has commented on Atwood's involvement with the visual arts, discussing photographic images and some early watercolours: "Camera Images in Margaret Atwood's Novels" in *Margaret Atwood: Reflection and Reality*. Ed. by B. Mendez-Egle. Texas: Pan American University Press, 1987. 29-57; and "Sexual Politics in Margaret Atwood's Visual Art" in *Margaret Atwood: Vision and Forms*. Eds. K. Van Spanckeren and J. Garden Castro. Carbondale: Southern Illinois University Press, 1988. 205-14.

6. Margaret Atwood. *Cat's Eye*. Toronto: McClelland & Stewart, 1988. All page references will be to this edition.

7. There is a third mini-retrospective as well, when Elaine at her mother's house after her father's death finds the cat's eye marble in her old red plastic purse (398).

8. De Man, "Autobiography as De-facement." 920.

9. Ibid., 926.

10. Ibid., 930.

11. Ibid., 920.

12. Ibid., 922.

13. For definitions of these terms, see Stephen Hawking, *A Brief History of Time*. London: Bantam, 1988, a book to which Atwood draws attention in her Acknowledgements.

14. See Lola Lemire Tostevin's interview with Christopher Dewdney, *Poetry Canada Review*, vol. 3 (1989). 1-3, 29.

15. In my thinking about the way that objects work in texts, I am indebted to Simone Vauthier's exemplary essay, "Images in Stones, Images in Words" in *Critical Approaches to the Fiction of Margaret Laurence*. Ed. C. Nicholson. London: Macmillan, 1990. 46–70.

16. Atwood, "Instructions for the Third Eye." 62.

17. For a brief discussion of subjectivity, see Toril Moi, *Sexual/Textual Politics*. London: Methuen, 1985. 9–11.

18. Atwood, "Instructions for the Third Eye." 62.

19. Bryson, *Word and Image*. 13: "A sign is always divided into two areas, one which declares its loyalty to the text outside the image, and another which asserts the autonomy of the image: a ratio of the sign which is as important a fact of art history as any of its discoveries about the individual styles that form variables within this overall sign-format – the typical sign-format of painting in the West."

20. Dennis Lee's definition, quoted by Helen Tiffin, "Post-Colonial Literature and Counter-Discourse." Kunapipi, vol. 9, no. 3 (1987). 17–34.

21. For a glimpse into this territory, see Hawking, *A Brief History of Time*. 155–69.

22. De Man, "Autobiography as De-facement." 922.

23. Ibid.

24. Elaine's final words echo Stephen's (104); see also Hawking, *A Brief History of Time*. 28.

Questioning the Triple Goddess

Myth and Meaning in Margaret Atwood's **The Robber Bride**

JENNIFER MURRAY

Myth is one of those terms which has been pushed in so many directions in recent years that its definition has become somewhat vague. Margaret Atwood's 1978 definition of myth does not go very far towards remedying this problem: "Myths mean stories, and traditional myths mean stories that have been repeated frequently. The term doesn't pertain to Greek myths alone. Grimm's Fairy Tales are just as much myth or story as anything else" (*Conversations* 114).[1] Personally, I have no argument with this vagueness, as, indeed, two of the forms of mythical intertext which I will discuss in relation to *The Robber Bride* are, precisely, Greek myths and fairy tales. These domains of discourse, which are closely related in the novel to the characters Charis and Roz, are two elements in a three-fold structure which also includes history, whose field of discourse is related to Tony.[2]

However, it is essential to address the ways in which mythical intertextuality functions. Atwood's *The Robber Bride* calls upon mythological intertexts in two different ways: first of all, by echoing pre-existing texts, mythical references make actions, characters, themes and structures pleasantly recognizable to the reader. This is an open-ended mode of intertextuality whereby familiar content is reworked into a later moment of textual production. The second function of myth in Atwood's novel is to frame meaning: to frame it in the sense of keeping it within certain boundaries, but also to frame it in the sense of setting it up as something which it is not, namely, limited in its possibilities. This is intertextuality which takes over not so much the context as the structure of the work to which it refers. The principal intertexts which *The Robber Bride* uses in this way are the Triple Goddess and The Three Little Pigs. Because of the triple structure of each of these myths, underscored by the triple narrative of the characters' personal histories, this particular use of mythical intertext is, I will argue, the restriction which prevents the novel from opening up to the reader a range of potentially radical positions.

II

The question of myth in Atwood's work in general has been given considered attention by Sandra Djwa, notably in an article entitled "Back to the Primal: The Apprenticeship of Margaret Atwood." Therein, Djwa evokes the primary literary discourses to which Atwood was exposed during her formative years, especially during the period she spent at Victoria College in Toronto: amongst these influences were the poetry of T.S. Eliot and his conception of "'the mythical method,' that is, literature structured by developing a continuous parallel between classical myth and contemporary reality" (Djwa 19). Other influences included Robert Graves's *The White Goddess* which argued that patriarchal myths are in fact derivative of an earlier, matriarchal goddess myth. Finally, argues Djwa, the influence of Northrop Frye's perspective on myths and archetypes, as well as Atwood's acquaintance and discussions with Jay Macpherson, a writer who practiced the "mythical method," were also important elements:

> Macpherson was a guru to a group of younger poets who read, admired, and talked about her difficult, Blakean poetry, which com-

149

bines snippets of Greek, Roman, and Biblical myth, fairy tale, and ballad in a style that moves from the formal to the colloquial voice. (29)

It is therefore no surprise to find traces of classical mythology in Atwood's writing, but it is more specifically the myth of the Triple Goddess, the goddess of the three ages – Maiden (Persephone), Matron (Venus) and Crone (Hecate) – which is the dominant mythical component of her work.

Readers of Atwood's work have already discussed this aspect of *The Robber Bride*: both Sandra Djwa and Hilde Staels point to the figure of the Great Goddess to clarify aspects of Zenia's identity and come to associate her more closely with the figure of Hecate (Djwa 41, Staels 201). I would suggest that the myth of the Triple Goddess is an intertext which is invoked far more extensively than its connection with Zenia would suggest: it contributes much to our understanding of the triad structure to which Tony, Charis and Roz belong. It is not, however, the only intertext which informs the triadic structure; other dependencies are also hooked onto this framework which is sufficiently well-anchored to carry their weight. For the Triple Goddess is not a myth of action or odyssey, it is a myth of presence, a presence which is constructed so as to appear, at one and the same time, to precede those who receive it, and to live on beyond those who reactivate it through their story-telling.

As myth, the Triple Goddess is a chosen meaning-producing structure which Sandra Djwa sees as offering a universal site of identification for women: "For women the myth of the mother goddess is emotionally charged, expressing as it does the primal aspects of female experience: sexual initiation (the descent), followed by gestation and new birth" (16). What is presented here as universal experience captured by myth works at least as much the other way around. It is myth which is telling women what their experience of themselves should be, notably, that their sexuality involves a fall, and that sexual reproduction is the appropriate form of redemption from this fall. For many women today, sexuality is experienced differently and is far less strongly bound to the reproductive aspect. Djwa colludes, unconsciously I would like to think, in the tendency to see myth, and especially myths about women, as eternal. Roland Barthes refuses this view:

> Y a-t-il des objets *fatalement* suggestifs, comme Baudelaire le disait de la Femme? Sûrement pas: on peut concevoir des mythes très anciens, il n'y en a pas d'éternels; car c'est l'histoire humaine qui fait passer le réel a l'etat de parole, c'est elle et elle seule qui règle la vie et la mort du langage mythique. Lointain ou non, la mythologie ne peut avoir qu'un fondement historique, car le mythe est une parole choisie par l'histoire: il ne saurait surgir de la "nature" des choses. (216; Barthes's emphasis)

The type of speech in which the goddess myth participates is, as mentioned above, one which depends heavily on its structure, or in other words, on its internal organization which attempts to collapse the difference between the particular and the universal. It is "one" and it is "three," it is "always" and it is "now," it is all of life, and, at the same time, life carved up into three neat phases. It is, therefore, in every aspect of its sign, the promise of presence and fullness. In myth, long-term stability of form is often invoked as the proof and the guarantee of something beyond time, beyond reach, beyond human intervention. In Derrida's general and far-reaching attempt to wrest the concept of structure from the notion of a fixed centre or origin, he writes:

> Le concept de structure centrée est en effet le concept d'un jeu *fondé*, constitué depuis une immobilité fondatrice et une certitude rassurante, elle-même soustraite au jeu. Depuis cette certitude, l'angoisse peut être maîtrisée, qui naît toujours d'une certaine manière d'être impliqué dans le jeu, d'être pris au jeu, d'être comme être d'entrée de jeu dans le jeu. (410)

The Triple Goddess, it seems fairly clear, is just this sort of centered, presence-affirming framework which allows for "les répétitions, les substitutions, les transformations, les permutations" (Derrida 410) within its walls, without the essential unity of the structure being in any way at stake. Atwood plays brilliantly, joyfully, but the deck is, to some extent, stacked. The very structure of the Triple Goddess and its variants in *The Robber Bride* allows for only one outcome, to use Atwood's terminology. The structure will remain intact, and Atwood knows that from the onset.

III

The Triple Goddess belongs to the semiotic sphere of the mysterious. Like all divine trinities, beginning with the Father, Son and Holy Ghost who is / are more familiar to many of us, she is both one and several. She is three, in her three phases: maiden, matron and crone, and yet, unified as the muse, she is at once creator and destroyer. Whether evoked through the variations on her seemingly timeless names – the Great, the White, the Triple or the Mother goddess – or situated within the various cultures which have effected these transformations – the stability and immortality of the figure never come into question. A breech in the structure, and the structure would vanish. It is this structure of immortality which serves as the basis for the construction of Margaret Atwood's *The Robber Bride*.

The three-in-oneness of the Triple Goddess is worked into the choice and development of the characters, as well as into the narrative organization of their respective stories. Within the doubled framing chapters ("Onset" and "Toxique"; "Toxique" and "Outcome"), at the centre of the story, are the triple, parallel narratives of Tony, Charis and Roz. Each of these inner chapters also contains its own beginning, middle and end which are structured in a highly controlled manner. More precisely, the physical space in which each of these inner chapters begins and ends, as well as the objects present at those moments, indicates the domain of association for each character.

When, in the long inner chapter called "Black Enamel," Tony is to begin telling of her battle with Zenia, she goes into the basement and sits beside a "large sand-table" which "contains a three-dimensional map of Europe and the Mediterranean, made of hardened flour-and-salt paste" (125); she stays by it until her story has been told, and then she "turns out the cellar lights and climbs the stairs to the kitchen" (215). In this way, the presence of the map showing "the day of Otto the Red's fateful battle" (125) holds her narrative within the sphere of her function as historian. It is her role to evoke traditional history (Canadian and European essentially) and, in the process, to question whether traditional historical narratives have any value. The answers she provides at the end of the novel are tentative and ambiguous, as the response to the following question indicates: "But do the stories of history really teach anything at all? In a general sense, thinks Tony, *possibly* not" (518; my emphasis).

Through similar structural techniques, Charis will be associated with the mythological figure of Charon, the boatman of the Styx. This connection is provoked on the one hand by the homophonic relation between "Charon" and Karen, Charis's submerged, unhappy side, but also from the fact that, before telling her story, she boards a ferry-boat which takes her from the shores of Lake Ontario to her home on Centre Island, where, having finished the narrative of her personal history, she disembarks. Other references to the ferry-boat develop the allusion to the Charon myth in such a way that it is both visible and invisible within the overall scene described. Let us consider the following passage which recounts the last time Charis sees her companion Billy:

> When she reaches the dock, the ferry is already boarding. People are going on, singly and in twos; there's something processional about their entrance, in the way they step from land to water. Right here was where she last saw Billy; and also Zenia, in the flesh. They were already aboard, and as Charis came heavily running, gasping, hands on her belly to hold it attached to her, it was dangerous for her to run like that, she could have fallen and lost the baby, the ferry men were hoisting up the gangway, the ferry was hooting and backing out, the deep water churning to a whirlpool. She couldn't have jumped. (58)

Fairly indirectly, the general atmosphere and certain details call upon the intertext of the myth of Charon. The description of the procession, for instance, suggests the solemnity which might be associated with a funeral, Charis, who is carrying a life, is excluded from the trip, and she will never see the beloved departing person again. Structurally, this creates a division between those "living on the earth" and those who have undertaken a water voyage. The water, clearly dangerous, is also associated with the river Styx because of the whirlpool which forms as the boat is leaving the harbour, recalling the whirlpool Charybdis (a name which is close to Charis in its form). Finally, the named presence of actual "ferry men" allows us to bridge the symbolic gap between practices of contemporary life and mythological beliefs.[3]

Once the significant domains of history and mythology have been anchored in the characters of Tony and Charis, it is Roz's turn to go and find an appropriate setting to tell her story. Like Tony, she goes into the basement,

> sits down on the cellar floor . . . pulls books off the shelves at random . . . There on the cover is the dark forest, the dark wolfish forest, where lost children wander and foxes lurk, and anything can happen;

there is the castle turret, poking through the knobby trees. *The Three Little Pigs*, she reads. The first little pig built his house of straw. *Her house, her* house, shout the small voices in her head. (380)

In this extract, the illusion of randomness is offered, but the design is retrospectively apparent. The book which comes into Roz's hands will provide another far-reaching intertext to echo that of the mythical goddess in its tripleness and in its ostensible permanence: the fairy-tale mode has in Roz its ascribed godmother, and its key tale, *The Three Little Pigs*. In its economic density, the quotation cited above interlaces analeptic references to the ways in which Tony and Charis have entered into the overall structure of the fairy tale; the reference to the castle turret has already been associated with Tony ("Tony in her turret room" 211), and there have been references to the fragility of Charis's house on at least two previous instances ("her flimsy house that is still standing" 322, and "Charis wished there were a layer of straw under her . . . house" 307). In the attribution of relatively weak or strong houses to the characters, and through the conversion of male pronouns to female ones for the fairy tale characters, the text brings together key elements in the structuring of this intertext.

Moreover, as the guardian of the world of fairy tales, Roz has her own associated tales: she is, in her dreams, a confused Goldilocks in a lifeless house walking "through the white kitchen where nothing moves, past the table with the three chairs" (450). Yet, as other critics have pointed out, Roz is also very clearly associated with the Cinderella figure, the poor little girl who becomes rich. She is, however, an atypical Cinderella: just as Tony, the historian, is lacking in her field because she cannot uncover any real value in the practice of historiography, and Charis, with her repressed underwater self, is as much the passenger as the ferry-man in her own Charon myth, Roz lacks the prescribed beauty of her archetype, and must make do with a prince whose charm is not reserved for her alone.

The exploration of one aspect of the structural organization of *The Robber Bride* shows that each of the characters has a domain of human story-telling associated with her: for Tony it is history, for Charis it is mythology and for Roz it is the world of fairy tales. Beyond their attachment to a particular character, each of these domains receives in turn more extensive development within which the structural logic of the domain itself prevails. Hence, in the historical development of each character, time and the passing of generations shape the text. The starting point is the Second World War, marked clearly as "the past" through its association with the parental generation; then the story moves on to the "present" battles of the Tony-Charis-Roz generation (these battles are seen as being in some way related to the childhood experiences of the characters) and the novel finishes with speculative considerations about the next generation, through the children of Roz and Charis. The emphasis on cause-and-effect in historical narrative is tentatively affirmed, even if the future remains unpredictable.

Within the fairy tale structure, the three little pigs will all be bitten by the wolfish Zenia. There is no place which provides protection from her attacks, no house which is an absolute refuge. It is perhaps for this reason that the "three little pigs" do not run from their homes looking for shelter, but run to each other's house to offer aid and comfort to the most recent victim. When Tony is on her own after West leaves her for Zenia, Roz goes and stays with her. Tony and Roz do the same for Charis when she is pregnant and is devastated because Billy has left with Zenia. Finally, Tony and Charis go to Roz after she attempts to commit suicide, this following Mitch's desertion of her for Zenia, and his own subsequent suicide. According to Bettelheim, *The Three Little Pigs* in its traditional form teaches the reader that cumulative experience makes one wiser. Here, however, there is a sense of people going around in circles making consoling gestures towards each other. Nonetheless, and in spite of the transformations of the tale, the wolf gets boiled in the end, falling from her hotel balcony into the fountain / cauldron in the courtyard below. The reasons for this particular ending seem to arise, at least in part, from Atwood's decision to respect the overall structure of the fairy tale, a choice which, as I will argue further on, imposes limitations on the potential force of the novel.

I have very briefly summarized the discourses related to Tony and Roz so as to be able to focus more intensely now on that which is related to Charis, the sphere of mythology. While it seemed important to show that there are multiple and intricately developed intertexts at work in the novel, it is the discourse of classical mythology, the one which comes under the reign of the Triple Goddess which centers the text structurally. I will begin by looking at the triad in its fragmented form, through the characters of Tony, Charis, and Roz, in order to explore the range of play (in the form of transformations, inversions, subversions, and so on) which they are allowed within the limits of their attachment to their mythical model. I will then briefly examine the more dynamic function attributed to the goddess figure: that of the muse in her specific manifestation as Zenia.

IV
Miss Tony

Tony is, in the framework of the Triple Goddess, "the elusive Diana or Maiden figure, the young girl" (Atwood, *Survival* 199). This analogical relationship in *The Robber Bride* is not based, on one overriding element, but on the interweaving of intertextual suggestions throughout the novel. The "young girl" aspect of the mythological figure is associated with youthful beauty, hunting, chastity, and childlessness. In terms of appearances, Margaret Atwood attributes this "youthfulness" to Tony by describing her in comically inappropriate clothing: when she goes to her first university "bash" wearing "a dark green corduroy jumper with a white blouse under it, a green velvet hairband, and knee socks and brown loafers," a young man "gives her an unfocused look" and comments: "Shit, the Girl Guides" (140). Later, well into her forties, Tony is described as wearing "a forest green rayon outfit with small white polka dots that she bought in the children's section at Eaton's" (18). As these descriptions suggest, Tony's childlike appearance is, at least in part, a refusal to take on the dress codes of the adult world, and with it, the world of gendered sexuality.

Moreover, the youthfulness which characterizes Tony is not in any way that of fresh-faced innocence; indeed, she is described as looking like "a very young old person, or a very old young person" (19). She is not shown to be especially attractive to men, and does not enter into the illusory magic of make-up, feeling that "Lipstick is alarming on her" (19). The stereotypical beauty that we might readily associate with the Maiden aspect of the triad is subverted in these contradictory descriptions of Tony. Nonetheless, even as, within this comparison, the component of female beauty is being undermined, the descriptions of Tony's clothing seem to be shooting out associative filaments in the direction of another aspect of Diana, the forest huntress, through the words "forest green" (18) and "dark green" (140). Tony is, in many ways, a paradoxical Diana. Situated outside the stereotype of a seductive young goddess, she will have no suitors pursuing her and she will have to turn her hunting skills to the problem of tracking down a male partner.

Tony's potential lover is West; there is no other man on her horizon. Their relationship is initially situated on the plane of platonic friendship: "Drinking coffee, was about all Tony did with West" (137). In the absence of any sexual overtures, Tony is not forced to determine her own position in relation to her sexuality and, indeed, the classic position offered by her mythological role model is that of chastity. To this extent, Tony remains in line with "Diana." Moreover, "the thought of going to bed with anyone at all is terrifying" (200). However, unlike her mythological forebear, this refusal of sexuality is not born of an ideal to defend, but of her inability to see herself as a sexual being and to project herself into such a scenario.

However, when Roz suggests that Tony should take West to bed (200), and also provides her with a reason she can believe in, or in other words, an ideal to invest, Tony responds positively, since it is not about sex, it is "really" about "saving [West's] life" (201). Depressed after Zenia's departure, West is perishing and Tony decides that in such an extreme situation "heroism and self-sacrifice are called for. [She] grits her teeth and sets out to seduce West" (201). This ironic discourse also serves to keep the military strategist that Tony incarnates in view, since it is in the name of "duty" and by developing a "strategy" that she will undertake her mission.

Margaret Atwood thus creates a paradoxical situation where the Maiden, who should be pursued by a suitor, whom she is, in fact, expected to resist, finds herself confronted by a lover who is not one. Moreover, this potential lover is not chasing her, and in fact seems to be resisting her. Even when Tony makes considerable efforts to court and seduce him, "cooking a candlelight dinner" for example or "[taking] him to movies . . . that give her a chance to clutch his hand in the dark" (201), West remains impassive. The total inversion of the active and passive roles is accomplished when West seems to be dying, his "eyelids . . . curved and pure, like those on carved tombstone saints" (201), and

Tony employs the method which, in fairy tales, never fails: "[she] gives him a kiss; albeit "on the forehead" (201). Through the inversion of roles, it is the male character, put to sleep by a wicked witch (Zenia) who must await the kiss of salvation which comes from a woman. The sense of liberation nonetheless remains attached to Tony who, by her action, has freed herself from the obligation of chastity suggested by the Diana figure.

She and West make love and the experience is like a baptism for Tony:

> [it's] like falling into a river, because West is what other people call him, a long drink of water, and Tony is so thirsty, she's parched, she's been wandering in the desert all of these years, and now at last somebody truly needs her. (202)

The metaphor at work here is that of descent and rebirth, the mythical structure of female sexuality which we referred to earlier. The myth of Persephone who was swallowed up by the earth and given to the violent Hades is clearly softened in Atwood's version, where the violence of the mythical version is transformed into a tender, comfy sort of sexuality. Not an ideal, but a situation which allows the character Tony to free herself from her sense of sexual inadequacy.

Mrs. Roz

Roz, as the only one of the three women to hold a discourse which invests the body, conjugal love and children with positive values, can be associated with the Matron figure of the Triple Goddess, the guardian of the hearth and family values. This reference can be understood most clearly in Roz's self-image, communicated through internal focalization: "She tried so hard to be kind and nurturing"

(332). The spheres included in this desire to nurture are, of course, the world of her children, over whom "[s]he extends her invisible wings, her warm feathery angel's wings, her fluttery hen's wings, undervalued and necessary, she enfolds them. Secure, is what she wants them to feel" (341). But it is especially in the eyes of her husband, Mitch, that Roz must cultivate this image which is, in fact, the basis of their relationship as a couple: "In Mitch's cosmology, Roz's body represents possessions, solidity, the domestic virtues, hearth and home, long usage. Mother-of-his-children. The den" (335). Traditionally, in exchange for this affective security, Mitch should fulfill the role of hunter (or breadwinner), and protector of the family.

This schema is not, however, respected, since the couple lives off Roz's fortune, inherited from her father. Instead of being the hard-working husband tradition would have him be, Mitch is described mostly as a skirt chaser, and it is paradoxically Roz who is put in the position of the protector. Specifically, Roz saves Mitch from becoming entrapped by the situations he creates through his extra-marital affairs, by repeatedly taking him back into the fold of the family whose stability he has put in danger.

Yet, after a certain time, Roz no longer finds herself sufficiently rewarded by the limited and limiting role of the eternally forgiving and loving wife, and she begins to push back the moment when she will save Mitch until, finally, she refuses to do so altogether. When, because of Zenia, things fall apart around him and Mitch comes looking for comfort, Roz does not comply:

> "I want to come back," he tells her, gazing around the high, wide living room, the spacious domain that Roz has made, that was once his to share. Not *Will you let me come back?* Not *I want you back?* Nothing to do with Roz, no mention of her at all. It's the room he's claiming, the territory. He is deeply mistaken . . .

> Now he does finally look at her. God knows who he sees. Some avenging angel, some giantess with a bared arm and a sword – it can't be Roz, tender and feathery Roz, not the way he's staring at her. (426-27)

Roz, through Mitch's perception of her, sees herself transformed into a warrior woman, an Amazon figure closer to Diana. Since we have no access to Mitch's thoughts, he functions as a mirror for Roz, offering a reflection which Roz processes through mythological imagery. Roz is rendered insecure by the radical nature of the shift in her self-perception, and she must fight to resist the temptation to go back to more familiar modes: "[she] clenches her fists tight because she won't let herself be fooled like that again" (429). Roz achieves a form of self-affirmation here which is that of the victim confronting the victimizer, not so much as a person, but as a pattern of abuse in which both sides have colluded. She refuses to collude any longer, because the illusion which made that possibility attractive to her (the illusion that Mitch, through his unfaithfulness and return, had always been expressing a paradoxical form of love for her) has been shattered. Affirming her self-worth is, therefore, at the same time, an act which renders the comforting illusion which had also been a part of her self-definition, definitively inaccessible.

Ms. Charis

The final phase of the Triple Goddess is that of the Crone, the mystical figure who "presides over death and has oracular powers" (Atwood, *Survival* 199). Charis has already been associated with the realm of death through her proximity with the figure of Charon and she incarnates just as clearly the mystical aspect of the Crone phase. This reference is signalled on the level of "realism" since Charis's character is based to some extent on an affiliation with New Age beliefs. An example of the forms of mysticism involved can be seen in the following description of a very elaborate private ceremony which Charis carries out to give herself the courage to affront Zenia:

> She took the book and the gloves downstairs and put them on the small table under the main window in the living room – where the sunlight would shine in on them and dispel their shadow sides – and set her amethyst geode beside them and surrounded them with dried marigold petals. To this arrangement she added after some thought, her grandmother's Bible, always a potent object, and a lump of earth from her garden. She meditated on this collection for twenty minutes twice a day. (470)

The hoped-for result of this ritual would be to allow Charis "to absorb the positive aspects of her friends, the things that were missing in herself" (470). For, in the same way that Tony is a paradoxical Maiden and Roz a reformed nurturer, Charis, lacking strength of will, is a problematic Hecate figure.

Fatherless, beaten and raped as a child, Charis perceives herself as divided, and she only accepts the more peaceable side of herself. Her rejection of that part of herself which knows about evil occurred when she was a child, enduring abuse at the hands of her uncle:

> [H]e falls on top of Karen and puts his slabby hand over her mouth, and splits her mouth in two. He splits her in two right up the middle and her skin comes open like the dry skin of a cocoon, and Charis flies out. Her new body is light as a feather, light as air. There's no pain in it at all . . . What she sees is a small pale girl her face contorted and streaming, nose and eyes wet as if she's drowning – gasping for air, going under again, gasping. (294)

Although the violence of the uncle's sexual penetration of the child is suggested by the phrase "he splits her in two,"

163

this violence is immediately attenuated by the butterfly imagery ("cocoon," "flies out") which follows. This seems to be an attempt to attribute to Charis a defense mechanism which R.D. Laing describes under the heading of "the unembodied self." He writes:

> In this position the individual experiences his self as being more or less divorced or detached from his body. *The body is felt more as one object among other objects in the world than as the core of the individual's own being.* Instead of being the core of his true self, the body is felt as the core of a *false self* which a detached disembodied, "inner," "true" self looks on at with tenderness, amusement, or hatred as the case may be. (69; Laing's emphases)

The emotion attributed to Charis's unembodied self is that of "amazement" as she watches "the man [who] grunts, as the small child wriggles and flails as if hooked through the neck" (294-95). Atwood, while constructing this psychological way out for her character, nevertheless forces the reader to take fully into account the impact of the child being martyred by the sexual violence of an adult. Through the image of the little girl "drowning – gasping for air, going under again, gasping" (294), the reader is taken beyond Charis's amazement to the more critical perspective which we, as readers and members of society, need to keep in sight.

Charis's ritual of meditation maybe seen as part of her continuing attempt to negotiate her place in a world of violence. But it also has other connotations. Amongst the objects upon which Charis meditates is her Grandmother's bible, the book which first revealed Charis's oracular powers. Charis, choosing a passage in the bible with a pin, lands, on three separate occasions, on the story of Jezebel, the whore of Babylon. The grandmother, who initiates Charis into the practice of this "art" cannot see how this story could relate to Charis, and she says "Must be too far ahead"

(278). This impression is confirmed on the second occasion: "Ah," said her grandmother, squinting. "Jezebel again . . . Now that's a strange thing, for a little girl . . . You must be living ahead of yourself" (285). The repeated prediction eventually comes to be associated with the death of Zenia which Charis also "sees" from a distance: "'I saw it in the candle,' says Charis. 'I saw her falling. She was falling, into water. I saw it! She's dead.' Charis begins to cry" (500).

Unlike the situations of Tony and Roz, where the mythological roles offered can be transposed onto life patterns and psychological possibilities that are open to all of us (sexual awakening, nurturing), Charis's psychic powers require of the reader greater suspension of disbelief. Indeed, within the novel, the reality-effect accorded to this mystical experience is never contradicted; on the contrary, it is reinforced when Charis's premonitory vision turns out to be correct. At that point, for this reader, the mythological analogy is infringing on the realist boundaries to an untenable extent. This is not to suggest that *The Robber Bride* is simply, or even mainly, a realist novel, but its realist level, established by the spatial and temporal setting (Toronto in the 1990s) and by the characters whose lives are situated within recognizable limits for the contemporary reader, cannot be ignored. Within this perspective, the magical possibilities offered by the character of Charis are problematic.

Muse

In my discussion of character construction within a mythological framework, I have noted where the different characters both meet up with and diverge from their role models. We might note, in conclusion, that the points at which the characters fail to conform to their corresponding element of the Triple Goddess, Zenia gives every appearance of filling in that gap. Thus, the elements of the Maiden to which Tony can only correspond in a comic mode are fully present in their mythological form in Zenia in her relationship to West. For him, she is beauty ("Zenia is as beautiful as ever" (36) and paradoxically, chastity: "Zenia was frigid" (457). Similarly, while Roz can provide the form of the family structure, it is to Zenia that Mitch would like to give his undying love (424, 428), and where Charis is the incarnation of a fragile Hecate figure struggling to assemble strength and will, Zenia "is a cold and treacherous bitch" (424).

Zenia functions as a sort of inverted mirror figure for the characters in their Triple Goddess roles, but also for Charis, in her Charon aspect. This is especially striking in the following image which echoes, inverts and amplifies an earlier description of Charis on the ferry, "leaning on the railing, facing backwards" (225): "Zenia sweeps through life like a prow, like a galleon. She's magnificent, shs's unique. She's the sharp edge" (463). Zenia is up front, breaking new ground, claiming territory, while Charis, prudent, is looking back, trying to read the traces of the past. This comparison will later be extended to the triad of women when, at Zenia's "wake," the "three of them stand at the back of the ferry as it churns its way through the harbour, outbound towards the Island, trailing the momentary darkness of its wake" (522). They contemplate the "momentary darkness," which is also Zenia's passage in their lives, as if it were the trace of a disaster which had crossed their paths, a disaster which they had survived, and had also learned from. The rounded polysemy of the signifier "wake" comes into play here, signifying the farewell ceremony to Zenia, the churning water following the boat's path, and the overall effect of Zenia on the lives of the three women: she has "wakened" them to other ways of approaching conflict. Through their contact with Zenia, they acquire the power to recreate their self-images; instead of continuing to perceive themselves as innocent victims of circumstances beyond their control, they begin to understand and accept that they do have the power to react, intervene, protest, and even counter-attack.

Here, however, the reader needs to be wary of transforming Zenia into an ideal. Calling her the "good witch" as Bloom and Makowsky do (177) on the basis of the fact that the women do seem to gain in self-knowledge is not tenable. It is a form of "the end justifies the means" logic. Zenia is, for the women, a catastrophe. There is nothing in Zenia's constructed personality which could be seen as positive within the human contexts provided and for that reason, "Zenia remains a female villain – that is a toxic figure" (Bouson 162). It would require complete abstraction from context for us to be able to distil qualities such as the intelligence, cunning, perseverance, and strength of will which the character Zenia displays and to reinvest them positively. Such traits of character, empty of context, are meaningless. It is only to the extent that the other characters, at the end of the novel, can envisage, without guilt, the possibility of turning these traits to their own needs and desires that they take on positive potential.

V

We have had such pleasure in following the varying movements, transformations, hidden forms and reformulations of the Triple Goddess that it may seem ungenerous to question the very premises of the source of this pleasure. Let us begin by questioning instead what sort of pleasure we have been having. Has it been the pleasure of being "impliqué dans le jeu" as Derrida puts it, or has it been the pleasure of piecing together a puzzle which is exterior to us? We have watched the Triple Goddess take shape, shift about, be stretched in different directions, and turned upside down. We have attended the event of her modernization, and the confrontation of her unity and her fragmentation, but we have never really doubted that she would survive. Indeed, Tony's voice, setting the story up through hindsight in the prefatory section "Onset" allows us to know from the beginning that, whatever the dangers ahead, the voice which speaks for the "we" at stake, has come through the ordeal. Moreover, even the survival of Zenia is ensured: in the burst of energetic blue light as she returns to the underworld of collective memory (526), we recognize the same blue light which, associated with Charis and her grandmother, signifies mystical power (280, 296). We understand that Zenia is simply waving *au revoir* to us and she has no sooner disappeared than she is reinstated in iconic form as an artifact which Tony can contemplate: "an ancient statuette dug up from a Minoan palace" (527) [4] Tony is then reunited with the other two members of the human form of the goddess, Charis and Roz, so that the structure, both in its unified and in its fragmented configurations, is symbolically intact at the close of the novel.

The structure of the Triple Goddess is, I would conclude, the basis upon which the dominant possibilities of meaning in *The Robber Bride* rest. It is what serves to hold the text in place, and it is in place before the play of signification can begin; it is a form of "sure play," "[c]ar il y a un jeu *sûr* celui qui se limite à la *substitution* de pièces *données et existantes, présentes*" (Derrida 427, his emphases). I have tried, in this interpretation of *The Robber Bride*, to focus on the play of signification, remaining open to the possibility that it might, at some point, undermine the structural expectations attached to the intertext of the Triple Goddess. For example, it might have killed off the mother goddess. It might have broken up the parallelism of the women's lives, one of the women might have joined Zenia, Zenia might have actually loved one of the men, one of the women might have killed Zenia and been forced to face the consequences of transgression . . . That of course, would have been a radically different story, you might say. Clearly the novel is not concerned with questions of probability, but with resolving, within a predetermined framework, the questions it raises, much as fairy tales do.

But why not, we might ask ourselves? Should we not read fairy tales? It is of course an option, as long as we recognize them as fairy tales, structures of reassurance which presume that we are not yet capable of facing life without magical intervention. Indeed. Bruno Bettelheim comments on the function of such stories. He notes the importance of magic in the psychological structuring of children, but also the role these stories play in helping the child "to relinquish his infantile dependency wishes and achieve a more satisfying independent existence." In other words,

> the more secure a person feels within the world, the less he will need to hold on to "infantile" projections – mythical explanations or fairy-tale solutions to life's external problems – and the more he can afford to seek rational explanations . . . On the other hand, the more insecure a man is in himself and his place in the immediate world, the more he withdraws into himself because of fear or else moves outward to conquer for conquest's sake. (51)

If someone who is insecure is prone either to turn to conquest or to social withdrawal as a form of self-defense, in *The Robber Bride*, it is Zenia who seems to incarnate the conquering spirit. In contrast, the female triad is characterized by the desire of its members to withdraw within themselves, and while they do gain an ounce of courage at the end, they are in fact finally delivered from Zenia and the threat that she represents to them by the magical resolution of her timely accident. The genie goes back into the bottle, the wolf is boiled, and in this way, anxiety is temporarily mastered.

One might argue that the comforting resolution the novel offers is in fact tempered by its realist strain. The women do not find all their personal problems resolved, they have just taken a small step forward in terms of personal self-knowledge. Yet, as I argued earlier, the realist level is not the strongest one in the novel. What stands out most clearly for the reader is the impression of a congregation of the women, who will, "increasingly in their lives, tell stories" (528). It is the completion of the structure, the affirmation of the three-in-oneness which dominates meaning. It is, indeed, the reaffirmation of the mythical structure of the trinity, given (or given back) to matriarchal designs. Personally, I subscribe whole-heartedly to the point of view expressed by Angela Carter who, in *The Sadeian Woman*, wrote:

> All the mythic versions of women from the myth of the redeeming purity of the virgin to that of the healing, reconciling mother, are consolatory nonsenses; and consolatory nonsense seems to me a fair definition of myth, anyway. Mother goddesses are just as silly a notion as father gods. If a revival of the myths of these cults gives women emotional satisfaction, it does so at the price of obscuring the real conditions of life. This is why they were invented in the first place. (5)

This function of "obscuring the real conditions of life" is also underlined by Roland Barthes: "Nous sommes ici au principe même du mythe: il transforme l'histoire en nature" (237). The use of myth, or rather the imposition of myth as a structuring framework, and the maintaining of the integrity of this structure beyond the reaches of possible disruption is a strategy which attempts to do away with history: "En passant de l'histoire à la nature, le mythe fait une économic: il abolit la complexité des actes humains, leur donne la simplicité des essences ... [I]l fonde une clarté heureuse: les choses ont l'air de signifier toutes seules" (Barthes 252).

In *The Robber Bride*, the impoverishment of the human possibilities of the characters and their world may be seen as the result of the illusory reassurance created by Atwood's triple frame of effects: the intimations of permanence which the myth structure offers, the assurance of survival promised by the fairy tale ending, and the budding nostalgia on which the realist level finishes create an almost oppressive sense of closure. This is not to deny that Atwood's use of traditional structures is innovative. On the contrary, her blending of the different realms of discourse does produce something new which is, at times, joyfully poetic. Yet, as the novel explores these new possibilities, it never manages to evacuate the centring force, the anchoring presence, the fundamental logocentrism which these discursive traditions carry with them. Even as *The Robber Bride* attempts to offer women a way of reconstructing their identity more positively, acknowledging the fear and the risk of pain which the process involves, the novel cushions the reader against any such journey on the ontological level. The ending of *The Robber Bride* tries to evacuate the conflictual tension between the painful exploration of new ways of being on the one hand, and structures of reassurance on the other. The book favours the latter and thereby impoverishes, retrospectively, an important part of the reader's experience of the novel.

NOTES

1. Interview with Karla Hammond, "Articulating the Mute." Atwood, *Conversations* 109-20.
2. The frequent association of the words "history" and "story" in the novel (198, 383, 403,) generally grants history the same discursive status as Greek myths and fairy tales.
3. Another intertextual association which emerges here from the processional aspect of the described scene is that of Noah's ark. Here, it

is Charis who is "not wanted on the voyage," to quote Timothy Findley. One intertext suggests her exclusion from death, the other her exclusion from life. These are productive contradictions which feed the ambiguity of Charis's divided self.

4. In her conversation with Victor-Levy Beaulieu concerning the end of *The Robber Bride*, Atwood is quite clear about Zenia's potential for resurrection: "Why scatter her ashes like that? That's a little obscure . . . At the end of a lot of vampire movies, the vampire is burned and its ashes are scattered. In a Christopher Lee movie, you know that, after a certain amount of time, the ashes of the vampire will come back together and form the vampire again. That's the image I wanted to create." *Two Solicitudes*, 96.

WORKS CITED

Atwood, Margaret. *Conversations*. London: Virago, 1992.

——. *The Robber Bride*. Toronto: McClelland and Stewart, 1993.

——. *Survival: A Thematic Guide to Canadian Literature*. Toronto: Anansi, 1972.

Atwood, Margaret and Victor-Lévy Beaulieu. *Two Solicitudes*. 1996. Trans. Phyllis Aronoff and Howard Scott. Toronto: McClelland and Stewart, 1998.

Barthes, Roland. *Mythologies*. Paris: Editions du Seuil, 1957.

Bettelheim, Bruno. *The Uses of Enchantment: The Meaning and Importance of Fairy Tales*. 1975. London: Penguin, 1991.

Bloom, Lynn Z. and Veronica Makowsky. "Zenia's Paradoxes." *Literature, Interpretation, Theory* 6. 3-4 (1995): 167-79.

Bouson, J. Brooks. "Slipping Sideways into the Dreams of Women: The Female Dream Work of Power Feminism in Margaret Atwood's *The Robber Bride*." *Literature, Interpretation, Theory* 6, 3-4 (1995): 149-66,

Carter, Angela, *The Sadeian Woman: An Exercise in Cultural History*. London: Virago, 1979.

Derrida, Jacques. *L'Ecriture et la différence*. Paris: Editions du Seuil, 1967.

Djwa, Sandra. "Back to the Primal: The Apprenticeship of Margaret Atwood." *Various Atwoods: Essays on the Later Poems, Short Fiction, and Novels*. Ed. Lorraine York. Toronto: Anansi, 1994. 13-44.

Graves, Robert. *The White Goddess: A Historical Grammar of Poetic Myth*. 1948. London: Faber and Faber, 1961.

Laing, R.D. *The Divided Self: An Existential Study in Sanity and Madness*. 1960. Hamondsworth: Penguin, 1965.

Staels, Hilde. *Margaret Atwood's Novels: A Study of Narrative Discourse*. Basel: Francke, 1995.

I Am Telling This to No One But You

Private Voice, Passing, and the Private Sphere in Margaret Atwood's Alias Grace

STEPHANIE LOVELADY

> When you are in the middle of a story it isn't a story at all, but only
> a confusion; a dark roaring, a blindness, a wreckage of shattered glass
> and splintered wood; like a house in a whirlwind, or else a boat
> crushed by icebergs or swept over the rapids, and all aboard power-
> less to stop it. It's only afterward that it becomes anything like a story
> at all. When you are telling it, to yourself or to someone else. (298)

Alias Grace brims with references to the act of narration.
Susan Sniader Lanser has noted that private narration, in
which a narrator addresses another character in the text, is
much more likely to contain "considerable commentary on
communication itself" than public narration because "the
immediate communicative context of the private narrator"
(*Narrative* 139) is represented in the text. In classic cases of
private narration, the narrator is speaking directly to another character, either aloud or, in epistolary novels, in letters.
Public narrators, by contrast, either directly or implicitly
address "a reader-figure or audience 'outside' the text"
(138).

As Grace Marks narrates her life story to Dr. Simon
Jordan from her jail cell, she must carefully modulate what
she says because Simon is no casual conversationalist. He has
been asked by a clergyman who believes in Grace's innocence to interview her and write a letter to the Governor
on her behalf. Though she rarely mentions the underlying
purpose of their meetings, she is always mindful of and
motivated by it. In her conversations with Simon, Grace

finds an opportunity to participate in shaping her own representation, power this "celebrated murderess" (22) lacks in court or in the press. Her narration is private; she narrates specifically to Simon, and their relationship shapes what she says. At the same time, she has a broader implied audience which is quite public and which cannot help but shape her discourse. *Alias Grace* is based on an actual 1843 Canadian murder case and examines mid-nineteenth-century immigration as well as gender and class relations from a late-twentieth-century perspective.[1] Grace, a lower-class Irish immigrant at the centre of a sensational murder trial, is the subject of others' scrutiny and is figured as a dangerous force to be contained, frequently seen filtered through characters of higher social status like Simon. Grace also narrates a good part of her own story. Private and public narration intersect in Grace's tale, which cannot be said to be truly private or public, but which moves along a continuum between these two poles.

The nineteenth-century notion of gendered public and private spheres is also influential in the novel. Grace, whose previous life as a household servant remained circumscribed within the domestic and the private realms of most nineteenth-century women's lives, moves squarely into the public sphere when she becomes a household name and an object of collective fascination and horror. However, even before "Grace Marks" became synonymous with monstrous and uncontrolled criminality, as a member of several subservient classes of people, if not as an individual, she was *already* in the public sphere, the object of several forms of cultural anxiety, most notably the "Irish Question" (80) and the "Woman Question" (22).[2] While Atwood did not invent her name, Grace is aptly named. The mark she bears is not the "Mark of Cain" (105), as her aunt suggests in cursing Grace's father, but a question mark. She is the subject of earnest Victorian social questions about ethnicity and gender. Moreover, she is an amnesiac who has forgotten the key to a compelling mystery, a victim of possession who cannot know, or a charlatan who knows all and will not tell. The private and the public, the hidden and the exposed, all intertwine in *Alias Grace.*

In three realms, narrative transmission, her perception of her ethnic identity, and her adoption of gender roles, there is a movement away from the public toward the private. This movement does not represent a natural affinity for the private sphere, or a cowed surrender to it, but rather a strategic, if compromised, move to make the best of available roles. The private sphere is both stifling and liberating for Grace, while the public sphere, often attractive for the poor Irish serving girl, ultimately proves too perilous.

Telling It to Yourself or to Someone Else

Not only does *Alias Grace* contain both public and private narration but there is also a notable intermixing of these modes. Simon is represented by a public narrator, who describes his thoughts and actions in the third person for an audience outside the text. Simon serves as a focalizer, or a character to whose thoughts and feelings readers have access (Prince 31–32) in these scenes, the second most common kind of narrative situation in the text, which is also liberally sprinkled with epigraphs, poems, and letters. The most common and most complex narrative situation is Grace's narration. When she speaks she is often narrating her life story to Simon, sometimes for chapters at a time without interruption. These are fairly straightforward cases of private narration, despite Grace's very public secondary audience. However, this narration is interspersed with Grace's observations about Simon's reaction to her story and her description of her activities in prison between their sessions. She always reports her own thoughts and actions in the first person whether she is telling him her story, breaking away from this story to record thoughts she does not report to him, or relaying incidents that occur while he is not present. Presumably she acts as a public narrator in the latter two cases, because her audience is outside the text. Therefore, she is not speaking to a specific character. In many cases, however, what seems like public narration is shifted back into the private realm, or into an intermediate zone by a key phrase, as I will demonstrate.

Grace several times refers to telling stories to herself, noting that in prison there is "a lot of time to think, and no one to tell your thoughts to; and so you tell them to yourself" (161), and that a story is not a story until "you are telling it, to yourself or to someone else" (298). These statements raise the possibility that her seemingly public narration is not in fact directed outwards at a hypothetical public audience, but exists only as a record of Grace's interior monologue. If she is her own intended audience, narration would remain private because she is a character in the text and speaks only to herself when she is not speaking to Simon. This split between Simon's public narration and Grace's private narration would seem to mirror the Victorian construction of a male public sphere and a female private sphere. However, such a near opposition cannot be sustained because of Atwood's use of homodiegetic, heterodiegetic and autodiegetic narrators. A homodiegetic narrator also acts as a character within the text while a heterodiegetic narrator does not. An autodiegetic narrator tells his or her own story, as opposed to an observer narrator (Prince 9, 40-41). Simon is never a public narrator, only a focalizer; he is represented by a public narrator but he is not one himself. He is on occasion a private narrator, in his letters for instance. Meanwhile Grace, an autodiegetic narrator, has more narrative privilege than Simon. Moreover, I will argue that Grace's narration can be considered public, at least in places. Narrative voice not only alternates between public and private, but often takes unexpected turns. Thus, the public / private, male / female association is challenged as much as it is upheld in narrative terms.

The novel begins with a series of epigraphs, then the following description: "Out of the ground there are peonies growing. They come up through the loose grey pebbles, their buds testing the air like snails' eyes, then swelling and opening, huge dark-red flowers all shiny and glossy like satin. Then they burst and fall to the ground" (5). Because there is no explanation of narrative context, no frame narrative, no quotation marks to mark this text as spoken dialogue, it appears to be public narration. By the third paragraph, which starts "I tuck my head down while I walk" (5), it is clear the "narrator is homodiegetic, while it is not yet clear whether or not she is autodiegetic. The fourth paragraph gives some orienting information about the narrator; "It's 1851. I'll be twenty-four years old next birthday. I've been shut up in here since the age of sixteen. I am a model prisoner, and give no trouble" (5). Eventually, clues that the scene is a dream, a hallucination or a vision begin to emerge: "I watch the peonies out of the corners of my eyes. I know they shouldn't be here: it's April, and peonies don't bloom in April" (5-6), is followed by "this time it will be different, this time I will run for help . . . none of it will have happened" (6). After two pages of description, there is some extra spacing and this startling sentence, which ends the chapter: "This is what I told Dr. Jordan, when we came to this part of the tale" (6). Narration that seemed public is rendered private by this explanation. What we have been reading has not been narrated principally for a "reader-construct" (Lanser, *Narrative* 137), but to another fictional character, to whom we have

177

not yet been introduced. Yet, on the other hand, someone, a public narrator or the implied author, has chosen to begin with this excerpt of Grace's narration, to present it out of order and first. The sentence that alerts us to the fact that the narration is private – "This is what I told Dr. Jordan" – seems to imply that this organizer is Grace herself, who acts in her arranging capacity as a public narrator, even as she narrates privately. These two pages are public and private at once.

Eventually, Simon begins to shape Grace's narration. While he listens and takes notes she feels "as if he is drawing me; or not drawing me, drawing on me" (69). She imagines him writing on her body in a vivid demonstration of his shared authorship in the story he is allegedly merely recording. Simon's influence extends even into scenes in which he is not present. Grace plans her stories for him, wondering: "What should I tell Dr. Jordan about this day?" (295). That this narration takes place in the context of their relationship, that she crafts it specifically for him, moves what might be considered public narration closer to the private pole of the continuum, even though Grace is not technically telling this story to another character. When Simon ceases to visit Grace altogether she continues the story, complete with direct addresses, composing it in her mind as if he were still listening and anticipating his desires: "What should I tell him, when he comes back? He will want to know about the arrest, and the trial . . . I could say this" (353). When it becomes apparent that Simon is not returning she writes him a letter which she intends to smuggle out of prison, asking him to write the Governor on her behalf. Receiving no reply, Grace continues to address him mentally for decades, and after her own release from prison and her marriage, she notes, "I've written many letters to you in my head" (441). In fact, the last twenty pages of the book consist of one of these mental letters, describing her new life. Simon, or rather the idea of him, has become a confidante for Grace: "as I have no close woman friend I can trust, I am telling you about it, and I know you will keep the confidence" (456), as well as someone with whom she can share an unorthodox Biblical interpretation: "I am telling this to no one but you, as I am aware it is not the approved reading" (459). The focus of these addresses to Simon is no longer on how to tell the story to please or interest him but on how telling the story to him will please or comfort Grace. She has internalized Simon as an audience, as someone who will hear her, something Grace is always seeking.[3] When he tells her, "I simply wish to know what you yourself can actually remember," she responds, "Nobody has ever cared about that before, Sir" (307). It is a subdued but nonetheless affecting moment.

Internalizing Simon, however, changes Grace's speaking voice. The carefully modulated voice she uses to speak to him, and later to herself, while imagining him, is not the angry, bitter voice she uses before she meets Simon. The bitter voice frequently incorporates the discourse of others in order to satirize it, as in this imitation of the visitors to the Governor's house where Grace is hired out:

> When I have gone out of the room with the tray, the ladies look at the Governor's wife's scrapbook. Oh imagine, I feel quite faint, they say, and You let that woman walk around loose in your house, you must have nerves of iron, my own would never stand it. Oh well one must get used to such things in our situation, we are virtually prisoners ourselves you know, although one must feel pity for such poor benighted creatures . . . Although naturally she can be here only during the day, I would not have her in the house at night . . . Oh I don't blame you, there is only so far one can go in Christian charity, a leopard cannot change its spots and no one could say you have not done your duty and shown a proper feeling. (24)

Or in this prediction:

I will shrivel, my skin will dry out, all yellow like old linen; I will turn into a skeleton. I will be found months, years, centuries from now, and they will say Who is this, she must have slipped our minds, Well, sweep all those bones and rubbish into the corner, but save the buttons, no sense in having them go to waste, there's no help for it now. (35)

Grace continues to display anger after she meets Simon, and sometimes even directs it at him, but in a much more restrained fashion.[4] When he asks her if she feels she has been treated unjustly, she responds mildly, "I don't know what you mean, Sir" (91). The blistering, mocking anger disappears from her tone once she adopts Simon as a permanent narrative audience. Crude or forthright thoughts do emerge in her dialogue after this point, but she always uses the cover of her friend Mary, either imagining what she would say or quoting something she did say. For example, "lady or lady's maid, they both piss and it smells the same, and not like lilacs neither, as Mary Whitney used to say" (216). Mary becomes a crutch to say what Grace cannot while Simon is listening. Habitually quoting Mary also is a way for Grace to keep her dead friend alive, to continue their dialogue, to retain her as an interlocutor alongside Simon.

The mixture of public and private voice in Grace's narration is not merely a curiosity, but demonstrates Grace's unfulfilled needs for privacy and intimacy, as well as for what the Governor's wife calls "an enlarged sphere" (82), both literally and figuratively. Lanser argues that as white women characters' voices first emerged in the eighteenth century, private voice in epistolary novels "channelled female voice into forms that contained and defused it" (*Fictions* 26). Female characters, often male-authored were not empowered to speak to the world, at large, but only within a private relationship. A novel like *Jane Eyre* (1847), with its bold use of personal voice and direct address to readers, represented a breakthrough. For African–American women authors, Lanser asserts, however, private voice may not be a restriction to escape but "a necessary first location of power" (*Fictions* 198) for people forced into servitude and denied power. To reclaim the private is also to assert power. She points to novels such as *Their Eyes Were Watching God* (1937) and *The Color Purple* (1982), which both rely on a sympathetic listener or letter reader to create a safe place from which to narrate. Grace stands somewhere in between these positions. She is closer to Jane Eyre, a young, white female servant from a genteel family fallen on hard times who has caught the eye of her prosperous employer. But Grace is younger, ethnically Other, a lower ranking servant from a poorer family. Mr. Kinnear might seduce her, but he will not marry her, as Grace has learned from his house-keeper Nancy's example and Mary's before her. The avenues that lead to power for Jane – a wholesome Englishness that contrasts with Rochester's mad wife's decadent Creoleness (see Spivak) – and to a genteel middle-class position of gov-erness, are blocked off for the impoverished Irish maid-of-all-work.[5]

Grace's life, first as a servant, then as a prisoner, lacks the privileges of both the private and the public spheres. She is constrained by the private sphere – the Governor's parlour where she is hired out is literally an extension of prison for her – without enjoying any real privacy, either as a prison-er or as public figure. She notes that in prison "nobody . . . does you the courtesy of knocking" (35), and she resents being treated as "a fascinating case, as if I was a two-headed calf" (32). She suspects Simon of being "a collector" (41) and another doctor of viewing her as "a sight that must be seen" (244). The reason for tourists' and doctors' interest is her status as an infamous criminal. As Sarah Robertson notes, "the individual Grace has been subsumed by the pub-lic Grace" (154). Grace, like her historical counterpart, is the subject of numerous newspaper articles. In the novel (as in real life), the chronicler of mid-nineteenth-century Canadian life, Susanna Moodie, devotes a chapter of *Life in the Clearings* (1853) to her. Atwood uses quotations from Moodie as epigraphs, and Simon and Grace both read her account and refer to it. It was Moodie who first described Grace Marks as a "celebrated murderess" (Moodie 195), a term Grace repeats many times. Grace suspects that the salacious nature of the murders plays no small role in the public's fascination with her: "They don't care if I killed anyone, I could have cut dozens of throats, it's only what they'd admire in a soldier, they'd scarcely blink. No: was I really a paramour, is their chief concern, and they don't even know themselves whether they want the answer to be no or yes" (27). Simon is also compelled by this question. When Grace is hypnotized, he immediately asks if Grace ever "had relations" with James, realizing only as he asks that this is "the one thing he most wants to know" (399). After they are married, Jamie, too, persuades Grace to tell him the story of what happened at Mr. Kinnear's over and over and "for his wicked purposes" (457).

Even before she becomes celebrity, Grace experiences intense scrutiny. As a child in a large, poor family she tries to hug herself tight to shrink herself "because there was never enough room for me, at home or anywhere" (33). At Mr. Kinnear's, when her afternoon idyll making daisy chains in the meadow with Jamie is watched by her employer and two other servants, she is angered and reports, "I feel as though my afternoon had not been mine at all, and not a kind and private thing, but had been spied upon by everyone of them . . . exactly as if they'd all been lined up in a row at the door of my chamber, and taking turn at looking through the keyhole" (263).[6] Grace explains that her need for privacy is the reason she withholds information from Simon. When he asks her to relay a dream from the previous night, she does, but only after the page-long dream has been narrated does the reader find that Grace has only remembered the dream silently, and then responded to Simon, "I can't remember, Sir" (101), adding to herself, "I have little enough of my own, no belongings, no possessions, no privacy to speak of, and I need to keep something for myself" (101). This trick, the withholding that initially looks like compliance, is possible because in Grace's narration, there are no quotation marks, so it is often unclear whether text is spoken or thought until a tag clause appears at the end.[7] Grace guards her privacy through silence, and by playing the part expected from her. "I have good stupid look I have practiced" (38), she confides to the reader, and uses it on Simon during their first meeting. Later, when she trusts him more, she tells him of her use of a similar tactic at Mr. Kinnear's: "I had now been a servant for three years, and could act the part well enough" (224).

But just as Grace desires physical and mental privacy of an escape from publicity (a greater entry into the private sphere), she also wants to escape from the restricted life of the prison (a greater entry into the public sphere). On one level this desire for release is literal. Grace wants out of prison. Early in her narration (pre-Simon), she mocks the prison authorities who have sentenced her to solitary confinement: "I'm being left alone to reflect on my sins and misdemeanors, and one does that best in solitude, or such is our expert and considered opinion, Grace, after long experience with these matters" (34). She longs to go outside. Simon presents her with an apple, she smells it and thinks, "It has such an odour of outdoors on it I want to cry" (39). Despite this very real desire for literal escape, as a reviewer has attested, the novel as a whole examines "the cramped, desolate, private spaces that served as the cauldron for stewing resentments and desires" ("Women on the Verge" 1). Nina Auerbach notes that Grace's imprisonment functions as a symbol of women's imprisonment in domestic roles as

183

well as immigrants' entrapment in poverty. Auerbach asserts that the prison "is only an extension of the rooms, houses and ships beyond the jail" (1). Consider the following passage, which refers literally to prison, but also to the restriction of all subordinate classes of people:

> Today when I woke up there was a beautiful pink sunrise, with the mist lying over the fields like a soft white cloud of muslin, and the sun shining through the layers of it all blurred and rosy like a peach gently on fire.
>
> In fact I have no idea what kind of sunrise there was. In prison they make the windows high up, so you cannot climb out of them I suppose, but also so you cannot see out of them either, or at least not onto the outside world. They do not want you looking out, they do not want you thinking the word *out*, they do not want you looking at the horizon and thinking you might someday drop below it yourself, like the sail of a ship departing or a horse rider vanishing down a far hillside. (237)

Grace's narrative false start here, which presents her fantasy of the sunrise as fact, is an example of the way she "thinks the word *out*." Simon, frustrated by the knowledge that Grace is withholding information from him, surmises that her "strongest prison is of her own construction" (362). There is some truth to this assertion, but with this statement and by dismissing the story of her childhood and immigration as "only the usual poverty and hardships, etc." (133), he ignores the material facts that conspire to trap Grace, the prisons not of her own construction which define her in the public eye. Two of the most prominent are Irish nationality and female gender. While Grace's Irishness is something she can make private if she chooses, passing by assimilation rather than by outright denial, gender proves a more difficult border to cross.

"When you cross over the border, it is like passing through air, you wouldn't know you'd done it; as the trees on both sides of it are the same" (266), Jeremiah tells Grace. He is speaking of crossing the U.S. / Canada border in order to escape paying customs, but Jeremiah is a seasoned border crosser.[8] He appears in the text as Dr. Jerome DuPont, "Neuro-hypnotist" (83), Jeremiah Pontelli, peddler, Gerald Ponti, magician, and finally, in the English translation of this symbolic surname, Gerald Bridges, medium. He identifies himself as an American of French Protestant descent or as an American of Italian decent. Other characters refer to his "trace of a foreign accent" (83) and his "gypsy doing" (155); they identify him as a "Jew peddler" (338), and accuse him of being "a heathenish sort of man" (197) and of having "a low foreign look" (270); but none can pin a specific ethnic identity on him. That he is a Jew or a gypsy are common guesses. Jeremiah has "the air of being able to see more than most could" (265), according to Grace, or "the deep liquid eyes and intense gaze of a professional charlatan" (83) according to Simon. His hair is usually dark but sometimes red. He wears a "sand-coloured" suit (305). Jeremiah slips through others' definitions of him like sand, escaping where Grace seems trapped.

Grace first develops a friendship with Jeremiah when he comes to peddle his goods at the house where she has her first position. When she begins to sense danger at Mr. Kinnear's, he makes her an offer: to run away with him as a "medical clairvoyant" (267). Jeremiah has previously told Grace, "You are one of us" (155), puzzling her. One possible meaning of her own identity. "You would need a different name, of course, a French one or something foreign, because people on this side of the ocean would find it hard

185

to believe that a woman with the plain name of Grace had mysterious powers" (268), he coaches her. Grace is tempted. As she says, in "a new country, friends become old friends very quickly" (264). The escape Jeremiah offers is not only from danger, but also from social class and nationality. If she follows his example she can jump the barrier, assume a French name, perform in the parlours of the middle and upper classes as well as in travelling shows for the lower classes, be accepted as a specialist in hypnotism one day and wander the byways of Ontario selling buttons and clothes the next. Ultimately, because he does not mean to marry her, Grace rejects the offer and shortly thereafter she finds herself in prison. Her imprisonment contrasts starkly with Jeremiah's physical and social mobility. Jeremiah makes another attempt to free Grace by hypnotizing her for the Governor's wife and her circle of friends who have been working for Grace's release. Grace feels this attempt represents "a pact" (306) that Jeremiah, now Gerald Bridge, celebrated medium" (455), at a performance, he winks at her and she gives him a discreet wave, which escapes the notice of her husband. She reflects, "I would not wish any here to learn my true name; but I know my secrets are safe with Jeremiah, as his are safe with me" (456). For now, like Jeremiah, Grace is also a name-changer, an "escape artist"[9] assimilated into society under a new name, no longer bound by her history as a celebrated murderess, her childhood poverty, or her Irishness.

Grace indignantly quotes the preface to her confession, which reads "*both of the accused were from Ireland by their own admission*" (103, original emphasis). She protests, "That made it sound like a crime, and I don't know that being from Ireland is a crime; although I have often seen it treated as such. But of course, our family were Protestants, and that is different" (103). Grace's comments reveal several important points. The phrase "by their own admission" associates Irishness with deviance, and simultaneously identifies it with something one could and might want to conceal. (The wording is reminiscent of today's "avowed homosexual.") Anti-Irish prejudice and Grace's lack of positive associations with Ireland or a strong Irish identity make passing an acceptable option for her. She suffers through a miserably poor childhood in the absence of the ethnic solidarity she might feel if that poverty were attributable to English oppression rather than her maternal grandfather's and her father's personal disgraces.[10] Separated almost immediately from any family that might have reinforced her national identity when her mother dies and she goes into service in Canada, Grace is left without much sense of national origin: "I don't recall the place very well, as I was a child when I left it; only in scraps, like a plate that's been broken. There are always some pieces that would seem to belong to another plate altogether; and then there are the empty spaces, where you cannot fit anything in" (103).

However, Grace has some ideas about the Irish. Her assertion that Irish Protestants are "different" (and presumably less worthy of slander) points to one assimilation strategy available to Grace, stressing her Protestantism over her Irishness. She takes advantage of this strategy almost immediately upon immigrating. The first time words are put in her mouth for her. When the twelve-year-old girl is being interviewed for a position as a scullery maid, the housekeeper conducting the interview wants to know "if I was a Catholic, as those from Ireland generally were; and if so she would have nothing to do with me, as the Catholics were superstitious and rebellious Papists who were ruining the country" (128). Later she needs no encouragement to disassociate herself from Catholics, as seen in her insistence on Protestant difference or in her distaste at seeing James act "so Papist" (332) when he crosses himself. While she does not go as far as her father, who has been involved in anti-Catholic terrorism in Ireland, Grace is quick to disassociate herself from Catholics when possible.[11]

But disassociation is not always so easy. The Reverend Verringer, one of the petitioners for Grace, notes to Simon that political factors hinder Grace's chance for release, as the "Tories appear to have confused Grace with the Irish Question, although she is a Protestant; and to consider the murder of a single Tory gentleman – however worthy the gentleman, and however regrettable the murder – to be the same thing as the insurrection of an entire race" (80). Like Grace, Verringer makes the distinction between the Catholic and Protestant Irish, although to his disappointment, others are not making it. Grace is marked as Irish in several ways. Simon notes a "trace of the Northern Irish accent" (133) in her voice. Her red hair is frequently commented upon and holds negative associations for many who do so. Quoting the newspaper descriptions of herself, Grace notes she has the "Red hair of an ogre" (33), the interviewing housekeeper fears she will be "bad-tempered, as redheaded people frequently were" (128), and prison guards assume she will be sexually available to them because "a little fire . . . comes with the redness of the hair" (240). Not only is Grace marked as Celtic by the colour of her hair,[12] in one instance a specifically Catholic identity is attached to her when her lawyer, sympathizing with Simon's difficulty in getting to the bottom of Grace's story, nicknames her "Our Lady of the Silences" (373).

Grace is Methodist. Her maternal grandfather was a minister who "had done something unexpected with the church money" (104), lost his position and left his family destitute. Her father was Anglo-Irish, and presumably Anglican, but not religious. As an adult, Grace attends a Methodist church. While this is an unsurprising choice, given her family background, it is also a very strategic, assimilationist one. Cecil Houston and William Smyth have noted that in mid-nineteenth-century Canada, Protestant churches, especially the quickly growing Methodist church, served as "forums for ethnic fusion" (169). In these churches, Irish Protestants met and intermarried with Scots, English, and American settlers. While the Anglican religion remained associated with English ethnicity, and Presbyterianism with Scotch heritage, the ethnicity of a Methodist was not as easily traceable. Protestant churches, Houston and Smyth assert, are part of the reason that in Canada, "the Irish have disappeared" (3), despite the immigration of half a million Irish to Canada from 1815 to 1845 and their status as "a pivotal charter group" (8) of Canadian settlement.[13] Simon notes the political advantages of Methodism when he suspects Reverend Verringer has converted from the Church of England to Methodism because of "the falling political star of the former in this country, and the rising one of the latter" (78). Methodism was safely Protestant but not too closely associated with England at a time when the Canadian identity was consolidating under the federation, which joined British Canada West and French Canada East.

Aside from church affiliation, marriage is another factor that affects the perception of ethnicity. In fact, if she takes her husband's name, marriage can obscure a woman's ethnicity to outside observers. As girls, Grace and Mary play a game throwing apple peelings to see what letter they will spell in order to divine the initials of their future husbands. Grace's peel falls into a J. Mary jokes Grace will marry Jim, the stable boy, or Jeremiah, and in fact several men whose names start with J – Jeremiah, Simon Jordan, and two others who share Jim's name – are potential sexual partners for Grace. James McDermott, the Irish Catholic servant who is hung for the murder of Mr. Kinnear, is widely believed to be Grace's lover, and to have been urged by her to commit the murders. Jamie Walsh, the neighbour boy who has a crush on Grace testifies against her at the trial, repents and marries her after her release. If a partnership with Jeremiah would have offered Grace a kind of flexible ethnicity, perceptions of her sexual relations with James reinforce her Irishness in the public eye, to the detriment of her image. Her eventual union with Jamie helps erase her national identity, even though he is probably Irish, and may even be Catholic by birth.

James and Jamie represent two distinct kinds of Irish identity. James represents the criminal, rebellious Irishman Anglo-Canadians so feared. He is a "surly black-browed rascal" (278) according to Mr. Kinnear and a self-described "scapegrace . . . never one to lick the boots of the rich" (226), endowed with a prodigious amount of physical energy. When he expends it in an ethnic-identified way, step-dancing in the barn loft, the noise sounds ominous to Grace. James is filled with ethnic resentment. Grace reports that "he hated all Englishman . . . they were all thieves and whores and stealers of land, and ground down the poor wherever they went (257). It is largely because of the perception that Grace is the paramour of the Catholic, Celtic-identified McDermott that she cannot escape the taint of Irishness during the trial. The association of Irishness with criminality and revolt plays an important part in the pre-trial publicity. As Grace's lawyer notes to Simon, the recently quashed populist Rebellion led by William Mackenzie, who "took the part of the poor Scots and Irish" (372), cast a political shadow over the scandal, though Grace was ten years old and still in Ireland at the time. Being Irish is enough to make her suspected of being anti-Tory – moreover, her murdered employer was a Tory, and also a Scot, but a lowland Scot, which according to James is "the same thing" (257) as being an Englishman.

Jamie Walsh, the pipe-playing youth who makes daisy chains with Grace, represents a considerably less threatening version of the Irish-Canadian, as his juvenile nickname implies. He is never explicitly named as Irish, but his Irish surname, his red hair and freckles all suggest such an identity. Walsh is not only an Irish name, but for the most part, an Irish Catholic name,[14] though Jamie's religion is never mentioned, except to note that after their marriage Jamie attends the Methodist church with Grace. If Jamie was born Catholic, his conversion to Methodism is notable since relatively few Catholics converted. Also remarkable would be Grace's acceptance of him, given her bias against Catholics. On the other hand, this distaste could be what prompts Jamie to convert, or evidence of Grace's lack of viable options when Jamie proposes.

Whether he is a convert or not, Grace and Jamie's married life is carefully conformist in order to protect Grace's identity and their privacy. Ironically, marriage to countryman does not bring Grace back her lost ethnicity, but rather helps Grace to assimilate more completely as Jamie is as bent on anonymity as she is. They name their cat Tabby and their dog Rex because "we don't wish to get a reputation in the neighbourhood for being too original" (455). The next sentence announces that they attend the Methodist church, presumably for the same reason. By successfully avoiding detection and by obtaining a house of her own, Grace gains the privacy she has always lacked, and entry to a more satisfactory version of the domestic sphere than the one she experienced as a servant. While she has greater access to the outside world than she did as a prisoner, her life is still for the most part circumscribed by the private sphere. Grace's chief pleasures are in keeping her own house, in quilting for herself and in her hopes that at forty-six she may be pregnant with her first child. Her marriage to Jamie, a man who is more suited to home life than

Jeremiah and more open to assimilation than James, makes this quiet, private life possible. They have heeded this advice from the conduct book *The Ideal Woman*: "Let's the woman's first requisite be a man who is domestic in his tastes, and the man's first object be a woman who can make his home a place of rest for him" (Melendy 47). Grace is neither the celebrated murderess she was nor the celebrated medium she could have been. Instead she sits on her porch and admires a scene "so peaceful you would think it was a picture" (453). Her passing, both in terms of ethnic assimilation and in hiding her identity, is not as flamboyant an escape from definition as Jeremiah's, but it is an escape of sorts, an escape into privacy.

Their Own Limited Space

Christopher Lehmann-Haupt writes that Grace's "subordinate role as a child, a poor person, a servant and a prisoner have bred in her a bitter sense of irony" (19). This is certainly true, but the reviewer leaves her gender off the list. This proves to be the subordinate identity most difficult for Grace to escape. By the end of *Alias Grace*, she is not a child, or poor, or a servant or a prisoner, but she is still a woman. She is freer than she was at the beginning of the novel, but she is not altogether free. Whether campaigning like Mrs. Quennell for "an enlarged sphere for women" (82) or cheerfully accepting their "own limited sphere" (429) like Simon's mother, all the women of *Alias Grace* live lives shaped by gender and by the long-lived Victorian concept of public and private spheres belonging respectively to men and women. *The Ideal Woman* explains women's role in the home as follows:

> If it be the man's part to lay the foundation and erect the building, it
> is woman's to beautify and enshrine music and the kindly arts with-

in them. It is his to build and hers to beautify. It is woman who informs the home with light and life. Her hand is that decorates and adorns, that culls and twines the flowers and leaves, and lets in "sweetness and light" into the rooms. Her touch is that of the purifying, transforming and beautifying angel in the home, or indeed to be a help-meet in every sense of the word. (Melendy 45-46)

Nine-year-old Grace, in charge of her younger siblings and taking care of a house inhabited by a continually sick and pregnant mother and an alcoholic father, may not succeed in purifying, transforming, and beautifying the home to the extent Mary Melendy envisioned. She does, however, understand from a very early age that the domestic sphere, whether in her own home or those of others, is her realm, never questioning this fate or wishing it could be otherwise. The third of the parents' nine surviving children, she sees her older sister go into service and her older brother go to sea while she is quite young. When she is almost thirteen she begins her own career as a domestic servant. It never occurs to Grace to even fantasize about following her brother's example instead of her sister's. She knows and accepts that poor boys leave home to take jobs that may be arduous and ill-paying but which at least lead them into the wider world, while poor girls go from their own homes to the houses of others and perform much the same domestic work they have already been carrying out from an early age. Grace inherits responsibility for the ever-increasing number of younger siblings at the age of nine, then passing it to the next youngest sister, who is nine and a half, when she goes into service herself. There is a deep sense of inevitability in this pattern. Her submissive mother, trapped into an abusive marriage by her first, illegitimate pregnancy, does not give Grace much to hope for in adult life:

She'd begun life under Aunt Pauline's thumb and continued the same way, only my father's thumb was added to it. Aunt Pauline was always telling her to stand up to my father, and my father would tell her to stand up to Aunt Pauline, and between the two of them they squashed her flat. She was a timid creature, hesitating and weak and delicate, which used to anger me. I wanted her to be stronger so I would not have to be so strong myself. (104-05)

This is a portrait of female weakness, but it is also one of female strength. Aunt Pauline has a force of will Grace's mother does not, as does Grace herself.

Grace senses the corrosive effect entrapment within the family sphere has on her mother, even to the point of mis-understanding a common turn of phrase:

When I was quite young, six or seven, I put my hand on my mother's belly, which was all round and tight, and I said What is in there, another mouth to feed, and my mother smiled sadly and said Yes I fear so, and I had a picture of an enormous mouth, on a head like the flying angel heads on the gravestones, but with teeth and all, eating away at my mother from the inside, and I began to cry because I thought it would kill her. (107)

Grace's mother does eventually die, eaten from within by a tumour in her uterus on the ship from Ireland. Grace's childhood, such as it was, ends here. But Grace learns from her mother's negative example. She has a power of cunning resistance and withholding that her mother lacks, as demonstrated in her conversations with Simon. She is something of a trickster figure.[15] The Eve, Pandora, and Scheherazade motifs running through the novel all under-score Grace's role as a transgressor. She is able to take advan-tage of the roles available to her, even when they are severe-ly limited, as she admits when she tells Simon she knows how to "act the part" of a servant. The role of murderess, which moves Grace out of the private domain into the public eye, is a surprise and more of a challenge. Early in the novel she muses:

Murderess is a strong word to have attached to you. It has a smell to it, that word – musky and oppressive, like dead flowers in a vase. Sometimes at night I whisper it over to myself: *Murderess, Murderess.* It rustles, like a taffeta skirt across the floor.

　Murderer is merely brutal. It's like a hammer, or a lump of metal. I would rather be a murderess than a murderer, if those are the only choices. (22-23).

In her more frank, pre-Simon voice, Grace is trying on the role that has been handed to her, trying to find some good in it, something she can use. There is of course a very practical advantage to being a murderess rather than a murderer. James is the one hanged. Grace's youth and gender allow her lawyer to argue she is "little better than a halfwit; and very soft and pliable, and easily imposed upon" (361) by the murderous McDermott, and to win her the clemency of a life sentence. Several options are open to Grace as a convicted murderess. She is sometimes tempted to act the brutal madwoman, reasoning that "If they want a monster so badly they ought to be provided with one" (33); and she does in fact spend several years in a lunatic asylum. By the time the book opens, however, Grace is committed to being the "model prisoner" in hopes of pardon and release. This is a role, she notes, that takes unseen strength to carry off, like hanging off a cliff. Tom LeClair sees Grace fitting herself into feminine roles Simon will understand by using the literary conventions of local colour and romance. Prone to fainting, or feigning this trait, she encourages Simon's self-described tendency to see her as "the heroine of a sentimental novel" (58) by describing the "genteel swooning" LeClair points out "was not expected of an Irish serving girl" (26). At the same time, she steers him away from believing she is merely playing the lady by making an argument for her own candidness. She asserts, "I have no reason not to be frank with you, Sir . . . A lady might conceal things, as she has her reputation to lose; but I am beyond that ... I was never a lady, Sir, and I've already lost whatever reputation I ever had" (90). By indicating she is beyond caring about her reputation and has forsworn all hope of release, Grace attempts to minimize any doubt Simon might have about the veracity of her story.

The story Grace tells Simon revolves around three women, all of them seduced and come to disastrous ends, all having failed one of the cardinal rules of Ideal Womanhood, to contain one's sexuality within the domestic, marital relationship. Though Grace herself does not get pregnant out of wedlock, these illegitimate pregnancies shape her life.[16] The cultural narrative of the fallen girl is a powerful force in her life. Aunt Pauline tells Grace her mother's story to warn her that "too many young women were caught in that fashion" (105). Their hasty marriage traps both of Grace's parents and their children into a life of unhappiness and poverty. After her mother dies, betrayed in death as in life by the female reproductive system, Grace finds a new mother-figure in Mary Whitney, with whom she works in the laundry at Grace's first domestic position.

Mary is three years older than Grace, also an orphan, part friend, part mother to the girl who has known little of friendship or mothering. "Mary took me under her wing from the very first" (151), Grace reports, and "comforted me better than my own mother could have done, for she was always too busy or tired or ill" (164). Mary provides Grace with her first opportunity to tell her story, to be listened to and to have her grief validated. Mary teaches Grace how to be a servant, not only how to do laundry, but also how to be "respectful and demure" to her employers while behind their backs "she made jokes about them and imitated their faces and walks and ways" (150). It is a lesson Grace learns well, though being more restrained than Mary, she does not fully apply her acerbic wit to her superiors until she is a prisoner, and then only in her own mind. Mary gives Grace new ways of looking at her position which undermine the dominance of master over servant: "In the end, she said, we had the better of them, because we washed their dirty linen and therefore we knew a great deal about them; but they did not wash ours, and knew nothing about us at all" (158). This, like Mary's habit of stealing candle stubs to extend the lighted portion of her day, is reclamation of the privacy and private time that are so scarce for servants.

As Richard Eder notes, Mary also initiates Grace into female sexuality, explaining menstruation to the terrified girl when she reaches her menarche and repeating warnings similar to Aunt Pauline's: "Grace, you will be a beauty, soon you will turn the men's heads . . . but you must be very careful what you ask, and you must never do anything for them until they have performed what they promised; and if there's a ring, there must be a parson to go with it" (164-65). Mary also gives Grace an idea of what sort of future she can reasonably hope for. She tells her they will save money from their wages for their dowries. Mary's vision is of Grace as mistress of a tidy farmhouse, and independent" (158). For herself she imagines she will

> marry a nice young farmer whose land was already cleared and a good house built; and if she could not get one of those, she would settle for one with a log house, and they would build a better house later. She even knew what kind of hens and cows they would have – she wanted white and red Leghorns, and a Jersey cow for the cream and cheese, which she said there was nothing better. (166)

If the level of detail about the house and the farm animals is greater than that about the husband, this is not surprising because girls like Grace and Mary are in training to excel in the domestic realm. Their hopes centre around transferring familiar domestic labour from an employer's home to their own. In Mary's ideal scenario, as in Melendy's, it is her husband's task "to build" the house before she arrives and hers "to beautify" it with the prettiest chickens and the best cheese and cream. The most obvious alternative to this role, that they continue as servants, is not attractive. Mary assures Grace they will not — "being a servant was not a thing we were born to . . . on this side of the ocean folks rose in the world by hard work, not by who their grandfather was" (157-58). Two other cultural roles for women who fail to become the Ideal Woman surface as well, when Mary tells Grace that wrapped in a sheet after a bath she looks "very comical, just like a madwoman" (152) and takes her down to the red-light district to "see the women who made a living by selling their bodies" (152). Wife, maid, madwoman and prostitute / criminal are the cultural roles open to Mary and Grace. They can be domestic and "independent" as mistresses of their own homes, domestic for pay in the homes of others, or exist dangerously outside of domesticity, out of their minds or outside the law, their sexuality threateningly unregulated. Grace inhabits all four female roles within her lifetime, beginning as a servant, thrust into the national spotlight as a celebrated murderess and suspected paramour, descending into (or feigning) madness, recovering and ending as a quiet, moderately prosperous wife. What makes her remarkable is her ability to move through these roles, between the private and the public sphere, to emerge from madness and sexual scandal and turn these common narrative ends into a mere interludes in her life, phases she can move beyond.

Mary is the key to Grace's movement through each of these roles. As she taught her how to be a maid while she was alive, after her death Mary teaches Grace how to fill other female roles. Grace calls Simon, "without her, it would have been a different story entirely" (102), and it would have. When Mary, ignoring her own warnings to

Grace, becomes pregnant and dies of a botched abortion, Grace is orphaned anew. After they play the apple peelings game to determine the identities of their future husbands and Mary's peel breaks three times in a row, foreshadowing her death before marriage, Grace dreams of her mother's burial at sea, substituting Mary's dark hair for her mother's auburn hair rippling out of the sheet. The conflation of mother / Mary in the dream indicates that the second loss is as crushing as the first to Grace.

Grace finds herself "depressed in spirits" (202) for years after Mary's death. When she meets Nancy Montgomery, a housekeeper whose joking manner reminds her of Mary who is looking to hire an additional servant, Grace, now almost sixteen, takes the job. Nancy hires Grace to provide cover for her affair with Mr. Kinnear, but she is also fearful lest he should turn his libidinous attention to the younger girl. As a result, she is alternately kind and sharp with Grace and Grace is disillusioned: "I thought we would be like sisters or at least good friends, the two of us working side by side, as I had done with Mary. Now I knew this was not the way it was going to be" (223). Despite her failure to fill Mary's shoes, Nancy continues to be linked with Mary in Grace's mind just as Mary was linked with Grace's mother. When Nancy asks Grace to brush her hair, Grace remembers how Mary brushed hers. Eventually James tells Grace that Nancy is Mr. Kinnear's mistress, and soon after she recognizes the symptoms of Nancy's pregnancy. Although there is little love lost between Nancy and Grace, the news hits Grace hard. "Oh no, Oh no . . . It cannot be" (279), she thinks, then wonders what Mr. Kinnear will do when he finds out:

> Boot her in the ditch. Marry her. I had no idea, and could not rest
> easy with either of these futures. I wished Nancy no harm, and did
> not want her cast out, a waif on the common highway and a prey
> to wandering scoundrels; but all the same it would not be fair and

just that she should end up a respectable married lady with a ring on her finger, and rich into the bargain. It would not be right at all. Mary Whitney had done the same as her, and had gone to her death. Why should the one be rewarded and the other punished, for the same sin? (276)

The mother-Mary-Nancy line is firmly established now. The two possibilities, a marriage or none, are the paths Grace's mother and Mary took when they found themselves pregnant. After she is rejected by the father of her child, Mary predicts that "no decent man would marry her and she would have to go on the streets, and become a sailor's drab as she would have no other way of feeding herself and the baby" (173). She and Grace explore the options of hiding the pregnancy and giving the child up for adoption or going to a workhouse, but nothing seems tenable. Having been down this road with Mary, Grace can only imagine disaster for Nancy if Mr. Kinnear will not marry her. The question is never settled because they are both murdered in short order. Characters who believe Grace was involved in the murders construe that Grace must have been jealous of Mr. Kinnear's involvement with Nancy, but by looking to romantic motives for an explanation, they go astray. It is Mary who makes this "a different story entirely" than what the courts and the press see.

During the hypnotism scene, after Simon identifies the mysterious voice emanating from Grace as Mary, "Mary" affirms:

> I told James to do it. I urged him to. I was there all along! . . . Grace doesn't know, she's never known! . . . You mustn't tell her! . . . Do you want to see her back in the Asylum? I liked it there at first, I could talk out loud there. I could laugh. I could tell what happened. But no one listened to me . . . I was not heard . . . You're the same, you won't listen to me, you don't believe me, you want it your own way, you won't hear . . . (402–03)

Sandra Gilbert and Susan Gubar have noted that Victorian women writers "almost obsessively create characters who enact their own, covert authorial anger" (77), often in the figure of the madwoman, who is sometimes taken for a ghost. Atwood returns to this trope of nineteenth-century female anger by reintroducing it in the familiar forms of mental illness or spiritual possession. After the hypnotism, Simon, Reverend Verringer and Jeremiah discuss what they have seen. "Two hundred years ago, they would not have been at a loss . . . It would have been a clear case of possession" (405), Verringer asserts. But the men settle instead on a psychological condition known as "*double consciousness*" (405) or "*dédoublement*" (406), which closely resembles today's multiple personality disorder, a still controversial condition believed to be brought on by trauma that causes the conscious self to fracture. If we accept the diagnosis, the moment of disassociation is easy to pinpoint. When Mary dies, Grace hears a voice crying "*Let me in*" (178), which she believes she has misheard because she thinks Mary's ghost would want to be let out the window, as a fellow steerage passenger told her when her own mother died. Grace faints soon after:

> when I did wake up I did not seem to know where I was, or what had happened; and I kept asking where Grace had gone. And when they told me I myself was Grace, I would not believe them, but cried, and tried to run out of the house, because I said that Grace was lost, and had gone into the lake, and I needed to search for her. They told me later they'd feared for my reason, which must have been unsettled by the shock of it all; and it was no wonder, considering. (180)

Grace reports hearing another voice shortly after her realization that Nancy is pregnant, which echoes the words of her own response: "I heard a voice whispering: *It cannot be*. I must have been frightened into a fit, because after I lost consciousness altogether" (279). As the day of the murders draws closer, Grace's narrative becomes fractured and vague. She loses consciousness over and over, sleepwalks and has vivid dreams, which may not be dreams at all. Presumably during these lost times, "Mary" is seducing James in order to gain his co-operation in the murder and helps him carry it out. "Mary" is in control again while Grace is in the Asylum. It is also quite likely that "Mary" influences Grace's bitter and sardonic voice early in the novel even after Grace has resigned control and outwardly become "the model prisoner." Even more dramatically than Grace has internalized Simon as her audience after he is gone, she has internalized Mary as a speaking voice. Sometimes this is clearly conscious, as when she quotes Mary or tries to imitate her: "I try to think of what Mary Whitney would say, and sometimes I can say it" (63). Other times Grace seems almost, but not quite, conscious of Mary's presence within her as when another inmate spills soup on her and she is chastised for protesting, then "I was suddenly very angry and I screamed, I did nothing, I did nothing! It was her, it was her fault!" (32). She is literally speaking of the soup, but on some level she may also be speaking of the murders. Grace's very mind seems divided into public and private zones to which she has varying access. As Hilary Mantel points out, "Grace can know and not know, she is good at that" (4). She is not only "utterly present and unfathomable" (Eder 2) to readers, but also to herself.

By having Verringer raise the possibility of possession, pointing out that in different contexts the same set of facts are interpreted quite differently, Atwood is keeping a supernatural explanation open. From a literary perspective there is not nearly as much difference between these two explanations as there would be from a psychological or religious perspective. "Mary" works as easily as a ghost as an alternate personality.[17] Her reference to speaking to Nancy could be taken as either evidence of the sprits' communication with each other in the afterlife, or the existence of a third personality that manifest itself only to "Mary" and not to Grace. Positing the existence of three separate personalities adds resonance to Grace's final act of stitching scraps of Mary's petticoat and Nancy's dress into a quilt and declaring she has done this "so we will all be together" (460).

Grace may have slightly more agency as a multiple personality than as a victim of possession, since the psyche of a multiple presumably splinters in order to shield the original personality from painful knowledge. The splintering is a self-protective move from within, not an invasion from without. A final possibility, and one in which she retains the highest degree of agency, is that Grace is faking everything. This option is open but improbable since even in her own interior monologue she never admits to the murders or even hints that she has any memory of them. Atwood has explored the theme of the suppressed, unknown self throughout her career, particularly in *Surfacing* (1972) and *Cat's Eye* (1988). That Grace knows all and doesn't tell seems unlikely, though she may certainly know more than she tells, or she may willfully alter the story as she does the song "Tom, Tom, the Piper's Son" since "I didn't see why I shouldn't make it come out in a better way" (238). It would be wrong, however, to impose any one of these three explanations – mental illness, possession, or outright deception – on *Alias Grace* as the authoritative one, because the novel is so committed to ambiguity, multiple narratives, and undecidability.[18] The novel's end, with Grace unsure if she is pregnant or if the heaviness in her stomach is a tumour like the one that killed her mother – "a life or a death" (459), is one more example of the withholding of certainty and stable meanings common throughout the novel.[19]

Rather than choosing between the common female narrative ends of madness, marriage, or death, *Alias Grace* calls attention to these limited choices by invoking all three, relegating madness to a narrative middle and ending at a fork in the road, one path leading to a few more decades of married life for the middle-aged newlywed, the other to an early death.[20] Grace's maturation as measured by conventional milestones goes into slow motion in prison. As she notes, in the Penitentiary "some of them stay the same age all the time inside themselves; the same age as when first put in" (380). Physically at least, this happens to Grace, who is said to look older than her age at sixteen when she is incarcerated and younger than her age after almost three decades in jail. According to Janet, Grace appears to be "almost a girl" (446). However, time has not stood still, and the twenty-nine years represent a real loss. When Grace associates the word "murderess" with a "musky and oppressive" smell "like dead flowers in a vase" (22-23), she invokes a traditional image of maidenhood, flowers, but these blossoms have been left to rot.

Grace's status as "almost a girl" at forty-five is no doubt partially due to her being unmarried. Prison temporarily halts the marriage plot for her. That she marries immediately upon her release from prison, saying simply "I did not have many other choices" (452), points to the near inevitability of marriage as the end of a woman's story. When it seems she would never be released from the prison, Simon thinks, "Her story is over . . . the thing that has defined her. How is she supposed to fill in the rest of the time?" (91) If the marriage plot defined most Victorian women's stories, Atwood seems to be asking, how did they fill in the rest of the time? The forced stasis that delays Grace's marrying until middle age may not be that much different than the arrested development of a woman who marries at twenty and suddenly finds her story over. When Grace observes that the new Governor's daughter Janet, who finds Grace's box of clothing and presents it to her on her release, is "too young to have realized what the effects of twenty-nine years shut up in a box might be" (445), she is referring not only to her rotted clothes, or to her own time in prison, but to Janet's own likely fate. Marriage, Grace points out once she has married, "is not what most girls imagine when young" (453).

Nonetheless, she makes the best of it. Marrying in her forties without romantic illusions, Grace thinks, "at least the two of us know what kind of bargain we have gotten into" (453). The conclusion of the novel is one of partial satisfaction. Grace has made a remarkable escape from many of the roles that seemed to have trapped her, from Irish serving girl, to sexually degenerate criminal, to lunatic. Yet her deliverance is into a somewhat disturbing marriage in which she has little say. Jamie sends for her when she is released from prison and she is brought to him without knowing the identity of the gentlemen who has agreed to provide her a home, or what that role in that home is to be. Grace agree to the marriage, but afterwards always calls Jamie "Mr. Walsh," indicating distance between them. She is "troubled" (456) by Jamie's insistence that she re-live the murders over, performing the role of McDermott's victim for him. Grace's release from a prison symbolizing women's constriction in domestic roles leads her into one of those very roles; it is an improvement, but not a triumph.

Conclusion

Grace sometimes wonders what would have become of her if she had run away with Jeremiah. She concludes, "my fate would have been very different. But only God knows whether it would have been better or worse; and I have done all the running away I have time in this life" (456).

Grace gains a measure of freedom by conforming, both in terms of assimilation and by creating conventional, domestically bound life for herself – in other words, by retreating as far as possible in both ethnic and gender terms into the private sphere.[21] She also contains the running narrative she keeps of her life within the context of a private relationship by addressing it to Simon, rather than to the public at large.

It is not surprising that she should do so. While Grace gives evidence throughout the novel of her discomfort with the constriction of the private sphere and the limited, culturally scripted roles available to her, she has ample motivation to blend into Canadian society by assimilating and following conventional gender roles. An already weak Irish identity and her Protestantism make shedding any associations with her Irish origins easy.[22] Moreover, Grace finds comfort and satisfaction in the private sphere, in her intimate friendship with Mary, and in the concrete pleasures of sewing and washing so lyrically described throughout the novel. Grace is never one to covet male privilege, accepting gender conventions as given. She does not consciously choose her two public roles, madwoman and criminal celebrity, and given the choice, she rejects another public role in which she would have been on display as a medicine show performer. Grace probably feigns her shock – "under their own names? . . . I would never be so brazen" (68) – when Simon tells her of the literary magazine female employees of his father's mill put out, but that it is a credible response demonstrates the degree to which women are expected to remain in the private sphere, and Grace does not veer very far from this expectation, at least not of her own volition. All the behaviour that thrusts her into the public sphere, as well as the most public aspects of her narration, come from the alternate personality or ghost, "Mary," who dares what Grace does not. "Mary" transgresses not only by acting sexually outside of marriage and committing murder, bur also by speaking freely – that is, publicly and outside the boundaries of acceptable female speech. That Grace needs "Mary" to perform these roles for her is a measure of her dissatisfaction with contemporary gender configurations.

Late in the novel Grace quotes the hymn "Amazing Grace":

> Amazing Grace! How sweet the sound
> That saved a wretch like me!
> I once was lost, but now I'm found,
> Was blind but now I see.
> I hope I was named after it. I would like to be found. I would like to see. Or to be seen. (379)

The hymn touches on many themes in Grace's life. Its authorship by a slave-ship captain whose conversion led him to turn his ship back to Africa recalls her traumatic sea voyage. The song also calls to mind Grace's unexpected release from prison, the blindness of her amnesia, and the extent to which so much of her story and her self is lost to her. She expresses a desire to have her true self found, seen by others and to see it herself. As Auerbach has pointed out, it is only by fulfilling the existing roles of "celebrated murderess, madwoman, victim and demon" that "a Victorian servant could turn a life of washing and quilting into a riveting public narrative" (3). But Grace would like to bring what is hidden and private out into the open in a way, which would be more genuine than the spectacle of her celebrity. It is an unrealized desire.

NOTES

1. Atwood's ability to recreate the Victorian world is widely praised. See especially Auerbach, Cameron, LeClair, Mantel, and Robertson. (Rubin dissents, claiming that Grace's acceptance of Mary's abortion is anachronistically feminist). Nonetheless, many of the issues treated in *Alias Grace* do have continued relevance in the present. The private / public distinction so fundamental to the novel, both in narrative and thematic terms, can be seen as a reflection of inner / outer binaries that have shaped twentieth-century thinking about psychology and literature. Some critics see *Alias Graces* form (the novel is long, partly epistolary, leisurely paced and contains multiple viewpoints) as a tribute to Victorian story-telling techniques. See Prose and reviews in *Publishers Weekly* and *Chicago Tribune Books*. If some of the social issues such as "the Irish Question" seem quaint as specific white ethnicities have lost much of their meaning in contemporary North American society, others remain quite relevant. The regulation of the sex lives of unmarried young women through sanctions on illegitimacy and abortion has continued, from late-nineteenth- and early-twentieth-century anti-prostitution campaigns and rescue home narratives to contemporary welfare reform debate and political skirmishes around access to abortion.

2. This and other references to Grace Marks are to the fictional Grace Marks and not the historical Grace Marks, unless otherwise noted. However, this statement could also be applied to the actual Grace Marks, which is no doubt why she made such a lasting mark on the Canadian and Atwood's imagination. Atwood has returned to the figure of Grace Marks several times. First in her poem "Visit to Toronto With Companions" in *The Journals of Susanna Moodie* (1970) and secondly in a television play, *The Servant Girl*, which aired on the CBC in 1974.

3. As Nina Auerbach notes, despite his manifest failures to understand, Simon is the only one who truly tries to hear Grace after her arrest.

4. Though I don't entirely agree with this characterization, this surface conventionality is what I believe Elspeth Cameron is reacting to when she contrasts Grace's "bland, prim, mealy-mouthed" spoken discourse with her "opulent and intense" (40) inner life.

5. That Rochester's wife, Bertha, is white but questionably so, is from a British colony and goes mad raises the possibility that Grace occupies the positions of Jane and Bertha at once.

6. This scene recalls what Nancy Armstrong calls Mr. B's "ocular rape" (122) of Pamela through spying, letter reading, and other violations of the servant girl's privacy.

7. In Simon's sections, by contrast, spoken dialogue is clearly differentiated from thought in the conventional way. In fact, in one chapter, which consists solely of Grace's narration without any introductory scene, interruption from him, or supplementary thoughts from her, the presence of quotation marks at the beginning of every paragraph is the only way to know that the point of view is Simon's – that what we have read is what she says as he remembers it, rather than as she does.

8. There are frequent references to crossing the U.S. / Canada border in the text as well as to Niagara Falls, a natural feature which spans the border. Not only does Jeremiah cross the border, but Simon is an American who comes to live in Canada and then returns, while Grace flees to the U.S. with James after the murders and is arrested there and brought back to Canada. These flights across the border echo William Lyon MacKenzie's flight to the United States after the failure of the 1837 Rebellion in Canada as well as the series of unsuccessful raids by the Irish nationalist Fenians who invaded Canada from the United States in 1866.

9. Coral Ann Howells discusses other "escape artists" in Atwood's fiction such as Joan in *Lady Oracle*, Lesje in *Life Before Man*, Offred in *The Handmaid's Tale*, and Elaine in *Cat's Eye* (69, 97).

10. These disgraces impoverish the formerly middle class family and inspire Grace's uncle to pay their passage to Canada in order to be rid of them. Most pre-famine Irish immigrants to Canada were, like Grace's family, Protestant and from families of moderate means. The pattern of more prosperous relatives pre-paying the passage of poorer relatives was a very common one. (See MacKay, and Houston and Smyth.)

11. Noel Ignatiev has argued that Catholic Irish-Americans overcame religious prejudice against them and gained access to mainstream American society, or "became white" by disassociating themselves politically from African-Americans, their natural class allies. It could be argued that in a Canadian context, Irish Protestants like Grace gained power by exploiting an existing religious divide in Canada that favoured Protestants over Catholics.

12. Some Irish Protestants are ethnically Celtic, but many are not. The important point is that Grace is believed to be.

13. Glazer and Moynihan note that in the United States, where Irish immigration was more Catholic than in Canada, Protestant Irish immigrants quickly "ceased being Irish" (240).

14. See baptismal, marriage, and cemetery areas on the Walsh Family Genealogical Home Page. Walsh is a well-researched surname and this site is quite comprehensive, providing a history of the name and historical information about thousands of mainly eighteenth- and nineteenth-century Walshes in the Irish diaspora worldwide. In cases

where religion is noted, an overwhelming majority of Walshes are Catholics, about 90% in the marriage listing section, for example. The historical Jamie Walsh testified at Grace Marks's trial, but their subsequent marriage is Atwood's invention. Given Atwood's painstaking historical research, it is not unreasonable too assume she has paid attention to the national, ethnic, and religious associations of the surnames of the historical figures she fictionalizes.

15. See Tom LeClair. Coral Ann Howells, writing before *Alias Grace* was published, also notes the prevalence of tricksters in Atwood's work.

16. Though it is more peripheral to the plot, the Governor's daughter Lydia also gets pregnant by a military officer and is forced into a hasty marriage with Reverend Verringer to cover it up.

17. Atwood takes a similarly ambiguous stance toward Elaine's vision or hallucination of the Virgin Mary in *Cat's Eye*.

18. This characteristic ambiguity has been the focus of early criticism of *Alias Grace*. Christie March explores the heteroglossia inherent in symbolic objects in the novel, or their power to mean different things to different characters. Margaret Rogerson in analyzing the quilt Grace sews for herself at the end of the novel finds it could be "an abject and terrified admission of guilt, an innocent desire to create a memorial to the only female friendships that she had ever experienced, or a brazen celebration of a crime for which she feels no remorse," in other words, a product of "memory, amnesia or madness" (21).

19. Atwood also thus avoids what she wryly identifies as the common Canadian literary phenomenon of the "Baby Ex Machina," whose appearance at the end of a book gives it more hope than its vision has previously been able to sustain (*Survival* 207).

20. Of course, as Atwood points out in her experimental short story, "Happy Endings," "The only authentic ending is the one provided here: *John and Mary die. John and Mary die, John and Mary die,* (*Good Bones* 55-56) or in this case, Grace and Jamie die. Grace and Jamie die, Grace and Jamie die, which of course, their historical counterparts have, at least a century ago.

21. Jane Marcus has noted a similar movement in the writing of many prominent turn-of-the-century women who turned to autobiography as a "deliberate resignation from the public world and patriarchal history . . . re/signing their private lives into domestic discourse" (114). However, Marcus argues that these women were motivated by a belief that they could retain their fame only through gender-appropriate domestic discourse, whereas Grace seeks to lose her fame, or rather her infamy, entirely.

22. In 1938, Marcus Hansen formulated three generational positions for immigrants. According to Hansen, second generation immigrants

seek assimilation while their children try to return to their ethnic roots. Many theorists of ethnic identity categorize child immigrants as second generation and Grace fits Hansen's assimilationist second-generation position nicely. Authors such as Werner Sollors and Mary Dearborn have rightly critiqued Hansen's schema for its rigidity, but it remains useful in some circumstances.

WORKS CITED

Rev. of *Alias Grace*, by Margaret Atwood. *Publishers Weekly* 7 Oct. 1996: 58.

Armstrong, Nancy. *Desire and Domestic Fiction: A Political History of the Novel*. New York: Oxford UP, 1987.

Atwood, Margaret. *Alias Grace*. New York: Doubleday, 1996.

———. *Good Bones and Simple Murders*. New York: Doubleday, 1994.

———. *The Journals of Susanna Moodie*. New York: Houghton Mifflin, 1997.

———. *Survival: A Thematic Guide to Canadian Literature*. Toronto: Anansi 1972.

Auerbach, Nina. "The Housemaid's Tale." Rev. of *Alias Grace*, by Margaret Atwood. *Women's Review of Books* Apr. 97: 1.

Brookner, Anita. "A Wretch Like Her." Rev. of *Alias Grace*, by Margaret Atwood. *Spectator* 14 Sept 1996: 36.

Cameron, Elspeth. "Alias Fiction." Rev. of *Alias Grace*, by Margaret Atwood, *Canadian Forum* Jan./Feb. 1997: 39-42.

Dearborn, Mary. *Pocahonta's Daaughters: Gender and Ethnicity in American Culture*. New York: Oxford UP, 1986.

Eder, Richard. "Her Truth is Scheherazade's." Rev. of *Alias Grace*, by Margaret Atwood. *Los Angeles Times Book Review* 15 Dec. 1996: 2.

Gilbert, Sandra M. and Susan Gubar. *The Madwoman in the Attic; The Woman Writer and the Nineteenth-Century Literary Imagination*. New Haven: Yale UP, 1979.

Glazer, Nathan, and Daniel Patrick Moynihan. *Beyond the Melting Pot: The Negroes, Puerto Ricans, Jews, Italians, and Irish of New York City*. 2nd ed. Cambridge: M.I.T. P, 1970.

Hansen, M.L. "The Third Generation in America." 1938. *Commentary* Nov. 1952: 492-500.

Houston, Cecil J. and William J. Smyth. *Irish Emigration and Canadian Settlement: Patterns, Links and Letters*. Toronto: U of Toronto P, 1990.

Howells, Coral Ann. *Margaret Atwood*. Modern Novelists. New York: St. Martin's, 1996.

Ignatiev, Noel, *How the Irish Became White*. New York: Routledge, 1995.

Lanser, Susan Sniader. *Fictions of Authority: Women Writers and Narrative Voice*. Ithaca: Cornell UP, 1992.

——. *The Narrative Act: Point of View in Prose Fiction*. Princeton: Princeton UP, 1981.

LeClair, Tom. "Guilty Verdict." Rev. of *Alias Grace*, by Margaret Atwood. *Nation* 9 Dec. 1996: 25-27.

Lehmann-Haupt, Christopher, "Did She or Didn't She?; A Tale of Two Murders." Rev. of *Alias Grace*, by Margaret Atwood. *New York Times* 12 Dec. 1996: 19.

MacKay, Donald. *Flight From Famine: The Coming of the Irish to Canada*. Toronto: McClelland and Stewart, 1990.

Mantel, Hilary. "Murder and Memory." Rev. of *Alias Grace*, by Margaret Atwood. *New York Review of Books* 19 Dec. 96: 4.

March, Christie, "Crimson Silks and New Potatoes: The Heteroglossic Power of the Object in Atwood's *Alias Grace*." *Studies in Canadian Literature* 22.2 (1997): 66-82.

Marcus, Jane. "Invincible Mediocrity; The Private Selves of Public Women." *The Private Self: Theory and Practice of Autobiographical Writings*. Ed. Shari Benstock. Chapel Hill: U of North Carolina P, 1988. 114-46.

Melendy, Mary R. *The Ideal Woman: For Maidens, Wives, Mothers*. N.p.: E.E. Miller, 1915.

Moodie, Susanna. *Life in the Clearings Versus the Bush*. 1853. Toronto: McClelland and Stewart, 1989.

Prince, Gerald, *A Dictionary of Narratology*. Lincoln: U of Nebraska P, 1987.

Prose, Francine. "Death and the Maid: Margaret Atwood's Latest Novel Revolves Around a Notorious Murder in 19th-century Toronto." Rev. of *Alias Grace*, by Margaret Atwood. *New York Times Book Review* 29 Dec. 1996: 6.

Robertson, Sarah, Rev. of *Alias Grace*, by Margaret Atwood. *Canadian Book Review Annual*. 1996. Ed. Joyce M, Wilson. Toronto: U of Toronto P, 1997. 154.

Rogerson, Margaret. "Reading the Patchworks in *Alias Grace*." *Journal of Commonwealth Literature* 33.1 (1998): 5-22.

Rubin, Merle. "Novel Approaches to History." Rev. of *Alias Grace* by Margaret Atwood. *Wall Street Journal* 15 Nov. 1996: A12.

Sollors, Werner. *Beyond Ethnicity: Consent and Descent in American Culture*. New York: Oxford UP, 1986.

Spivak, Gayatri Chakravotry. "Three Women's Texts and a Critique of Imperialism." *Critical Inquiry* 12.1 (1985): 243-61.

Walsh Family Genealogy and History Home Page. Internet. 10 March 2000. http:// homepages.rootsweb.com/~walsh/

"Women on the Verge; Two Novels of Madness and Mayhem." Rev. of *Alias Grace*, by Margaret Atwood. *Chicago Tribune Books* 19 Jan. 1997: 1.

The Blind Assassin

Myth, History and Narration

CATERINA RICCIARDI

> One need not be a Chamber – to be Haunted –
> One need not be a House –
> The Brain has Corridors – surpassing –
> Material place –
>
> Ourselves behind ourselves, concealed –
> Should startle most –
> Assassin hid in our Apartment
> Be Horror's least . . .

Emily Dickinson (670)

The Blind Assassin, Atwood's tenth novel,[1] opens with a mystery scene: is Laura Chase's plummet from the bridge[2] while driving out of Toronto, ten days after the end of World War II, a fatality, a suicide, or a murder? And just as we expect to know more about her death, we are introduced to a novel-within-the-novel written by Laura and published posthumously in 1947.[3] And then, through a 1947 newspaper clipping, we are also informed of the death of Richard Griffen who, too, perished in a mysterious accident.

In a typically dead pan manner, Atwood stages at the very beginning of the novel two deaths and a possible culprit. By "calling up the dead" (*Negotiating* 166), she ensnares the reader right on the threshold of a labyrinthine voyage through twentieth-century Canadian social history.[4] Yet, such a startling foreground may also be the narrator's device to divert the reader's attention from what might be the core of such an intricately crafted "node within a network"

(Foucault 23): a multilayered narrative structure. We must, however, reach the very last pages of the novel to discover the truth that lies behind the enigma, which appears to be centred not only on the untimely deaths of two main characters,[5] but also on authorship. Moreover, the entire narrative is, in fact, intended to shadow a trickster storyteller – or even a "forger," an "impostor" (*Negotiating* 51) – dealing with at least three different generic conventions: autobiography, romance and pulp science fiction, bedecked with snippets of poetry. The storytelling method – based on flashbacks, intertextuality, and on a detailed chronicle cast in the present tense – is studiously analeptic, and dense with clues, but "clues," as Atwood appears to warn us towards the end of the novel, can be deceptive (603). Because of such a textual ambiguity, the identity of the "blind assassin" is seemingly left undisclosed, remaining an unanswered question. If the novel is, however, viewed as a "system of references to other books, other texts, other sentences" (Foucault 23), as well as to other cultural discourses, the true answer to the question of identity is not its ultimate end.

The primary narrator, who is also a character and an "author" of *The Blind Assassin*, is an old lady, Iris Chase Griffen, who, in 1998, at the age of eighty-two, traces her life back to her childhood spent with her younger sister Laura in Port Ticonderoga at Avilion, an old "merchant's palace" (72) – the family wealth having been amassed through the manufacturing of buttons. The narration moves from Iris's pampered childhood to the fateful moment when the two sisters meet at a "pastoral" picnic a young man of obscure birth, Alex Thomas,[6] a Marxist agitator on the run. Due to her family's financial troubles caused by the Great Depression, Iris condescends to marry, in Toronto, the older, *noveau riche* Richard Griffen. Glamour and easy life at first, and then complacencies and lies against a background of social upheavals, wars in Europe and a rapidly changing

Toronto – Emma Goldman's exile, Jewish immigrants, Reds – finally break the fragile shell of her world. The sudden deaths of her sister and of her own husband, followed by the loss of her daughter Aimee and of Alex Thomas on the European front, turn her life downward into meagre survival and solitude. Her sole recompense in the following decades is a "trade in second-hand artefacts" (620) and the posthumous publication in 1947 of a pulp science fiction fantasy, *The Blind Assassin*. This successful book, woven into the frame of the chronicle of a clandestine (erotic?) love affair – reportedly in the tradition of Djuna Barnes, Carson McCullers, Elizabeth Smart (346) – makes Laura Chase a literary cult figure and her editor – her sister Iris – only "an appendage: Laura's odd, extra hand, attached to no body – the hand that passed her on, to the world" (350-51).

The final reprint of *The Blind Assassin* that Iris opens in 1998, published by Artemisia Press, constitutes one of the relevant analeptic messages. Named after "the raped Renaissance painter" Artemisia Gentileschi (346), the Press itself is a "tessera," leading to the centrality in Atwood's text of Ovid's *Metamorphoses*. Both of the Chase sisters, Atwood informs us, had studied Ovid's masterpiece of transformation in school and were familiar with such myths as the "rape of Europa by a large white bull, of Leda by a swan, (and) of Danae by a shower of gold" (199). With her forcedly curbed tongue Laura may recall Philomela who was raped by King Tereus – the husband of her sister Procne – and whose tongue was cut out by him in order to silence her (*Metamorphoses*, VI: 412-676).[7] And as a Core (a Proserpine) figure, Laura is recalled by Iris years later: "In a painting she'd be gathering wildflowers, though in real life she rarely did anything of the kind. The earth-faced god crouches behind her in the forest shade. Only we can see him. Only we know he will pounce" (509).

The Blind Assassin crosses generic boundaries, exploring diversified fields of discourse and entering the domain of mythology through literature. Along with a number of literary allusions, the novel stands as a challenging attempt at re-constructing the "textuality" of the past through documents, photographs, mass culture images and icons, popular fashion magazines and television news. Moreover, it textualizes life and history into art by means of narrative strategies, which make use of a number of mythological archetypes and the mystery story conventions. In fact, we may say that the "blind assassin" is concealed within the canvas of Atwood's construction like a "figure in the carpet," inviting disclosure, a solution of the enigma. In the pursuit of disclosure, the reader is also invited to participate in a process that involves collation of diversified texts, which primarily aim at offering a representation of reality outside mere fiction.

The structure of the *The Blind Assassin* resembles that of a Chinese box. The excerpts from "Laura's Novel," for example, dovetail into the main narrative. Spliced within the latter are newspaper clippings from *Mayfair*, *Mail and Empire*, *The Toronto Star*, which Iris culls from her scrapbook thus giving shape to a modernist collage, intermittently, using historical, literary and apocryphal documents.[8] In addition, the sub-story of the two unnamed lovers is interspersed with samples of the science fiction fables, which the male character (Alex Thomas?) – himself a writer of hardboiled literature – makes up and relates to his friend (Laura? Iris?) during secret trysts in dismal Toronto boarding rooms. Those stories speak of colonization, destruction of cities, class exploitation and tyrannical kings. One of them is of a particular interest to the unnamed girl as it describes a ruthless society in a city called Sakiel-Norn on the planet Zycron, which prospers because of slave child labour – young boys and girls are forced to weave beautiful carpets until they are blinded by the harsh work.[9] Once blind, they are turned into prostitutes and, eventually, into assassins. However, in one such instalment the assassin, hired by the Lord of the Underworld, falls quite unexpectedly in love with his victim, a vestal girl whose tongue, in observance to a local ritual, has been cut out. And just as he is at the point of killing her, he changes his mind and spares her life:

> The blind assassin begins very slowly to touch her, with one hand only, the right – the dexterous hand, the knife hand. He passes it over her face, down to her throat; then he adds the left hand, the sinister hand, using both together, tenderly, as if picking a lock of the utmost fragility, a lock made of silk. It's like being caressed by water. She trembles, but not as before with fear. After a time she lets the red brocade fall away from around her, and takes his hand and guides it . . . Touch comes before sight, before speech. It is the first language and the last, and it always tells the truth. (311)[10]

How does this sub-story relate to Iris's memoir and Laura's / Iris's secret love affair with Alex Thomas? It also asks the question weather Iris is a reliable narrator? Is she "blind"? Does she prefer "touch" to get at the truth? In her own narration she reconstructs the secret history of her family (betrayals, lies, sexual triangles, dubious paternities and maternities, stolen babies) up to what we may call a dramatic "recognition scene" (Ingersoll 550), and she does this reconstructing not merely for a better understanding of her own responsibilities in the ultimate tragic fate of the house of Chase, but also for justice's sake, to vindicate the many wrongs she herself has suffered. Her prospective reader is hopefully Sabrina, her estranged granddaughter. The outcome of Iris's painful narration (*The Blind Assassin*) is, at the end, called a "memorial" (626). It includes "Laura's Nnovel" (*The Blind Assassin*) along with Iris's "omissions" and "erasures." Thus the mystery of *The Blind Assassin*, its true mystery – forgery? authorship? death of the author *à la* Roland

Barthes? a Scheherazade death-deferring storytelling (Foucault)[11] – is eventually unravelled.

A Voyage to the Underworld: the Sibyl

"It seems I will not after all keep on living forever, merely getting smaller and greyer and dustier, like the Sibyl in her bottle. Having long ago whispered *I want to die*, I now realize that this wish will indeed be fulfilled, and sooner rather than later" (52). Aged, shaky and with an ailing heart, with bones that "ache like history" (71), Iris fears but also hails impending death. Hers is the same "*cupio dissolvi*" that the decrepit Sibyl of Cuma wishes for herself in the famous epigraph from Petronius's *Satyricon* of Eliot's *The Waste Land*. According to the myth, Apollo granted the Sibyl long life at her own wish, to live as many years as she held grains in her hand. But, carelessly, she forgot to ask for eternal youth and thus her body disintegrated into old age.

Like Petronius's Sibyl, Iris shrivels up day by day and fears that in time she will be lost to sight, becoming a mere "voice."[12] Scornful of her neighbours' "whispering" and the children's "derision and a little awe," she would rather stay inside her house, and just die. But before her time runs out, she intends to tell the story of her doomed family and of Laura's "Pontius Pilate's gesture," of her decision to wash "her hands of me. Of all of us" (4).

Atwood's "mythical method" [13] leads us directly into the Sibyl's abode, her cave on the very threshold of Avernus, namely Iris's kitchen at Port Ticonderoga close to old Avilion, which was in 1998 sadly transformed into "Valahalla" (71),[14] an old-age home. Like Virgil's Sibyl, Iris will be our guide on a voyage to the Underworld, while the narrative she is crafting is her own "negotiation with the dead."[15]

"You can go down into the land of the dead," Atwood argues in *Negotiating with the Dead*, "and then you can get out again, back to the land of the living. But only if you're lucky." To reinforce this observation, Atwood quotes the Sibyl's warning to Aeneas just as he begins his perilous journey in Book VI of the *Aeneid*: ". . . the way to Avernus is easy; / Night and Day lie open the gates of death's dark kingdom: / But to retrace your steps, to find the way back to daylight − / That is the task, the hard thing" (167). And for Iris to retrace her steps to the daylight is also her hard task. On this backward journey into her past Iris wishes to give body, public evidence, to her telltale, albeit almost disembodied, voice.[16]

At first, however, Iris thinks she has no one else as an audience for her "sibylline" memoir but, somewhat ambiguously, herself as her own "double." Moreover, at the age of eighty-two she is not as agile at writing as she used to be. Her fingers, she complains, "are stiff and clumsy, the pen wavers and rambles, it takes me a long time to form the words. And yet I persist, hunched over as if sewing by moonlight" (53). With this powerful image of Iris sewing by moonlight, Atwood not only allows us to see her character tormented by the inexorable passing of time, afraid of the untimely death of her narrative, but also gives us a text that is enlarged with further mythological reference. At this point, Iris fears that she might fail to complete her memoir: "I hasten on," she says, "making my way crabwise across the paper. It's a slow race now, between me and my heart, but I intend to get there first. Where is there? The end, or *The End*. One or the other. Both are destinations, of a sort" (272). If the question of time is strictly intertwined with the act of "spinning," then the act of spinning as narration becomes a prominent feature of the novel:

You must see the writing as emerging like a long scroll of ink from the index finger of your right hand; you must see your left hand erasing it.

Impossible, of course.

I pay out my line, I pay out my line, this black thread I'm spinning across the page. (345)

In "I pay out my line" Iris refers to a moment of release, to let out the thread of her life as well as her threadlike mark on the page. Iris, the Sibyl —"seeress," and guardian of the Underworld – has metamorphosed into a doomed Arachne, a Philomela,[17] or a Penelope figure (weaving and unweaving or "erasing"), or even into one of the Three Fates, the Moerae. According to Robert Graves, it was "Erebus (who) begot on Night" the three ancient Fates: Clotho, Lachesis, and Atropos" (Graves, *Greek Myths* I 48). Atropos, the smallest of the three in stature, is the most terrible. The thread of life, spun on Clotho's spindle, and measured by the rod of Lachesis, is snipped by Atropos's shears. By paying "out" her "line," Iris is alluding to the "theory of the linen-thread." "[T]he goddess tied the human being to the end of a carefully measured thread," as Graves described, "which she paid out yearly, until the time came for her to cut it and thereby relinquish his soul to death" (*Greek Myths* I 204). Furthermore, the Moerae, apart from being "credited by some mythographers with the first invention of the alphabet" (*White Goddess* 210), are also manifestations of the Triple Moon-goddess:

> *Moera* means "a share" or "a phase," and the moon has three phases and three persons: the new, the Maiden-goddess of the spring, the first period of the year; the full moon, the Nymph-goddess of the summer, the second period; and the old moon, the Crone-goddess of autumn, the last period. (*Greek Myths* I 48-9)

Atwood's familiarity with the Triple Goddess archetype (Murray 72-90) is obvious when she casts Iris to appear in the diverse roles of the Moon-goddess during the various phases of her life. First she is a Core figure, abducted and "raped" by Pluto / Richard Griffen. Then she becomes a Nymph-like young lady in her "public" married life. And, finally, she is transformed into an old Crone when we meet her in the last year of her life: a modern representation of the Sibyl of the Cumaean shrine dedicated to Triple Hecate.

The hand trope: Atropos

The Blind Assassin is obsessed with the act of writing connected with the body.[18] Prominent in that process is, quite naturally, the presence of the "hand" image (right or left)[19] and, in particular, a surrealistic "disembodied hand" (*Negotiating* 35),[20] always "tracing out the lines of the past" (Howells 115), conjuring ghosts, but also beckoning to the future.

After a concise report of Laura's death, Iris introduces her novel with its "*Prologue: Perennials for the Rock Garden*," in which the unnamed narrating I / eye picks up a photograph of a man and a woman from an envelope with newspaper clippings. The photograph shows "the two of them together, her and this man on a picnic" (8). They are sitting "under a tree; it might have been an apple tree" (8), and the man is described as

> holding up his hand, as if to fend her off in play, or else protect himself from the camera, from the person who might be there, taking the picture; or else to protect himself from those in the future who might be looking at him, who might be looking at him through this square, lighted window of glazed paper. As if to protect himself from her. As if to protect her. In his outstretched, protecting hand there is the stub end of a cigarette. (9)

The photograph — with that "protecting" hand — is all that remains now of a fragment of time that is irretrievably lost. The fictional I (Laura? Iris?) keeps scrutinizing the photo in search of "something she might have dropped or lost, out of reach but still visible, shimmering like a jewel on sand" (9). It is obvious that this image functions as a representation of a perfect, "perennial garden" of youth and happiness, located close to "Avalon," the "secret 'island of the apple-trees'" (*White Goddess* 254), Iris's and Laura's family estate at Port Ticonderoga. However, this torn souvenir does not give a complete picture of the event it was meant to immortalize. Some details are missing, since one of its two sides has been cut: Over to one side — you wouldn't see it at first — there's a hand, cut by the margin, scissored off the wrist, resting on the grass as if discarded. Left to its own devices. (8) "Left" (like a left hand) to "its own devices." To this hand — and we don't know yet, and probably never will, whether it is a right or a left hand — the narration owes a great deal of its intricate construction.

As the reader will eventually find out, the picture was taken the day of the "button factory picnic," when Laura and Iris meet Alex Thomas for the first time. Iris finds Laura sitting under an apple tree with a young man and she joins them. It is right at that moment that the local journalist takes the picture of the three of them together. Alex raises his hand "as if to fend him off" (217). The photo appears on the Port Ticonderoga's *Herald and Banner*, "me to the left of him," Iris specifies, "Laura to the right, like bookends. Both of us were looking at him and smiling; he was smiling too, but he'd thrust his hand up in front of him, as gangland criminals did to shield themselves from the flashbulbs when they were being arrested. He'd only managed to blot out half of his face, however" (234). When, a few days later, Alex is sought by the police on a charge of setting the Chase factory on fire, it is this photograph that appears in a "Wanted

poster." His face is obscured by his hand and, quite proper-
ly, Laura and Iris are "cut off at the side" (263). However,
Alex on the lam is rescued by the Chase sisters. They hide
him first in the cellar of Avilion and then in the attic. This
upward movement may be credited with symbolic under-
tones as the dinginess of the attic foreshadows the dismal
rooms of the Toronto trysts in "Laura's Novel." Yet it is
here, in the Avilion's attic, that a secret affair, a possible "love
triangle," is starting to sprout.

The picnic photograph is further mutilated, this time by
Laura who cuts its margins and donates one print to Iris
("Because that's what you want to remember" (269), and
keeps the other for herself. In Iris's copy Laura has "cut herself out of it – only her hand remained. She couldn't have
got rid of this hand without making a wobbly margin. She
hadn't coloured this picture at all, except for her own cut-
off hand. This had been tinted a very pale yellow" (269). The
sight of Laura's "light-yellow hand creeping towards Alex
across the grass like an incandescent crab" (269) is frightening to Iris.[21] And yet, there is more: in Laura's print it is Iris
who is cut out except for her hand (269)!

This is a game Laura – but also Atwood – is playing, a
trick with hands that is only partly unravelled at the end:

> The photo has been cut; a third of it has been cut off. In the lower
> left corner there's a hand, scissored off at the wrist, resting on the
> grass. It's the hand of the other one, the one who is always in the pic-
> ture whether seen or not. The hand that will set things down. (631)

To whom does this "disembodied" hand in the "lower left
corner" belong? Which one of the two sisters was on the
right and which on the left side of Alex Thomas at the time
of their innocent picnic? To deal with this question, we
should acknowledge the presence in the story of a triple
representation of a hand. One hand that cuts (or hand-tints,
adulterating the photo by covering its image with allusive

colours), the other that writes (or "spins," tying-up the narrative), and the third that "fends" or "protects," which is recognizably the hand of Alex. But the cutting hand undoubtedly belongs to Laura; that is, to Atropos, the most terrible of the Three Fates. It should also be pointed out that although *The Blind Assassin* may appear to have been written with the left hand, it is actually this very same hand that is said to have, paradoxically, "erased" the writing done by the right one (345). Does this hand, then, belong to the very "blind assassin" whom the detective reader is pursuing?

In order to disclose some of the mysteries of Atwood's novel, we must investigate its concealed historical subtext that can be accessed through a quotation from de Maupassant's *"L'histoire, cette vieille dame exaltée et menteuse"* (199), the work the Chase sisters had studied with Mr. Erskine, their English tutor.

Wars and Empires

To go back to the beginning of such a tightly constructed analeptic novel as *The Blind Assassin*, one of the questions that ought to be answered is why Iris drops in her terse report of a family death such a pointed reference as one to the end of World War II? And why is the novel interspersed with so many bitter allusions to other wars? In particular, to those that seemed to have played an important role in shaking off Canada's colonial status. In spite of the fact that monuments and War Memorials in the narrative are elevated to the nobility of high art, the dark shadow of war is cast upon the entire novel and is further intensified by the words of the poets. The "ancestral voices prophesying war" (410), heard by Kubla Khan at Xanadu in Coleridge's poem that Iris and Laura learn by heart, reverberate in the evocation of Tennyson's *Mort d'Arthur*, in Longfellow's *Evangeline*,

John McCrae's "In Flanders Fields," and, quite prominently, in Virgil's *Aeneid*.

Captain Norval Chase, Iris's father, loses his brothers in World War I at Ypres and at the Somme, and himself returns from the front with a "black patch over his right eye" (94). Handicapped by the war, Captain Chase, nevertheless, becomes richer because of it (87). Iris, too, comments on how the war in Europe was good at home, in Port Ticonderoga, "for the button trade. So many buttons are lost in a war, and have to be replaced" (88). Years later, Richard Griffen thinks of making "a lot of money" (478-79) out of the wars abroad, coming off, however, with "dirty hands" (586). Significantly, the Spanish Civil War plays a role in Iris's and Alex's love story and World War II eventually claims Alex's life. In 1999, while writing her memoir, Iris is depicted watching the television news report of "another war somewhere, what they call a minor one." This war, as Iris's rumination reveals here, obviously "isn't minor" for those who are caught up in it. The true horror, she goes on describing, is that "[t]hey cart the young men off and murder them, intending to forestall revenge, as the Greeks did at Troy. Hitler's excuse too for killing Jewish babies" (582).

Following the trail of other references to wars, there is a Hundred Years' War on the planet Xenor, which seems to terminate just when World War II ends, with the destruction of Sakiel-Norn: "It's as if one huge bomb has fallen on it, it's all in flames," everything is burning, "bursting like fireworks," the people dead. "Nothing will be left of it, he (Alex) says. A heap of stones, a few old words" (573). Sakiel-Norn, like Troy or – as we shall see later – Ticonderoga, falls into ruins, is "destroyed." The "posthumous" apocalyptic ending (with allusions to Hiroshima) of Alex Thomas's science fiction novel is turned by the forger (Iris) into a sort of *Iliad*. The unnamed girl "can't bear to look at the flames" as Sakiel-Norn burns. Who "did this?," she asks; and Alex /

Iris the forger answers: the "old woman," de Maupassant's "*L'histoire, cette vieille dame exaltée et menteuse,*" thus linking the pulp story to Mr. Erskine's old French lesson. "Never mind," Alex cynically retorts at the end, "[t]hey'll build it up again. They always do" (573), as if though he were hinting at the classic *topos* of the founding of new cities, of new empires.

With the wars projected into the future, *The Blind Assassin* in fact collates the wars of the age of myth – Troy, Tyre, Carthage – with Aeneas sailing away from Dido to fulfil "through warfare" (609) his destiny in Italy so that Rome could be founded, and the empires move westward. And Port Ticonderoga – recalling Troy and its two rivers, Jogues and Louveteau – takes part in the history of the westward march of the British Empire.

Thus, the reader gradually discovers that *The Blind Assassin* is not only a mystery story but also, and more importantly, a type of a historical novel, which Hayden White has defined in terms of "historio*graphic meta*fition" (White 6n). Canada is not a mere "secret window" onto the world (582), as Iris ironically implies, but a place fully immersed in the flux of time and historical events. Such an argument had been first introduced in an earlier chapter called "*The Weary Soldier,*" where Iris is portrayed describing the town's War Memorial while ruminating on Port Ticonderoga's past.

Along with the "field gun" that was "present at the Somme" (175-76), near the Town Hall, are two statues both commissioned by the Chase family; on the left the "Weary Soldier," and on the right "Colonel Parkman, a veteran of the last decisive battle fought in the American Revolution at Fort Ticonderoga, now in New York State" (176). It was Colonel Parkman, Iris explains, "who upped stakes, crossed the border, and named our town, thus perversely commemorating a battle in which he'd lost. (Though perhaps that's not so unusual: many people take a curatorial interest in their own scars)." The statue dedicated to him represents "every sculptor's idea of every cavalry leader." No one knows, Iris adds, "what Colonel Parkman really looked like, since he left no pictorial evidence of himself and the statue wasn't erected until 1885, but he looks like this now. Such is the tyranny of Art" (176). Neither did Colonel Parkman, as far as I was able to investigate, leave record of his life and deeds in the books of History. One wonders if he really ever existed![22]

The reader already knows that Iris's forbears, following the American War of Independence, or rather, the War of 1812, "had come up from Pennsylvania in the 1820s to take advantage of cheap land, and of construction opportunities" It seems, therefore, obvious that Port Ticonderoga, because of its war associations, is deliberately selected by the author as one of the principal settings for *The Blind Assassin*. The Iroquois toponym Ticonderoga, translated into English, means "between two lakes" (Webster), between Lake Champlain and Lake George, which are themselves connected with at least three wars.

Built by the French in 1755, Fort Carillon, located near the foot of Lake Champlain on route to Canada, was the site of several battles during the last French Indian War. As the two world superpowers, France and Britain, fought for imperial supremacy in North America, the Eighteenth Century Fort assumes strategic importance because of its location, controlling the major north-south "highway," also known as the "Mohican Trail." The great French victory over the British at Fort Carillon took place after another victory at Fort William Henry, which became the setting of James Fenimore Cooper's *The Last of the Mohicans*. The following year, with Montcalm confronting Wolfe at Quebec, the British, marching from New York captured Fort Carillon and renamed it Ticonderoga. At the outbreak of

227

the Revolutionary War the fort was pillaged by the colonial rebels, the Green Mountain Boys, on May 10, 1775, and seized by General Montgomery in September. Then the British recaptured Ticonderoga on July 1777 and held it until their major defeat at Saratoga on 17 October, 1777, when General Burgoyne ultimately surrendered (Weisenberger 431–433; 942–948).

The July battle is possibly the one Iris is referring to, also because it is mentioned by Cooper in *The Last of the Mohicans*. While lamenting the siege and loss of Fort William Henry, a defeat that was due to the then scanty knowledge of wilderness tactics, Cooper argues that the "carelessness engendered by these usages descended even to the war of the Revolution, and lost the States the important fortress of Ticonderoga, opening a way for the army of Burgoyne into what was then the bosom of the country" (Cooper 135).

The ill-fated story of Ticonderoga is partially conjured up by Atwood in connection with the War of 1812, when several towns such as York (Toronto), Newark (Niagara-on the Lake), Buffalo and Washington were burned down. The new, fictional Port Ticonderoga, supposedly between Lake Ontario and Lake Eire in Canada, might have been virtually burned out during the Battle of Lundy's Lane on 25 July, 1814, the battle that turned back the American attempt to invade Canada (Weisenberger 1198–1202).

A renowned hero of the War of 1812 was the American general James F. Miller, described in 1846 by Nathaniel Hawthorne as the "Collector" (Hawthorne, *The Scarlet Letter* 310) in the dilapidated rooms of the Salem Custom-House. Three times, in the course of a couple of pages, Hawthorne mentions the "indestructible ramparts of Old Ticonderoga" (312) as a glorious symbol of the "spirit of New England hardihood" (314). In creating her own pseudo-myth of new Port Ticonderoga, where the Chase family takes roots after the War of 1812, Atwood appears to bear in mind Hawthorne's following passage:

> To observe and define his character, however, under such disadvantages, was as difficult a task as to trace out and build up anew, in imagination, an old fortress, like Ticonderoga, from a view of its gray and broken ruins. Here and there, perchance, the walls may remain almost complete; but elsewhere may be only a shapeless mound, cumbrous with its very strength, and overgrown, through long years of peace and neglect, with grass and alien weeds. (311)

Quite ironically, Hawthorne seems to imply that the ruins of Ticonderoga are indestructible, and that any attempt – including an imaginative one – to rebuild the fortress anew as, according to Atwood, a ghostly Colonel Parkman did, is actually only "a difficult task." Is Atwood challenging Hawthorne by anchoring her imaginary Port Ticonderoga in the history of Fort Erie?[23] Her new Port Ticonderoga, in fact, is said to have been burned down during the War of 1812, possibly by that very general Miller who fought at Fort Erie in the last battle for the "imperial" possession of the continent.

The burning of cities is a frequent *topos* in and outside the western culture of war and of empire building. It is not by chance, then, that the most memorable names of cities conquered or destroyed by fire are mentioned or alluded to in *The Blind Assassin*: from Troy, Tyre, Carthage, Babylon (421) and Jericho (422), to Tenochtitlan (422), Ticonderoga, York (Toronto), Hiroshima, Kapuscinski's Persian Kermàn and Sakiel-Norn. Sakiel-Norn, the city of the future, is doomed to disappear from "Laura's Novel" due to imperialistic wars amongst planets: Zycron, Xenor and Earth. Thus, Alex's words – forewarning that such a planetary catastrophe would wipe out "entire culture" from "the universe" (423) – are significant also in the context of Iris's memoir, and of her criticism of belligerent colonialism.

At the end, before her final invocation to the Furies, Iris quotes from Kipling's imperialistic "Recessional," written for Queen Victoria's Jubilee in 1897: "*Lest we forget. Remember me. To you from failing hands we throw.* Cries of the thirsty ghosts" (621). Such a reference is obviously meant to explain why Iris wrote "Laura's Novel." She did it not to forget her sister by creating "a memorial of some kind" (621). Yet, what Iris really wants is vengeance: "Without memory, there can be no revenge" (621). Revenge! That is her ultimate, rightful objective. She is possibly following Dido's invocation to Hecate and the "avenging Furies," with Dido's dreadful prediction of the wars between Rome and Carthage (*Aeneid*, VI: 607-629), or she may be highlighting the moving plea of the drowned Phoenician sailor in the Carthaginian epigraph of *The Blind Assassin*.[24] Remembrance against forgetting, a "memorial" that – along with justice and revenge – is what, explicitly, Iris's *The Blind Assassin* is about.

Iris's evocation of Kipling's departing hymn "Recessional" serves as a reminder to us that the English Empire still holds, in 1897, "[d]ominion over palm and pine" beneath God's "awful Hand" (Kipling 327). The poet's plea to the "Lord God of Hosts" is now, quite unassumingly, to "be with us yet," to "spare us yet, / Lest we forget – lest we forget!" Notwithstanding the glorious past, and the deeds done by the British among "the lesser breeds without the Law," it is in these lines that the divided voice of the poet realizes – dismissing what would customarily be a eulogizing tone – the precarious character of what has been achieved. The "Kings depart," the "navies melt away" and "all our pomp of yesterday / Is one with Niniveh and Tyre!" (Kipling 327). "Recessional" is not, indeed, a celebration but a reminder of the uncertain future of the Empire: "lest we forget!"

The Blind Assassin seems to enclose Atwood's "answering back" to the Empire at the close of another century of great displacements: lest the history of the former colonies – the glorious exodus of the Loyalists to Canada, the French Indian Wars, the "imaginary" (and yet, according to Hawthorne, impossible) re-foundation of lost Ticonderoga, the Canadian dead in the Boer War or at the Somme – should be "forgotten."[25]

The Blind Assassin: "Whodunit"

If *Alias Grace* "may be read as a variety of anti-detective novel which draws readers in with the expectation that they might discover the extent of Grace's culpability, only to leave them in the end without any confidence that she is clearly guilty or innocent, *The Blind Assassin* is on one level a 'whodunit' – with a vengeance" (Ingersoll 543).

In fact, Iris herself gives a number of possible explanations for unveiling the identity of the "blind assassin." But that identity is, after all, a spurious mystery. With respect to "Laura's Novel" (also a spurious mystery), Iris admits at the end that Laura "didn't write a word of it" (626). Instead, she wrote it while waiting (a Penelope figure) for Alex to return home. Afterwards she would say: "I thought of myself as recording. A bodiless hand, scrawling across the wall." She wanted a "memorial" for Alex and herself (626). And yet, Iris positively asserts that the "real author" was neither of the Chase sisters, but a "fist" (626). Laura "was my left hand," she says, "and I was hers. We wrote the book together. It's a left-handed book. That's why one of us is always out of sight, whichever way you look at it" (627).

Why has Iris contrived such a tricky game, such a forgery? It seems that she did it primarily for the sake of Laura, lest she be forgotten. And, then, for the sake of justice, both for Laura's and her own sufferings, which explains her extreme invocation to the Furies: "Stand by me now, as we near the end!" (607). The "end" here is her own "*end*" as well.[26] Thus, according to Iris, a "well-wrought invocation to the Furies can come in handy, in case of need. When it's primarily a question of revenge" (607).

But Iris wants justice also for herself as an "artist" and "author." At the end, after her voyage to the Underworld, she actually resolves to "tie the papers up" (636). What Laura had cut, she collates into a "history" – implemented by her sister's mutilated photos and enigmatic notebooks – the history of her family and of her country. From a Sibyl figure, Iris has metamorphosed into Calliope, the Muse of Epic, or Clio, the Muse of History. The fleeing leaves of the Sibyl of Cuma are bound into an epic book, her *Aeneid*, which is somewhat reminiscent of Ovid's "stone," the "memorial" that Aeneas promises to erect to honour the Sibyl once he returns from Hades ("*Templa tibi statuam*," *Metamorphoses* XIV, 128). In *Negotiating with the Dead*, referring to Ovid's version of the myth, Atwood explains the significance of the "stone": And Virgil did the same thing, as did Dante after him, thus becoming "the first writer to have given us a full account of the Underworld in his function *as a writer*" (*Negotiating* 173). Hence, Iris's high-sounding, almost stilted diction: *The Blind Assassin*, is her "memoir" and "memorial," her artful, literary monument.

As for the "blind assassin" mystery, the answers may be numerous. Emily Dickinson in poem 670 ("One need not be a Chamber – to be Haunted –"), quoted in *Alias Grace* (46), offers an excellent explanation. The "assassin," Dickinson points out, is within the "corridors" of our own mind: "Ourselves behind ourselves - concealed" (Dickinson 333). In Atwood's terms it is our own "double," Laura / Iris. Possibly, in our own "right hand."[27]

The Blind Assassin, however, has a few more traditional culprit figures to propose: blind Cupid and blindfolded Justice. "Eros with his bow and arrows is not the only blind god," Iris maintains, "Justitia is the other one. Clumsy blind gods with edged weapons: Justitia totes a sword, which, coupled with her blindfold, is a pretty good recipe for cutting yourself" (607-08). It is quite significant that the novel should end on such an ambiguous note, without a closure. The reader may, however, go beyond traditional iconography and identify a variety of similarly plausible offenders or accomplices. Time, War and History (de Maupassant's "*vieille dame exaltée et menteuse*"), Colonialism and Empires, may all be credited of being, unfortunately, clumsy "blind gods with edged weapons," still ruling over what is left of modern civilization.

NOTES

1. Winner of the Booker Prize and the Dashiell Hammett Award.
2. One cannot but think of the obsessive, threatening image of the bridge in *Cat's Eye*. The last section of that novel is called "Bridge" (just as the first chapter of *The Blind Assassin* is called "The Bridge"). At the end, Elaine Risley returns to the bridge of her Toronto childhood and realizes that in the ravine below her tangled past is buried: "Stephen's jar of light is buried down there somewhere" (418). She also ruminates on what it would be like a fall from the bridge: "I rest my arms on the concrete wall and look down through the bare branches that are like dry coral. I used to think that if I jumped over, it would not be like falling, it would be more like diving; that if I died that way it would be soft, like drowning. Though far below, on the ground, there's a pumpkin, tossed over and smashed open, looking unpleasantly like a head" (418). One should remember that Iris's beloved dead are all, albeit symbolically, "drowned now. // Drowned, but shining" (8). Actually, soon after their mother's death, a five-year-old Laura plummets into the Louvetau River; had it not been for Iris's hauling her out she would have drowned (183-84). Sabrina too seems to be irretrievably lost in a shipwreck: "She could be dead. She could be at the bottom of the sea" (476). The "death by water" motif is recurrent in *The Blind Assassin*.
3. From now on I will refer to the novel-within-the-novel as to "Laura's Novel."

233

4. This is particular of the Depression years. After the publication of Sinclair Ross's *As For Me and My House* (1941), the Depression, Atwood argues, "became part of the social mythology" (*Conversations* 53).

5. The enigma is carried on throughout the novel up to the end. For example: "Who killed Laura, then?" (453), Iris asks Winifred. In turn, Aimee charges Iris with Laura's death: "and you killed her" (532). And with respect to Richard's case, Iris imagines herself explaining to Sabrina: "I doubt she (Winifred) ever said to you that I murdered Richard, however. If she told you that, she would also have had to say where she got the idea" (625).

6. He is a modern Heathcliff. But also a Thomas of Erceldoune (*Thomas the Rhymer*), a renowned Scottish prophet (1220-1297), protagonist of a popular ballad. Due to the Carthaginian epigraph of *The Blind Assassin*, Alex may also be a sort of "Phlebas," the Phoenician sailor.

7. The correspondences between the Ovidian episode and the Chase sisters are numerous.

8. Among them one finds also a captivating record of what could be termed a history of ladies' fashion in the Thirties.

9. As the first of the epigraphs of the novel shows, Atwood seems to draw part of her oriental fable from Ryszard Kapuscinski's *Shah of Shahs* (1982), a first hand account of the fall of the Iran "Imperium" (1980) and the evils of despotism and dictatorship.

10. The reader, however, should not forget the silk "lock." It will surface again at the end of *The Blind Assassin* (607-611), in connection with Virgil's *Aeneid*.

11. Both Foucault ("Le langage à l'infini") and Barthes (*Le bruissement de la langue. Essais critique IV*) have often argued on the relationship between "writing" and "death" (i. e.: the so-called "death of the author;" the process of writing as a way of "entering his [the author's] own death;" "writing not to die;" the "death of narrative and narration," and so on). Actually, *The Blind Assassin* closes with the death of the "author."

12. The story of the Sibyl's ill-fated "handful of dust," of her shrinking body until she becomes invisible, and a bodiless "voice" ("nullique videnda, / Vocem tamen noscar; vocem mihi fata relinquent" (XIV: 152-53) is also told in Ovid's *Metamorphoses* (XIV: 134-153). The most relevant lines are quoted by Atwood in *Negotiating With the Dead* (2002). See below footnote 15.

13. On Atwood's conception and use of the "mythical method" see Jennifer Murray's essay on the "Triple Goddess" archetype in *The Robber Bride*.

14. Relevant here is Robert Graves's identification of Avilon with "Avernus" as proposed by Kenneth Dutfield. In *The White Goddess* Graves argues "that *Avernus*, the abode of the dead, which the Latins incorrectly derived from the Greek *a-ornis*, "birdless," is the same word as *Avalon*; which would identify the Elysian Fields with Avernus. Lake Avernus near Cumae (sic) apparently won its nick-name from the unhealthy airs of the surrounding marshes and from the near-by shrine of the Cumaean Sibyl who conjured up the spir-its of the dead" (254).

15. The point I am making is based on the last chapter of *Negotiating with the Dead* –Atwood's "Empson Lectures," and voyage into the myths and traditions of western literature – called "*Descent*: Negotiating with the dead. *Who makes the trip to the Underworld, and why?*" Atwood's lifelong interest in the Sibyl and Aeneas' trip to the Underworld is attested by Linda Sandler's 1976 interview when, talking about the maze figure in *Lady Oracle*, Atwood explained: "But the maze I use is a descent into the underworld. There's a pas-sage in Virgil's *Aeneid* which I found very useful, where Aeneas goes to the underworld to learn about his future. He's guided by the Sibyl and he learns what he has to from his dead father, and then he returns home. It's a very ambiguous passage and scholars have spent a lot of energy analyzing it" (47). To this respect, one should also mention the poem, and collection, called *Procedures for Underground* (1970).

16. By calling upon Ovid's *Metamorphoses* (XIV: 104-154), in Atwood's concluding words to *Negotiating with the Dead*, the Sibyl's voice becomes a figure of art also thanks to the "stone" (a "temple") Aeneas promises to erect once he returns from the Underworld: "I will give the last word to the poet Ovid, who has the Sibyl of Cumae speak, not only for herself, but also – we suspect – for him, and for the hopes and fates of all writers: // But still, the fates will leave my voice, / and by my voice I shall be known" (*Negotiating* 180) ("*voce mihi fata relin-quent*"). It should be remembered that the Sibyl of Cuma is also the author of the so-called "Sibylline Books," which are said to be the foundation of the "Constitution" of ancient Rome. Incidentally, Ovid's "stone" may also connect this passage with the "memorial" Iris thinks she herself has built at the end of her narration. Thus, *The Blind Assassin* would be Atwood's "monument" as well.

17. According to Ovid, tongueless Philomela cleverly weaves purple designs on a white canvas, revealing Tereus's crime (*Metamorphoses*, VI: 574-78). Incidentally, in Ovid's masterpiece the myth of Procne and Philomela shortly follows Arachne's, the "spider" (VI: 1-145).

18. Ingersoll argues that "it is Iris's body which appears to become the writing instrument, recording this narrative" (547). But Iris feels also her own body to be "written on." For example, by Richard: "I sometimes felt as if these marks on my body were a kind of code, which blossomed, then faded, like invisible ink held to a candle. But if they were a code, who held the key to it? // I was sand, I was snow - written on, rewritten, smoothed over" (455).

19. In 1989 Constance Rooke dedicated an insightful study to "Atwood's hands." "Hands are everywhere in Atwood," she argues, "I'm aware of the hazard attached to looking for them, and they proliferate and swell in significance for that very reason. But I have collected an astonishing number, several thousand of them, and they don't look innocent to me" (163). In 1981 George Bowering too had focused his attention on hands, suggesting, quite interestingly, that Atwood's hands often "grapple with one another as emissaries of the bicameral mind" (48). Both arguments are relevant to the "hand trope" in *The Blind Assassin*.

20. See, for instance, the following passage: "To the task at hand. *At hand* is appropriate: sometimes it seems to me that it's only my hand writing, not the rest of me; that my hand has taken on a life of its own, and will keep on going even if severed from the rest of me, like some embalmed Egyptian fetish or the dried rabbit claws men used to suspend from their car mirrors for luck. Despite the arthritis in my fingers, this hand of mine has been displaying an unusual amount of friskiness lately, as if tossing restraint to the dogs. Certainly it's been writing down a number of things it wouldn't be allowed to if subject to my better judgement. // Turn the pages, turn the pages. Where was I? April 1936" (457). The "disembodied hand" image appears also in *Negotiating with the Dead*: "Now, what disembodied hand or invisible monster just wrote that cold-blooded comment?" (35). Actually, in that book (so close to the material dealt with in *The Blind Assassin*) a whole chapter ("*Duplicity*: The jekyll hand, the hyde hand, and the slippery double") is devoted to hands and to the writer and his own "doubles." "All writers are double" (37), Atwood maintains, connecting their "duplicity" with hands. Particularly intriguing in regard to *The Blind Assassin* is her discussion of William Fryer Harvey's *The Beast with Five Fingers*, a story that shows "The Double as Cut-Off-Body-Part" (43), and a hand that, among other things, is "a writing hand that has become detached from any writer" (44). Also worthwhile highlighting in that chapter is the epigraph from Matthew 6: 3-4: "But when thou doest alms, let not the left hand know what the right hand doeth; / That thine alms may be in secret; and thy Father which seeth in secret himself shall reward thee openly" (29).

21. It is of interest to mention that only a few pages onward Iris will describe her plodding way of writing as "making my way crabwise across the paper" (272).

22. Atwood may be playing with the name of the famous American historian Francis Parkman, well known for his works on the history of the Jesuits in Canada and the colonial wars. By the way, the reader comes to learn the first name of Colonel Parkman ("Henry") only through the mention of the Port Ticonderoga's high school ("The Colonel Henry Parkman High School Home").

23. Since Iris had pointed out that old Ticonderoga is now in New York State, it is worthwhile recalling that there is a city called Erie on the United States side of the lake.

24. "I swam, the sea was boundless, I saw no shore. / Tanit was merciless, my prayers were unanswered. / O you who drown in love, remember me."

25. Significantly, Kipling wrote a moving poem called "Two Canadian Memorials" (1919), dedicated to the Canadian dead in World War I.

26. It is interesting that Iris dies "peacefully" in her garden. Somewhat, she regains her lost paradise: namely, her "rock garden" with its "perennials," the "button factory picnic" with Alex and the "apple tree."

27. In her review of Lewis Hyde's *Trickster Makes This World: Mischief, Myth and Art* for the *L.A. Times,* Atwood argues that Hyde is an "asker of naive questions that turn out to be the reverse of naive, fascinated by why we behave the way we do, and why our right hand is often so blind to what out left hand is up to do." Constance Rooke, too, had already suggested that "Atwood repeatedly connects hand with blindness" (171).

WORKS CITED

Atwood, Margaret. *Alias Grace.* Toronto: McClelland & Stewart, 1996.

——. *The Blind Assassin*. London: Virago, 2001.

——. *Cat's Eye*. London: Virago, 1990.

——. *Conversations*. Ed. Earl G. Ingersoll. London: Virago, 1992.

——. *Negotiating with the Dead. A Writer on Writing*. Cambridge: Cambridge U P, 2002.

——. "Ophelia Has a Lot to Answer For" (Lecture). http://www.web.net/owtoad/ophelia.html

——— "*Trickster Makes This World: Mischief, Myth and Art,* by Lewis Hyde" (Book Review). http://www.web.net/owtoad/trickste.html

Bowering, George. "Margaret Atwood's Hands." *Studies in Canadian Literature* 6.1 (1981): 39-52.

Cooper, James Fenimore. *The Last of the Mohicans*. New York: Airmont Books, 1962.

Dickinson, Emily. *The Complete Poems*. Ed. Thomas H. Johnson. London: Faber and Faber, 1975.

Foucault, Michel. *The Archeology of Knowledge*. Trans. Sheridan Smith. New York: Harper and Row, 1976.

Graves, Robert. *The Greek Myths*. 2 vòls. London: Penguin, 1960.

——. *The White Goddess. A Historical Grammar of Poetic Myth*. London: Faber and Faber, 1986.

Hawthorne, Nathaniel. *The Portable Hawthorne*. Ed. Malcolm Cowley. New York: Viking, 1969.

Howells, Coral Ann. "Lest We Forget." Rev. of *The Blind Assassin*, by Margaret Atwood. *Canadian Literature* 173 (Summer 2002): 114-16.

Ingersoll, Earl. "Waiting for the End: Closure in Margaret Atwood's *The Blind Assassin*." *Studies in the Novel* XXXV 4 (Winter 2003): 543-558.

Kipling, Rudyard. *Complete Verse*. New York: Anchor Books, 1989.

Longfellow, Herny Wadsworth. *Poems*. Ed. Thomas Byrom. London: Dent, 1983.

Murray, Jennifer. "Questioning of the Triple Goddess: Myth and Meaning in Margaret Atwood's *The Robber Bride*." *Canadian Literature* 173 (Summer 2002): 72-90.

Rooke, Constance. "Atwood's Hands." *Fear of the Open Heart: Essays on Contemporary Writing*. Toronto: Coach House, 1989: 163-174.

Weisenberger, Bernard A. et all. Eds. *Family Encyclopedia of American History*. Pleasantville: The Reader's Digest, 1976.

White, Hayden. *Metahistory*. Baltimore: The Johns Hopkins University Press, 1973.

Interview with Margaret Atwood

BRANKO GORJUP

B.G. I wonder if you are still writing for that "great critic in the sky?" In Graeme Gibson's interview you described him or her as "a personification of some ideal that is unattainable? "

M.A. I don't think the ideal reader, for me, is in the sky anymore. The ideal reader is located somewhere on earth but we don't know where he or she is because we never really meet our readers. Writers, unlike opera singers, can't create their art in the same time-space with their audience. Writers work in solitude. When the book is finally finished and published, a few years have gone by and you've grown older, you're no longer thinking about it. The book is now on its own, sent out into the world to meet people. At that meeting, you are not present and will never know whether your work has connected with the ideal reader. It's like being stranded on a deserted island: you put a message into a bottle and throw it into the sea, hoping that it will float to shore, and that someone will perhaps find it and read your message.

B.G. Literature has sometimes been thought of as a tool for social change. In Canada, at the end of the nineteenth century, literature was expected to be at the service of nation building. At different times and in different places, it has also meant propaganda, entertainment, testimony, aestheticism, and so on. On a number of occasions, you have said that writing is a political act. Do you mean that it is always and inevitably a political act, or that it is that for you? Can you expand this idea?

M.A. All I mean is that language embodies choices. This is something that's built into the language itself and it's very hard to get away from it. You may remember Alain Robbe-Grillet, who tried to purify fiction of character, plot and moral result, but he ended up essentially with the description of objects. That's as far as he could go. When I say that the table is red I already have the table and the colour red, a noun and an adjective, both of which possess a certain "frequency." No matter what, people will attach certain emotions to the word *table*, and *red* will present its own range of associations, which are different from those of the colour blue. Once you have a novel with characters in it, whether or not the author makes judgments about those characters, the reader will. As soon as you have a plot, you will also have an outcome to that plot, and the reader will again make judgments about that outcome. Chekhov has often been used as an example of a writer who does not judge his characters. As it turns out, he did judge his characters. It's very hard to avoid judgment, because that's what we do in real life all the time.

Do I mean that writing as a political act should be agitation propaganda? No, I don't. Human beings make moral choices whether we like or not. How can we, then, have such a thing as a novel that contains people and events and does not present the reader with an opportunity to participate in making moral choices? In fact, that never happens. There is the story of Oscar Wilde who was taking an examination in the classics. He was asked to translate orally, verbatim, from the New Testament, which was in Aramaic. After a while, the examiner told him, *Thank you, Mr. Wilde, that will do*. But Wilde kept on going. The examiner said again, *That's sufficient, Mr. Wilde*. At this point, Wilde cried out: *Oh! Oh! Let me go on, I want to see how it will come out*. So, if we are engaged in a piece of fiction, we want to see how it comes out, because we have an opinion about the outcome. There are characters that we like and approve of, and if they get rewarded we are happy. Such an ending is comic. If they are not rewarded, we're very upset, which makes the ending ironic or tragic.

B.G. So the idea of the *political*, in that sense, is predicated on human relationships . . .

M.A. . . . which are, in essence, human arrangements embodying various degrees of power. In that sense they are political. We are not talking here about the Liberal or the Conservative parties, or about the Republicans or the Democrats, although they may be involved. We are not talking about whether Tony Blair is going to be elected again. Political novels like that do exist, but they are usually not long lasting because the political situation that they deal with disappears. If such novels reappear again, they do so as historical political novels, like Don DeLillo's novel about the death of J.F. Kennedy. Generally, politics does not make a very good subject for a novel because many readers are not going to understand the local situation. One could write an interesting novel about how David Miller, the Mayor of Toronto, won the election, but it wouldn't be of interest to a wide readership. Those in Toronto already know the story; and those outside won't care about it. That's what *political* means — it means power structures. It would be impossible to write about characters who have the *same* degree of power because the end result of such a work would be lack of dynamism. Novels always involve osmosis. Energy leaks from one segment to another. Why is that so? Because novels take place in time — they are accounts of events in time. Time *is* change.

B.G. For me there is a kind of religious feeling in your work, arising from an individual's faith in the possibility of transcendence, from some re-imagining of the world as a different place from the one we've inherited. (The heroine of *Surfacing* is one such person.) Can you speak about that a bit? Is religious altogether the wrong word?

M.A. I don't know exactly what we mean by religious. What is usually meant by it is that somebody has adopted a particular set of practices and beliefs. What is interesting to me about the whole complex is that mythology precedes religion. What we usually mean by religion is theology and ritual. If we can talk about mythology instead of religion, then we'll be probably on a firmer ground. If we can talk about the kinds of stories that human beings have told for a very long time, then we'll be talking about those stories that are always concerned with the origins of the world. Sometimes they contain within them stories about how individuals should or should not behave, but those stories are not consistent. Some people behave very well and they have awful experiences, and some people behave very badly, and nothing particularly terrible happens to them – *The Bible* is full of such examples.

The desire to know is very much part of being human. We are the species that asks questions and continues to play into adulthood. We invented grammar, which includes the past tense, allowing us to say where we've come from, and the future tense, allowing us to imagine where we are going. As far as we know, other animals don't ask such questions on a large scale, although they may have languages and reason. I don't know if dogs have a mythology about the origins of the first dog. Maybe they do, but I doubt it.

B.G. Do you think that the invention of the tenses makes our perception of life fundamentally elegiac?

M.A. The fact that we can envision a future, which grammatically may be said not to exist – I would say that it does make it elegiac. Likewise, it is grammatically almost impossible to make the statement "I will not exist" and have the "I" vanish from that statement. It continues to be somehow present. You can say "I will not be here" but the "I" is still in the sentence, so where will you be? Possibly somewhere else, and most stories have that "somewhere," whether it is mentioned or not. As far as I know, there is only one culture in which the dead are never mentioned, which doesn't mean that no one ever thinks of them.

B.G. Aren't we really talking about our uniquely human ability to project ourselves into the next stage of our life, into tomorrow, summer, old age, eternity . . . ?

M.A. . . . into another story in which we don't have to be present at the moment. But we can envision ourselves in another different story – something human beings do. They've been asking all those questions as far back as we can remember: "Who made us?" "What is life?" "Why is there death and how can we get around it?" The first recorded poem sequence, written in Sumerian, asks exactly those questions, and does so much before the Biblical narratives.

B.G. When I spoke of the "religious" feeling that your work evokes in me, I didn't think in terms of a specific dogma . . .

M.A. . . . It's human. It's part of the human story. For instance, there are many different kinds of origin myth. You could say they involve some kind of a sexual act, giving birth to a world. You could say that a giant clam shell gave birth to the people or that the people come out of an egg. You could have a world that is spoken or danced into being. You could have a world that is made – the turtle dives down and brings up mud and creates the world. You could have people that are made like cookies and are baked into life – the first lot gets burned and they are black, the second lot didn't get cooked enough and they are white, and the third lot got cooked just right. In the Mayan creation myth gods make the world but first they worry and worry and it takes them a great deal of time before they create a single thing. They are not sure whether or not it is a good idea. Ordinary human beings are always doing something like this, even if it's just turning to the horoscope in the daily newspaper, asking what my day will be like today. And, then, there is the science story: the universe was created by a Big Bang. And what was there before the Big Bang? There was a Singularity. And what is a Singularity? We don't know. You like that one?

B.G. Yeah!

M.A. Why are we on earth? What created life and the rules by which all the elements are combined? We don't know. I'm afraid we always end up saying that.

B.G. And that's the mystery of it all, I guess.

M.A. Yes. Wouldn't it be awful if we knew everything?

B.G. Ours is an imperfect world, no matter where we live. There are people who manage somehow, even prosper with a modicum of happiness. Others don't. They feel abused, victimized, dispossessed. This, it is believed, is usually caused by forces beyond individual control. In your fiction, there are numerous characters who get stuck, like Rennie in *Bodily Harm* or Offred in *The Handmaid's Tale*, but who seek and find a way out. In the process, they are mentally and spiritually invigorated, reaching a new level of awareness that strengthens their hope for change. How does this transformation happen? What propels these characters and others like them to act? In what way are they different from those who remain paralysed?

M.A. There are two kinds of stories. There are lots of other kinds too, but let's mention these two. They are both about Beowulf. In the first story Beowulf battles and overcomes a monster, and not only that, he battles and

244

overcomes an even worse monster, namely the mother of the first monster, and does away with both. He emerges triumphant after a ferocious struggle in the dark. But there is more to the story of Beowulf. Later on in life Beowulf battles a dragon and the dragon does him in. What can we draw from this? Sometimes you win, sometimes you lose.

Some people prefer to tell the same story over and over again. They prefer the story of Elizabeth who meets Mr. Darcy and everything comes out fine. They prefer the Cinderella story, which is probably one of the oldest stories we know anything about. But if it's always the same story, we would get bored. People like different stories and they also don't like to know how the story they are in at the moment is going to come out. If we look for absolute certainty, we buy a piece of genre fiction. We know that the Elizabeth character will marry the Mr. Darcy character. We just wait for the proposal and we are very happy when it arrives. Likewise, in an Agatha Christie story we are certain, no matter how difficult the puzzle may appear to be, that Hercule Poirot will solve it in the end.

B.G. In your fiction, the reader is often left suspended in a state of ambiguity. The world your characters occupy is dangerously unpredictable. Anything can happen.

M.A. Because it's truer to life. It's less like the kind of fiction we had in the nineteenth century, in which the reader was told at the end of the book what happened to everybody. The bad characters at the end of a Dickens novel most likely got punished, and the good characters – if they were very good and very young – got to die, just like the bad ones. But they died in a beautiful way and the audience cried, and the bad characters didn't get any crying. That's the only difference. The medium-good characters, those we are rooting for, came out all right, with enough money to have a pleasant life, and they got to marry the right people. And that was what the readers wanted to know in those days. If you didn't tell them that, you'd have riots in the streets. Whereas in the sentimental novels of the eighteenth century, the heroine was put through the most dismal suffering and torture because the whole idea of the book was to make you cry through another's misfortunes.

B.G. And that was considered to be ennobling.

M.A. It meant that you had sensibility. It showed that you had a heart and that you were a person with sentiments, empathizing with the poor, suffering, virtuous character.

B.G. So we are talking about the types of stories and the types of characters that would embody the sensibilities of the age.

M.A. Yes, we are. And today you couldn't actually write a very convincing period novel about those days unless you were making fun of the form, saying: Now dear reader, bear with me, I'm going to tell you that in the end Minnie got out of her awful predicament and married a person called Fred and they lived happily in a house in the Annex and had couple of beautiful children and a dog. At the end of a book of mine, at this point in time, nobody would believe in such an ending. They would think it was a joke. Marshall McLuhan once said that art is what you can get away with. What does that mean? It means that the author's job is to be plausible. Not necessarily realistic up to the last detail, and not necessarily telling the truth, the whole truth and nothing but the truth. If this is the story we are in, this is the way we believe the story would happen.

B.G. This takes me back to my earlier question about characters' transformation. In your work there are certain characters, like the unnamed heroine in *Surfacing*, who rise to a higher level of awareness, while others, like

Anna in the same novel, remain static. Anna's story gets "stuck" – or Anna gets stuck inside her story. She just can't make it to the next level.

M.A. Remember, Anna is a secondary character and as such she has a thin time of it because she doesn't get to speak for herself. We never hear what the secondary characters think about except what they may say it through the primary ones. They don't have inner monologues or a narrative voice. And we always believe the person with the narrative voice. Once the story is told from the heroine's point of view, the same story could be told from the point of view of the secondary character.

B.G. As Tom Stoppard's play *Rosencrantz and Guildenstern Are Dead* in which Shakespeare's story is narrated from the point of view of the two luckless friends of Hamlet.

M.A. Exactly. Let's have the story told from a different point of view so that we can see it in a different light. Imagine telling the story from Bluebeard's perspective: Why can't I find the perfect woman? Time and again, I just have to keep chopping off their heads. It's tedious . . .

B.G. In a conversation with Geoff Hancock you described your own work as "somewhat eccentric." You also said it was strange that you had acquired the audience you did. Were you perhaps thinking of the more experimental character of your writing, going back to that early period when you were still associated with the Anansi group, or did you mean something else? Would you still use the word eccentric to describe your work?

M.A. My work is entirely eccentric – and, by the way, there really wasn't an Anansi group – although *The Edible Woman* is somewhat less so. When you get to *The Blind Assassin* you do have a publisher say – I'm not telling which one – that the reader might get confused at the beginning of the novel because there are several stories going on at the same time. I said I would take that chance. If anything, my work is becoming more eccentric. I don't know whether or not you've read *Oryx and Crake*. *The Handmaid's Tale* was a completely eccentric book at the time I wrote it. Now people no longer look at me the way they used to in those days. Now they ask: how did you know? But I am saying *eccentric* only from the point of view of publishing and in relation to general kinds of books that might appear. I never tell my publishers ahead of time what I am writing. If I did, they would freak out, they would say: you are writing *what*? You are writing a book about a bunch of women in long red dresses and white hats and you think anybody is going to want to read that?

B.G. I would like to back-track a bit to the point where I made reference to the Anansi group of writers. I didn't really mean to suggest that you constituted a group in the strictest sense of the word, but rather that you were a group of young aspiring writers who introduced something new, something fresh to the existing literary establishment. Writers such as yourself, Graeme Gibson, Michael Ondaatje, Dennis Lee and so on, re-defined Canadian writing in a way that hadn't previously been attempted. You introduced experimentation that, by and large, had been absent from what was still largely a colonial literary culture.

M.A. Yes, but there is a great deal more experimental writing produced in those days. If you go back and look at *Groundwork*, the anthology we put out a year and a half or so ago, you will see that we assembled a list of books from the late 1960s and early 1970s in which there was a great deal of quite eccentric writing as, for example, *Five Legs* and *Communion*. It would be hard to get books like that published today. Publishers probably wouldn't touch them — they would consider them too weird. The reason for this is that the whole publishing industry, as we know it today, has become much more consumptive of money. It is much more costly to publish books these days and it is much harder to get them distributed because big chains control distribution outfits. Therefore, a great deal of talent is filtered out because the distributors think that there is no market for it. Whereas, we could really do anything we wanted because there was no market at all.

B.G. A great deal of that work is still around, isn't it?

M.A. That's true, but the book world has become so commercialized that it is harder to do those kinds of things now and have them move into the mainstream audience. If *Five Legs* sold out, it was because there were hardly any Canadian novels. So here you have one and it was, strange though it may sound, well reviewed and people went out and bought it. It would be hard to do that now with a book so unusual. You are going to get many wonderful books but they are going to be more conventional.

B.G. I agree with you. There seems to be now a certain kind of book, which is well constructed, very sensitive, poetic . . .

M.A. And that's not exactly what I write. I can't say that I've never written that kind of work; I probably have. But that's *not* how I would characterize my work in general.

B.G. This brings me to a more general question about your writing. Every author produces something unique, yet we often speak of it in terms of a literary tradition or sensibility. Some writers may produce work that is more readily recognizable as national, local, ethnic or whatever, belonging to a specific sensibility. In what way do you perceive your work as Canadian? Would the adjective "eccentric," to go back to my previous question, qualify? Very often my colleagues in Europe are baffled, asking me how it is that so many "weird" things happen in Canadian books . . .

M.A. . . . because they've never been here . . .

B.G. . . . whereas the country's image as projected by Canadians they meet has remained decidedly straight.

M.A. I don't understand it. O.K., here is an interesting questions. An Australian said to me that when Australians send their movie stars to Hollywood, they tend to be hunks. When Canadians send them, they tend to be comedians. Why is that?

B.G. Why is it?

M.A. I don't know. As children we were constantly making fun of everything. Parody was the big form. As for "strange," I can only quote Robertson Davies, who said "I know the dark folkways of my people." During WW II we had a Prime Minister who was dullness incarnate – there couldn't be a duller man and he was, all this time, running the country according to his belief that the spirit of his mother inhabited his dog. He was receiving messages from his dead mother through his dog. And not only that, he would not make a decision in the Parliament unless both hands of the clock were pointing to the same number. Maybe it has to do with all that.

B.G. If you were to write a new critical work about the Canadian literary tradition as it stands today – a sequel to *Survival* – what might it say? Is there a thesis you could imagine now that would encompass what is characteristically Canadian about our literature today?

M.A. By a great coincidence, Anansi recently published a new edition of *Survival* in which I say why it would be impossible for me to write such a book today or why I myself wouldn't do it. So the answer is in that introduction. For one thing, too much has been published, which would make it theoretically if not practically impossible to produce such a work. Likewise, the reason for doing it wouldn't be the reason for which I did it. It simply wouldn't be necessary anymore. I wrote *Survival* in order to say that there was such a thing as Canadian literature, at the time when people thought there hadn't been.

B.G. Is Canada, in your opinion, a microcosm of a global-ized world? Has the national or ethnic environment dis-appeared? It seems quite obvious that our literature has not only responded to Canada's extraordinary ethnic mix, but has also embodied its various constituencies as they produce their own fictive environments. In the wake of globalization, are national literatures becoming obsolete? Aren't we all becoming international while the local in our culture remains a mishmash?

M.A. How local was opera in the eighteen century? How national? Actually, it was neither. It was very Italian at that point – Italy was the standard and people learned opera from Italians who went to other countries to do opera there. When the Italians went to Germany, for instance, you couldn't say that the product was com-pletely German. You also couldn't say that it was com-pletely Italian. What is Mozart anyway? It may interest you that the very national coloured sash that the Quebecois adapted as one of their symbols came from New England. Cultures are always borrowing things from one another and cultural artefacts are always making their way via trade routes to places where they didn't originate. So where does it come from, this idea that things originated in one place and stayed in that place forever? It was probably born in nineteenth-cen-tury Europe when nationalism replaced religion as an organizing force. I think it is a rather recent idea and not proven to be very stable because countries change their borders a great deal. The idea of owing allegiance to a nation has its origins in medieval times. First of all you were supposed to owe allegiance to your God and religion and second to your local prince, which was for military purposes. Your responsibility was to help the prince defend the territory held in common. But your allegiance to him, although bound by oaths and so on, was a worldly one. When such territories amalgamated into larger units you got nations under kings. Then the kings took on some of the attributes of God, resulting in such huge multinational and multiethnic empires as the Holy Roman Empire or the Muslim Ottoman Empire. After they dumped the kings, which they started doing in the eighteenth century, and the power got transferred into the hands of the countries' governments, individuals were supposed to swear their allegiance to a flag.

How valid are these ideas of nationhood and nationalism? How permeable are borders? They have always been permeable to other cultures. Artists have always been influenced by other artists who were from somewhere else.

B.G. This was true even during the darkest moments in history. When the curtains between nations fell, cultures still travelled.

M.A. Yes, they travelled underground, finding new incarnations.

B.G. So for you local cultures don't necessarily disappear when they meet foreign influences. Instead they are transformed by absorbing those influences into something new, into something different. Isn't that so?

M.A. You may encounter, for example, someone with a radio transistor in the Sahara Desert, but that person will be listening to something that you could not even imagine. The same technology that we use here finds a new purpose. People will always adapt new things to themselves, to their needs and situations. You may find the same objects all over the world, but people's attitudes to them will be different.

B.G. You have twice written about the world of dystopia. In both *The Handmaid's Tale* and *Oryx and Crake*, the worlds you depict are frighteningly real, strangely familiar. Whether they take place in the future or the past or in some collapsed fictional time, the experience one gets is that virtually everything in them takes place in the reader's present time. Is our world, one wonders, so deeply troubled? How significant it is that both novels are recognizably set in the United States, a society that had promised so much and now seem to be delivering so little in terms of essential human liberties?

M.A. Well, it is actually delivering a lot in terms of essential human liberties for many of the people in it. You know what St. Paul said? He said, I am a Roman citizen. This statement implied that there was one set of rules for Roman citizens and another set for peoples who weren't, but madly wanted to become Romans because they knew they'd get a better deal as the citizens of the Empire. This is what still propels many people, legally or otherwise, into the United States. In spite of everything, they want to be its citizens because they too believe they'd get a better deal. For reasons of security it is always more beneficial to be on the inside of an empire than to be on its fringes. All empires typically expand their borders past the point where they can defend them, as the peoples from outside are always pushing against them trying to get in.

Bibliography

Novels

The Edible Woman. Toronto: McClelland & Stewart, 1969; London: Andre Deutsch, 1969; Boston: Atlantic Little-Brown,1970. *Surfacing.* Toronto: McClelland & Stewart, 1972; London: Andre Deutsch, 1973; New York: Simon & Schuster, 1973. *Lady Oracle.* Toronto: McClelland & Stewart, 1972; New York: Simon & Schuster, 1972; London: Andre Deutsch,1976. *Life before Man.* Toronto: McClelland & Stewart, 1979; New York: Simon & Schuster; New Jersey: Cape,1980. *Bodily Harm.* Toronto: McClelland & Stewart, 1981; New York: Simon & Schuster; New Jersey: Cape,1981. *The Handmaid's Tale.* Toronto: McClelland & Stewart, 1985; Boston: Houghton Mifflin, 1985; New Jersey: Cape,1985. *Cat's Eye.* Toronto: McClelland & Stewart, 1988; New York: Doubleday, 1989. *The Robber Bride.* Toronto: McClelland & Stewart, 1993; London: Bloomsbury, 1993; New York: Doubleday,1993. *Alias Grace.* Toronto: McClelland & Stewart, 1996; London: Bloomsbury, 1996; New York: Doubleday, 1996. *The Blind Assassin.* Toronto: McClelland & Stewart, 2000; London: Bloomsbury, 2000; New York: Doubleday, 2000. *Oryx and Crake.* Toronto: McClelland & Stewart, 2003; London: Bloomsbury, 2003; New York: Doubleday, 2003.

Short Fiction

Dancing Girls. Toronto: McClelland & Stewart, 1977; New York: Simon & Schuster, 1977; New Jersey: Cape, 1979. *Murder in the Dark.* Toronto: Coach House Press, 1983. *Bluebeard's Egg.* Toronto: McClelland & Stewart, 1983; Boston: Houghton Mifflin,1985. *Wilderness Tips.* Toronto: McClelland & Stewart, 1991; New York: Doubleday, 1991; London: Bloomsbury, 1991. *Good Bones.* Toronto: Coach House Press, 1992; London: Bloomsbury, 1992; New York: Doubleday,1994.

Poetry

The Circle Game. Bloomfield, Mi.: Cranbrook Academy of Art, 1964; Contact Press, 1966; Toronto: Anansi, 1967. *The Animals in That Country.* Toronto: Oxford University Press, 1969; Boston: Atlantic Little-Brown, 1968. *The Journals of Susanna Moodie.* Toronto: Oxford University Press, 1970. *Procedures for Underground.* Toronto: Oxford University Press, 1970;

Boston: Atlantic Little-Brown, 1970. *Power Politics.* Toronto: Anansi, 1971; New York: Harper & Row, 1973. *You Are Happy.* Toronto: Oxford University Press, 1974; New York: Harper & Row, 1975. *Selected Poems.* Toronto: Oxford University Press, 1976; New York: Simon & Schuster, 1978. *Two-Headed Poems.* Toronto: Oxford University Press, 1978. *True Stories.* Toronto: Oxford University Press; 1981. *Interlunar.* Toronto: Oxford University Press 1984. *Selected Poems II: Poems Selected and New,* 1976-1986. Toronto: Oxford University Press, 1986; Boston: Houghton Mifflin, 1987. *Selected Poems 1966-1984.* Toronto: Oxford University Press, 1990. *Margaret Atwood Poems 1965-1975.* London: Virago Press, 1991. *Morning in the Burned House.* Toronto: McClelland & Stewart, 1995; Boston: Houghton Mifflin, 1995; London: Virago Press, 1995. *Eating Fire; Selected Poems, 1965-1995.* London: Virago Press, 1998.

Non Fiction

Survival: A Thematic Guide to Canadian Literature. Toronto: Anansi, 1972. *Days of the Rebels 1815-1840.* Toronto: Natural Science of Canada, 1977. *Second Words: Selected Critical Prose.* Toronto: Anansi, 1982. *Strange Things: The Malevolent North in Canadian Literature.* Toronto: Oxford University Press, 1995. *Two Solicitudes: Conversations* [with Victor-Lévy Beaulieu]. Toronto: McClelland & Stewart, 1998. *Negotiating with the Dead: A Writer on Writing.* Cambridge: Cambridge University Press, 2002; New York: Anchor Books, 2003; London: Virago Press 2003.

Books about Margaret Atwood

Bouson, J. Brooks. *Brutal Choreographies: Oppositional Strategies and Narrative Design in the Novels of Margaret Atwood.* Amherst: U of Massachusetts P, 1993. Beran, Carol. *Living over the Abyss: Margaret Atwood's Life before Man.* Toronto: ECW, 1994. Cameron, Elspeth. *Atwood- The Edible Woman: Notes.* Coles Notes. Toronto: Coles, 1983. Carrington, Ildiko De Papp. *Margaret Atwood and Her Works.* Toronto: ECW, 1985. Coles Editorial Board. *Atwood-Surfacing: Notes.* Coles Notes. Toronto: Coles, 1982. Davey, Frank. *Margaret Atwood: A Feminist Poetics.* Vancouver: Talonbooks, 1984. Davidson, Arnold E. and Cathy N. Davidson, eds. *The Art of Margaret Atwood: Essays in Criticism.* Toronto: Anansi, 1981. Fee, Margery. *The Fat Lady Dances: Margaret Atwood's Lady Oracle.* Toronto:

ECW, 1993. Grace, Sherrill E., *Violent Duality: A Study of Margaret Atwood*. Montreal: Véhicule, 1980. Grace, Sherrill & Lorraine Weir, eds. *Margaret Atwood: Language, Text and System*. U of British Columbia P, 1983. Hengen, Shannon. *Margaret Atwood's Power: Mirrors, Reflections and Images in Select Fiction and Poetry*. Toronto: Second Story, 1993. Howells, Coral Ann. *York Notes on The Handmaid's Tale*. Harlow, Essex: Longman, 1993. Howells, Coral Ann. *Margaret Atwood*. New York: St. Martin's P, 1996. Ingersoll, Earl G., ed. *Margaret Atwood: Conversations*. Princeton, New Jersey: Ontario Review Press, 1990. Irvine, Lorna. *Collecting Clues*: *Margaret Atwood's Bodily Harm*. ECW, Toronto, 1993. Keith, W.J. *Introducing Margaret Atwood's The Edible Woman: A Reader's Guide*. Canadian Fiction Studies 3. Toronto: ECW, 1989. Mallinson, Jean. *Margaret Atwood and Her Works*. Toronto: ECW, 1984. Mendez-Egle, Beed. *Margaret Atwood: Reflection and Reality*. Edinburgh: Pan American UP, 1987. Mycak, Sonia. *In Search of the Split Subject: Psychoanalysis, Phenomenology, and the Novels of Margaret Atwood*. Toronto: ECW, 1996. Nicholson, Colin, ed. *Margaret Atwood: Writing and Subjectivity*. Houndmills, Eng.: Macmillan, 1994; New York: St. Martin's, 1994. McCombs, Judith, Editor. *Critical Essays On Margaret Atwood*, G.K. Hall & Co., Boston, 1988. McCombs, Judith, and Carole L. Palmer. *Margaret Atwood: A Reference Guide*. Boston: Hall, 1991. Rao, Eleonora. *Strategies for Identity: The Fiction of Margaret Atwood*, Peter Land Publishing, New York, 1994. Rigney, Barbara Hill. *Margaret Atwood*. Houndmills, Eng.: Macmillan, 1987. Totowa: Barnes, 1987. Rosenberg, Jerome. *Margaret Atwood*. Boston: Twayne, 1984. Staels, Hilde. *Margaret Atwood's Novels: A Study of Narrative Discourse*. Transatlantic Perspective. Tubingen: Francke, 1995. VanSpanckeren, Kathryn, and Jan Garden Castro, eds. *Margaret Atwood: Vision and Forms*. Carbondale: Southern Illinois UP, 1988. Wilson, Sharon R. *Margaret Atwood's Fairy-Tale Sexual Politics*. Jackson: U of Mississippi P, 1993. Wilson, Sharon R., and Thomas B. Friedman, and Shannon Hengen, eds. *Approaches to Teaching Atwood's The Handmaid's Tale and Other Works*. New York: MLA, 1996. Woodcock, George. *Introducing Margaret Atwood's Surfacing: A Reader's Guide*. Toronto: ECW, 1990. York, Lorraine M., ed. *Various Atwoods: Essays on the Later Poems, Short Fiction, and Novels*. Anansi Press, 1995.

Contributors

Branko Gorjup is the chief editor of the Peter Paul Bilingual Series of Contemporary Canadian Poetry (English/Italian) in which the following authors have appeared: Irving Layton, Gwendolyn MacEwen, P.K. Page, Al Purdy, Margaret Atwood, Michael Ondaatje, Margaret Avison and Dennis Lee. He edited a number of anthologies of short fiction by English Canadian authors, a selections of stories by Leon Rooke and Barry Callaghan, and a book of essays by Northrop Frye, *Mythologizing Canada*. In 2003 he assembled a special issue, *Oceano Canada*, for Mondadori's *Nuovi Argomenti*, introducing Canadian contemporary writing in English to the Italian readership and in 2004 *White Gloves of the Doorman: The Works of Leon Rooke*. Gorjup has taught Canadian Literature in universities in Canada and Italy. Presently he resides in Los Angeles and Toronto.

Gayle Greene, professor of English and Women's Studies at Scripps College, has published several books on women writers and feminist theory. Her most recent book is a biographyof British radiation epidemiologist Dr. Alice Stewart. She has written a memoir about growing up in Silicon Valley, and is currently at work on a book called "Insomniac," which is part memoir and part scientific investigation, to be published by University of California Press.

Barbara Hill Rigney is Professor of English at Ohio State University. She is the author of *Margaret Atwood: A Critical Inquiry* in the Women Series published by Macmillan Education Ltd., 1987. Her other books include *Madness and Sexual Politics in the Feminist Novel: Studies in Brontë, Wolff, Lessing and Atwood,* 1980' Lillith's Daughter: Women and Religion in Contemporary Fiction, 1982 – both containing chapters on Atwood –, *The Voices of Toni Morrison,* 1981 and *Exile: A Memoir of 1939,* co-edited with Bronka Schneider and Erika Bourguignon. She has also written numerous articles on Feminist theory.

Coral Ann Howells is Professor of English and Canadian Literature at the University of Reading, England. Her books include *Private and Fictional Words* (1987), *Margaret Atwood* (1997. Revised 2nd edition 2005); *Alice Munro* (1998), and Contemporary *Canadian Women's Fiction: Refiguring Identities* (2004). She is editor of *Where Are the Voices Coming From? Canadian Culture and the Legacies of History* (2004) and of *The Cambridge Companion to Margaret Atwood* (2006). She has lectured extensively on

Atwood and contemporary Canadian women's fiction in Canada and the U.S.A., U.K., Europe and India.

Lorna Irvine is Professor of English and a member of the Cultural Studies and Women's Studies programs at George Mason University in Fairfax Virginia. She is the author of *Sub/Version: Canadian Fictions By Women*, *Collecting Clues: Margaret Atwood's Bodily Harm* and *Critical Spaces: Margaret Laurence and Janet Frame*. She has published many essays and book chapters on a variety of Canadian writers, and frequently teaches courses devoted to their work. Most recently, she has been working on the fiction of Carol Shields.

Stephanie Lovelady specializes in literature of the Americas and women's literature. Her research explores the role of narrative structures in women's coming-of-age stories that are also stories of immigration. She has taught at The University of Iowa, The University of Maryland and George Washington University.

Susan Jaret McKinstry, Helen F. Lewis Professor of English, teaches courses on the Victorian novel, Victorian poetry and painting, narrative theory, film adaptation, and literary theory. She edited *Feminism, Bakhtin, and the Dialogic* (1991), and has published articles on Jane Austen, Emily Bronte, Charles Dickens, Emily Dickinson, T. S. Eliot, Toni Morrison, Faye Weldon, Ann Beattie, and others. She is also a poet. Her current research explores the "sister arts" of poetry and painting in the work of the Pre-Raphaelites.

Jennifer Murray has written numerous articles. "Questioning the Triple Goddess: Myth and Meaning in Margaret Atwood's The Robber Bride" first appeared in *Canadian Literature* 1973 (Summer 2002).

Caterina Ricciardi teaches American Studies at the University of Roma Tre. She has extensively written on American Modernism and Canadian contemporary authors (Alice Munro, Margaret Atwood, Michael Ondaatje, Timothy Findley, Jane Urquhart). She has also translated into Italian (Atwood, Al Purdy and Dennis Lee). Her books include *EIKONE: Ezra Pound e il Rinascimento* (Napoli 1991) and *Northrop Frye e le finzioni supreme* (Roma 1992). She has recently edited *Voci dagli Stati Uniti: prosa & poesia & teatro del secondo Novecento* (Roma 2004).

Roberta Rubenstein is a Professor of Literature at American University in Washington, DC, where she teaches literature by Modernist and contemporary women writers and feminist literary theory. She is the author of more than thirty articles and book chapters and three books: *The Novelistic Vision of Doris Lessing: Breaking the Forms of Consciousness* (1979); *Boundaries of the Self: Gender, Culture, Fiction* (1987) — which includes a chapter on Margaret Atwood's fiction; and *Home Matters: Longing and Belonging, Nostalgia and Mourning in Women's Fiction* (2001). She has co-edited with Charles R. Larson an anthology of international short stories, *Worlds of Fiction* (1993; 2nd ed. 2001). At American University, she has been honored with awards for teaching and scholarship, including the College of Arts and Sciences Award for Outstanding Teaching (twice) and the Senior Scholar Award. In 1994, she was named the university's Scholar / Teacher of the Year.

Marquis Book Printing Inc.

Québec, Canada
2008